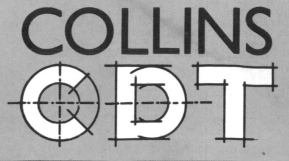

COLLINS CDT

Craft, Design and Technology

Design and Communication

Written in association with
Lincolnshire County Council

Authors: K. Crampton
M. Finney
Editor: A. Breckon

COLLINS
EDUCATIONAL

© Lincolnshire County Council 1988

First published 1988 by Collins Educational
8 Grafton Street, London W1X 3LA

ISBN 0 00322033–8

Design and cover by Sands–Straker Studios Limited, London

Artwork by Tim Cooke, Sam Denley, Peter Harper, Illustrated Arts, Kevin Jones

Typeset by The Word Shop, Rossendale, Lancashire
Printed in Spain by Mateu Cromo Artes Graficas, S.A.

CONTENTS

ABOUT THIS BOOK

This book seeks to cover the appropriate material for courses based on the National Criteria for CDT under the endorsed title of Design and Communication. The book is based on the principle that CDT is an activity focused area of the curriculum concerned with designing and making artefacts and/or systems to meet a specific purpose. This book provides the information necessary to tackle a wide range of design problems. It does not seek to solve them, but offers support and guidance in the process of transforming your ideas into reality. An important feature of the book is to place CDT in the context of the world in which we live. Most sections end with a range of questions based on the chapter, arranged so they become progressively more difficult. Finally, the book is intended to stimulate those studying the course to extend their interest in designing and making either by appreciating and/or improving the man-made environment, or by studying the subject further and perhaps pursuing an associated career.

TEACHER'S PREFACE

The material in this book is part of a comprehensive curriculum development programme for CDT in Lincolnshire. This began in 1981 and led to the publication of the CDT Foundation Course and its companion Teacher's Guide in 1986. Initially the material was written by teachers in the form of pupil guide books, which have now been evaluated and completely rewritten by the authors. This Design and Communication book is a natural progression from the Foundation Course book, as well as providing a comprehensive text for the full range of GCSE courses in CDT: Design and Communication.

   Design and Communication is one of a series of three GCSE textbooks for CDT. They have been written by a team of six teachers. The principal authors of *Design and Communication* are Kevin Crampton, Head of CDT at Charles Read School, Corby Glen, and Michael Finney, Head of CDT at William Farr CE Comprehensive School, Welton. They were ably assisted by Colin Chapman, Peter Fowler, Michael Horsley and Melvyn Peace. I am indebted to them for their commitment and professionalism in working so successfully as a team on this venture. I would also like to express my gratitude to the wives and children of these teachers for their patience and understanding throughout the absorbing but very demanding task of writing this book.

   This book was made possible by the encouragement of the former County Education Officer, Mr F G Rickard and the continued support of the former Director of Education, Mr D G Esp. Their professional support has been encouraged by enthusiastic members of Lincolnshire County Council, in particular Councillors W J Speechley and P Newton, whose positive approach to the development of CDT have greatly benefited the education of many pupils in Lincolnshire and hopefully, through this book, many others.

   Finally, I would like to thank the many pupils and teachers who, through their interest and enthusiasm, have such a positive contribution to the creation of this book.

A. M. Breckon.
Education Inspector (CDT)
Lincolnshire County Council.
Member of Secondary Examinations Council
GCSE and 18+ CDT Committees.

DESIGN AND DESIGNING

fig 1.1. 1987 camera

fig 1.3. Common logos

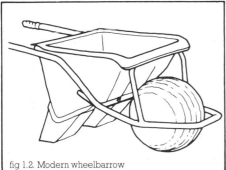

fig 1.2. Modern wheelbarrow

fig 1.5. Food packaging

Design plays a very important part in our lives. It controls and affects much of what we do in our everyday lives and we are all capable of designing.

You may design the pattern of your day, the layout of your bedroom or the way you travel to see a friend. From this you can see that design is always with you whether it is the shelter you live in, your means of travelling, or the clothes you wear.

This chapter looks at design and designing which are central to the whole subject of Craft, Design and Technology (CDT). It illustrates the different forms of designing related to CDT courses, and offers two frameworks which can help you to solve the design problems central to your course.

The rest of the book provides the necessary information and some helpful ideas for tackling a wide range of design problems.

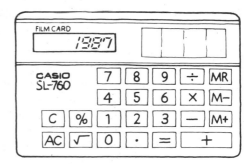

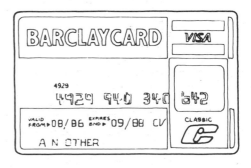

fig 1.4. Calculator and credit cards

fig 1.6. JCB excavator

fig 1.7. Lloyd's building

DESIGN AND DESIGNING

WHAT IS DESIGNING?

Designing is an activity which uses a wide range of experience, knowledge, and skills to find the best solution to a problem, within certain constraints.

Designing involves identifying and clarifying a problem, making a thoughtful response, and then creating and testing your solution. You can then usually start to modify your solution, so that the process of designing begins again.

Designing is a creative activity. You may often use known facts or solutions, but the way you combine these to solve your own particular problem requires creative thinking.

Designing is far more than just problem-solving. It involves the whole process of producing a solution, from conception to evaluation. This includes elements such as cost, appearance, styling, fashion, and manufacture.

Designers work in almost every area of life – textile design, product design, graphic design, interior design, engineering design and environmental design. Each area requires a different type of knowledge, but they all involve a similar design activity.

fig 1.8. Modern clothing

WHY DESIGNS CHANGE

There are various reasons why designs change. One is the change in the needs of society. An example of this is the fairly recent change to smaller cars. These were designed in response to the demand for economical, easier-to-park vehicles as our cities became more congested. You might argue, however, that the designer creates the change, and society then reacts to this change (as with fashion for example).

A second reason for change is the development of new technology which can be applied to traditional products. The new designs of computer have only been possible because of the development of 'microchip' technology. This was itself stimulated by people's desire for space flight.

HOW DESIGN AFFECTS OUR LIVES

A world without calculators, televisions, trains, aeroplanes, house insulation, advertising, shopping precincts and microwaves is difficult to imagine. These products have by and large benefited us. Few people would like to do without all the products designed in the last 20 years. However, designers have responsibilities to society because of the way their designs can affect us.

As well as solving the problem, designers may also work under timing, financial, and political pressures. However they must always place people first.

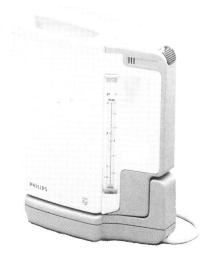

fig 1.9. Cordless kettle

LOOKING AT DESIGN

These first two pages show various designs which illustrate the fashion, style and technology of today.

Design is all around us and the next three pages illustrate three different aspects. Page 3 looks at the historical development of the telephone, page 4 looks at how designers have developed differing solutions to the same problem and page 5 looks at how designers communicate ideas, images and information. There are many other examples which you may also wish to investigate.

fig 1.10. Interior design of kitchen

DESIGN CHANGES THROUGH TIME

The telephone was invented over 100 years ago. It is a vital part of our lives which we use all the time to communicate.

Its function has remained almost identical over the years, but new technology has allowed changes from metal to wood to plastics, and from mechanical switches to electrical switches.

The flexibility of modern electronics allows the designer to create almost any shape of telephone. This page shows some of the external changes. At the same time there have been many improvements in the telephone's performance, which cannot be shown here.

fig 1.14. Telephone c.1927

fig 1.18. Viscount Super 4

fig 1.11. Ericson magneta table telephone c.1895

fig 1.15. Telephone c.1937

fig 1.19. BT Sceptre – memory and clock

fig 1.12. Desk telephone c.1907

fig 1.16. Telephone c.1968

fig 1.20. One piece wall mounted telephone

fig 1.13. Strowger calling dial c.1905

fig 1.17. British telephone 1960s to 1980s

fig 1.21. Remote control telephone

DESIGN SOLUTIONS TO SIMILAR PROBLEMS

This page shows some solutions to the problem of providing a portable source of light. Most have been designed to meet other needs as well, but they are all design solutions to the same basic problem.

When looking at a problem, designers think about how their solutions will be used. A torch has two principal uses – to provide light to see, and to act as a warning device. Sometimes both these functions are required at once. For example, you cannot cycle safely along country roads at night without a front light which does both.

When developing a new torch, the designer is likely to be constrained by the size of the batteries and bulbs. Another constraint for a cycle lamp is likely to be the means of attaching it to the cycle frame. These things are fixed because the designer is unlikely to be able to demand a specially designed battery or bicycle frame. There may be additional constraints, such as making the torch waterproof. Can you think of other possible constraints?

There are many other torch designs besides those shown here. Can you think of some other design solutions to this problem?

fig 1.25. Ever Ready cycle torch

fig 1.26. Motorist's lantern

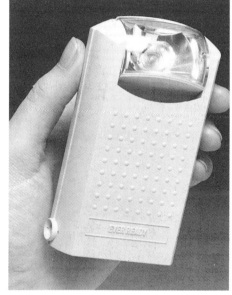

fig 1.22. Ever Ready swivel head torch

fig 1.24. Ever Ready small torch

fig 1.27. Dual purpose torch

fig 1.28. Pifco waterproof torch

fig 1.23. Durabeam torch

fig 1.29. Ever Ready rechargeable torch

DESIGN IN COMMUNICATION

You are constantly being bombarded by the communications industry creating images – either television, newspapers, magazines, posters, shop displays or exhibitions.

These images are created to communicate – to get a message across. The message may encourage you to buy a product or service, or it may provide entertainment or information.

The designers who create these images must be very sensitive to people's feelings, because they want to catch the eye of the consumer without offending.

The designer will use colour, texture, cartoons, pictures, and printed letters to get the message across. The development of computer graphics has also made the communication of information more effective.

Look carefully at some of the images on this page to see what messages or information they are getting across.

fig 1.31. Communicating through cartoons

fig 1.30. Company trademarks

fig 1.35. International communication symbols

fig 1.32. Communicating weather forecasts

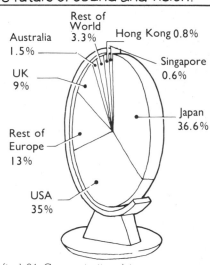

fig 1.34. Communicating data

fig 1.36. Advertising through carrier bags

fig 1.33. Comic strip

FRAMEWORKS FOR DESIGNING

OUTLINE DESIGNING FRAMEWORK

In your CDT course, designing is concerned with the whole process from identifying a problem, through to creating a solution and then testing it. This process requires you to consider many factors, and make a number of decisions.

There are many different methods or routes for doing this, and the one you choose will depend on the nature of the problem. This chapter introduces the idea of a framework which will support you in your design work.

A framework is a series of linked stages which will help you solve your problem. At each stage you will need to refer back to earlier stages.
This chapter looks at two frameworks, although it is quite feasible to use others. Equally, these two frameworks can be adapted to suit your own particular problem.

This page looks at the **outline designing framework**. This gives simple guidance on solving straightforward problems, or problems where time is very limited.

The following pages then look at the **integrated designing framework** which gives a lot more detail. This is suitable for more complex problems, and problems for which you have more time.

When designing, points you might consider include:

1. What is the problem I am trying to solve?
2. What is the purpose of my solution?
3. How will my solution be used?
4. How realistic are my suggested solutions?
5. Are the materials available?
6. Is my solution economical?
7. Is there sufficient time to make it?
8. Is this design task a challenge?

NOTE: Specific syllabuses may have a defined design process or framework. You should check this before tackling a design task as the framework may be linked to the assessment scheme.

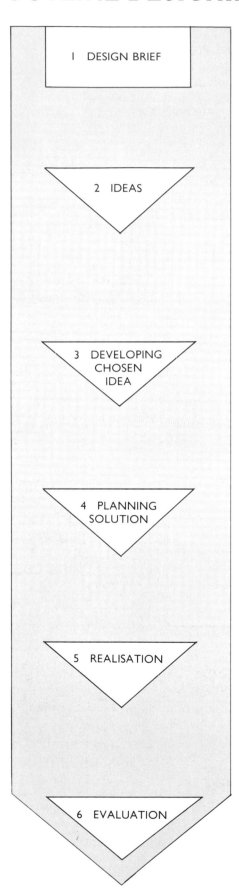

fig 1.37. Outline designing framework

1 The **design brief** is a clear description of the problem you are going to solve. You may have to form the brief from either a situation (such as the layout of your kitchen) or a theme (such as storage). Before finalising the brief you may need to do some investigations.

2 From the design brief you should get some initial **ideas** for your design. You may then need to carry out research before beginning to sketch these ideas.
It is wise to sketch a number of realistic ideas so you have some choice about the solution.
On completion of the ideas you should decide which one to carry forward, giving your reasons.

3 It is important to **develop the chosen idea** into a practical solution. This may involve further drawing of how it fits together, or modelling to see how it will work. At the end of this stage you should have a sound idea of what your are going to make.

4 The **planning of the solution** involves two stages. First, you need to make some drawings from which your solution can be made.
These are often called working drawings. Secondly, you should plan how your solution is to be made and which materials and components are required.

5 **Realisation** means making – either a scale model, a prototype or the final product. It is the realised model or product which will be evaluated, so the quality is very important. The realisation is one of the most exciting stages, but if the work in the previous stage has been poor, you may have difficulties.

6 **Evaluation** means finding out how well your solution works, and comparing it with your initial brief. Your evaluation should also suggest possible improvements.

INTEGRATED DESIGNING FRAMEWORK

Stage 1. Brief
Recognition of problem
Identification of needs
Recognition of situation
Formation of design brief

Stage 2. Investigation
Research into topic
Collation of useful information
Analysis of topic
Specification of requirements

Stage 3. Ideas
Generation of realistic ideas to satisfy
design brief

fig 1.39. Thinking and sketching an idea

Stage 4. Evaluating
Evaluation of ideas against the
specification
Identification of a proposed solution

Stage 5. Developing
Modelling, developing and refining
the proposed solution

Stage 6. Planning
Drafting drawings from which it can
be realised
Planning and organising of prepared
realisation

Stage 7. Realisation
Realisation of solution in the form of a
model, prototype, artefact or system

Stage 8. Testing
Testing to see if it works and how
well it works

Stage 9. Evaluation
How does it meet the brief?
How can it be improved?

fig 1.38. Integrated designing framework

fig 1.40. Modelling card

7

INTEGRATED DESIGNING FRAMEWORK

Designing becomes a lot easier if you have a framework to follow. The following pages explain how the integrated designing framework can be used. It is important to recognise that this should not be followed laboriously, but should be modified for specific problems. Various design methods and techniques are covered, but they are only suggestions which might be helpful.

STAGE 1: BRIEF

Where do you begin when you write a design brief? In some cases you might begin by recognising a problem, for example, how to get books to stand upright on shelves.

Another starting point might be seeing the need to improve something, like the instructions for fitting a burglar alarm.

A third starting point might be recognising an area where things are not working well because of layout – for example, in the kitchen. In this case you might have to do some research to find the real need.

From these differing starting points you will need to write a design brief. Design briefs range from the simplistic (**Design a seat**) to the more precise (**Design a garden seat which will be used by elderly people who may wish to sit in pairs**). This second brief is more useful because it sets out clear guidelines. The brief could go on to define more clearly details of colour, or describe the environment in which it would be situated.

The amount of detail given in the brief will decide the amount of freedom the designer has to experiment. If for instance, a design brief stated '**Design a brithday card**', the designer would have difficulty, because it could be for an 8-year-old or a 90-year-old. However, '**Design a birthday card for a teenager**' states the target without restricting ideas.

It is important not to give too much detail in a design brief, otherwise the designer can do little creative work. There are therefore four key points to remember about your design brief:

1 Identify a task which you are keen to work on.

2. Make sure the brief has a purpose.

3. Do not begin with such a vague brief that you have no idea where to start.

4. Do not define the brief so precisely that there is no room for innovation.

STAGE 2: INVESTIGATION

Investigation leads to a clearer understanding of the limits of the design problem. First of all you should read and understand the key words in the brief.

Consider the brief, '**Design a storage unit for kitchen roll, cling film and aluminium foil, which will take up a visible position in the kitchen and will dispense the material easily**'. The key points are storage, the three rolls, dispensing ability and appearance. These give a useful starting point for your design. Having analysed the brief you then need to research into the problems. For example:

1. Visit shops or exhibitions to view current products.

2. Draw up a questionnaire to discover further information.

3. Interview people about the problem.

4. Visit libraries and read magazines and books to find further information.

5. Write to and/or visit industry to discover more information.

6. Take a similar existing product or system and analyse it carefully.

Having carefully researched the topic, it is important to sort through the information and decide what is most useful. You should then have a good understanding of the task and can set out the exact limits and constraints for the designer. This is called a **specification**, and helps to focus towards the key

fig 1.41. A situation with many design opportunities

Fig 1.42. A new package for these biscuits

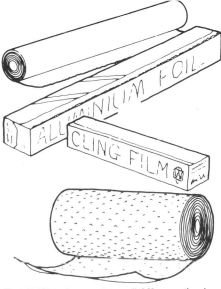
Fig 1.43. What sizes are these rolls? How can they be sto

aspects of the problem. A simple, systematic way of seeing if you have created a good specification is to check whether key factors are covered. These may not all be appropriate to any one problem, but having checked them, at least you will know the point has been considered: For example:

size	function	appearance	storage
cost	safety	environment	materials
manufacture	ergonomics	shape	reliability
maintenance	finish		

The order and priority will change according to the design problem. For example, the design of a 'pop-up' brochure would place low priority on safety, whereas a child's toy would give high priority to safety.

The design factors will often result in a series of conflicting points being raised. However, balancing these points is the essence of good design and it is now that you move into the third stage of creating ideas.

STAGE 3: IDEAS

Generating ideas which solve the problem is the most creative area of the whole designing activity. The quality of these ideas is one of the key elements in CDT work. Ideas can be generated through thinking and sketching. At this stage you might want to draw complete artefacts very precisely. This is a mistake, as it tends to create rigid, isolated ideas. It is far better to make quick sketches of outlines and rough forms which you can easily modify.

Different problems will lead to differing approaches. For example, if you are designing a car jack, the functional operations will be a key part of the design. However, if you are designing a piece of jewellery, the starting position may be looking at shapes and forms. The sketches should be a means of thinking on paper, using notes where appropriate, and ensuring your rich ideas are recorded. With complex problems, ideas may be created for parts of the problem rather than the whole solution.

It should be recognised that ideas do not automatically appear when you wish. Ideas may come at any time, and you must sketch or note them when they occur, because they can easily be mounted in your folder at a later stage. However, solutions to design problems cannot wait for ideas to just arrive, they must be worked at to determine solutions. There are several ways of working at the generation of ideas and different methods can be used, depending on the problem. The following may be helpful:

1. **Observation and adaptation** Look at existing solutions to similar problems, and then from these you can usually develop ideas. Look at nature to see how it solved the problem and then consider how this can be adapted. Remember that design is about solving problems in the best form, rather than always creating original ideas.

2. **Ideas from drawings** The creation of ideas from drawings is particularly useful for work in creating the shape and form of a product. This method may begin from shapes such as lines, circles, cubes, prisms or pyramids, which are then cut, rotated or combined to generate a new shape. These visual investigations are a very effective way of creating ideas.

3. **Brainstorming** This is usually a group activity where everyone thinks of ideas to solve the problem. The ideas are shared, which often stimulates further ideas or adaptations.

4. **Checklists** The use of a checklist can provide more starting points to stimulate ideas. A word or phrase in a cheklist can help you think about the problem from another viewpoint. The checklist may be as at the top of this page or it may be in the form of questions:
   What is the purpose of what I am trying to design?
   Who may use it?
   Where is it going to be used?
   Can it be modified?
   What is the important part of the design?

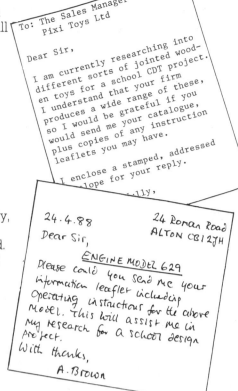

Fig 1.44. Letters requesting information

Fig 1.45. Use nature as a source for ideas

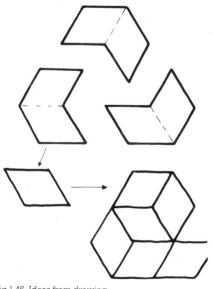

Fig 1.46. Ideas from drawing

STAGE 4: EVALUATING

The evaluation of ideas is a critical phase because it is at this stage that the proposed solution is first identified. It is wise to look carefully at all the ideas, but you need to be clear what you are looking for when choosing an idea to develop. These points may be helpful:

1. Does the idea meet the brief you started with?
2. If not, does it satisfy the need better?
3. Does it meet the specification?
4. Is it possible for the proposed solution to be made with the resources of time, materials and equipment available?
5. Is it financially viable?

In your design work it is wise to write down your reasons for making choices. At the end of the project it may be interesting to know the exact reasons for the decision-making at this critical stage.

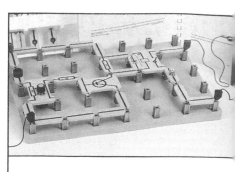

STAGE 5: DEVELOPING

Developing and refining the proposed solution is the stage when you convert the idea into reality. A key part of this stage is the modelling of the proposal to see how it works and how it can be improved. The models can use specialist kits or modelling materials. There is no doubt that a good model can be most helpful in developing and refining a proposal. At this stage, a number of factors are likely to arise and require you to make a decision.

fig 1.47. Modelling solutions

Materials

Materials provide a major constraint. First, you must know how you wish the various parts of your solution to behave. You can then begin to identify an appropriate material for each part. Properties of materials which you might consider are:

weight   strength   toughness   feel   resistance to heat/corrosion
colour   hardness   conductivity   appearance   flexibility

Having identified the properties of the material, you should then consider its availability. This will depend on both the material (e.g. acrylic, mild-steel, beech, card), and also its form (e.g. sheet, tube or block). When you specify the form you should give accurate sizes. In choosing materials you should also consider the cost. For example the cost of precious metals or specialist electronic components might lead you to reconsider.

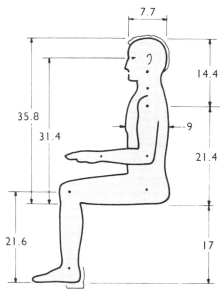

fig 1.48. Anthropometric data

Size and shape

These key points will greatly influence your final design. You will almost certainly need to consider how your proposed solution will come into contact with people. This will affect sizes, ranging from printed letters that can be read easily, to the height of a table.

The study of how objects, systems, and the environment can be designed to fit in with people is called **ergonomics**. It is important for deciding such things as the best height for a computer screen, or the smallest size for calculator buttons which can easily be pressed one at a time.

In order to design solutions which fit in with people, you will need to know human body measurements. These are called anthropometric data.

It is also important to consider how your proposed solution will look in its environment. When designing your solution you will therefore need to consider its overall size in relation to other objects.

Appearance

A highly functional product which looks awful is unlikely to sell, as is an attractive product which doesn't function. The visual qualities which give a sense of beauty to a product are called **aesthetics.** Aesthetic values vary with different cultures and within cultures, and fashion and styles change. It is wise to recognise fashion and style, but remember that there will always be differing tastes and opinions.

Safety

When developing any product, it is important that safety is considered throughout. Appropriate safety standards must be applied to the design.

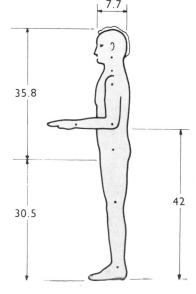

fig 1.49.

STAGE 6: PLANNING

Once the developing and refining of the proposed solution is completed, it is necessary to plan the realisation. Planning is done in two parts.

The first is concerned with the creation of working or production drawings, and the second involves planning to realisation. The working drawings are usually of a formal nature, perhaps in orthographic projection. They should show each part and how it fits together, and give details of all dimensions. This detailed planning through drawings is crucial, and it is essential that such drawings can be understood by others. As well as the working drawings there may sometimes be a presentation drawing which helps to convey the complete idea in its final form. With the final drawings there should be a list of materials to be used, and their sizes. This was traditionally called a **cutting list** and is now called a **parts** or **component list.**

Planning and organising the realisation requires considerable thought. At this stage it is wise to recognise the amount of time available for realisation, because working to a time limit is crucial in stage 7. It is important to write out a procedural flow chart for realisation and a time schedule. These may then need adjusting to fit your time limit. It may help to set a short time limit for each part. Planning can help you identify in advance materials and equipment required.

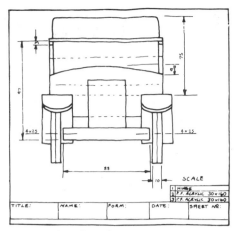
fig 1.50. A working drawing

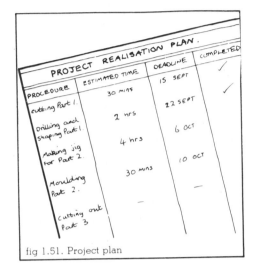
fig 1.51. Project plan

STAGE 7: REALISATION

This is one of the most exciting but time-consuming stages. It can also be one of the most frustrating if the planning stage has not been done thoroughly. The methods of realisation in CDT will vary from paint and ink on some dimensional graphics, to heavy construction in perhaps timber, to an electronic system using mass manufactured components. Good design will often involve the use of several different media together to create a sound solution.

The realisation of the solution could include models, prototypes, artefacts or systems. Throughout the realisation there are likely to be problems which were not envisaged, and this can often lead to redesigning parts of the solution.

In the realisation stage it may become necessary to design special tools to help you make the solution. The following are common examples:

Templates are made so that they can be marked around or cut around to repeat a shape several times.

Jigs are tools which are made to allow an operation to be repeated accurately, for example drilling or sawing.

Formers are shapes which are made to allow materials to form around them. This is especially common in plastics.

Moulds are shapes into which materials are usually poured to repeat the shape. It is often necessary to make a pattern first from which the mould can then be made. The pattern is almost identical to the required component.

The making of these specialist tools takes time, but if they are well made it is usually worthwhile. If a project is part of the course work for your examination, you must keep these tools for assessment.

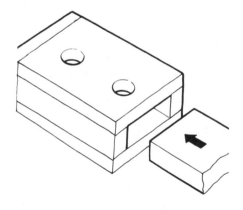
fig 1.52. A jig

When carrying out the realisation there are some common ground rules:

1. Use tools, equipment and processes in a careful, safe manner.

2. Use materials economically, for example, do not cut material from the centre of a sheet.

3. Always measure and mark out materials accurately.

4. Aim for a high quality finish at all times.

5. On completion, always treat the end product with care.

6. Record briefly the procedures for making in a diary. This will help you learn from your errors and should help you in the future.

7. Try to set yourself small tasks within the project, so that you can assess your progress more easily.

8. Realisation of your solutions should be exciting, so enjoy it.

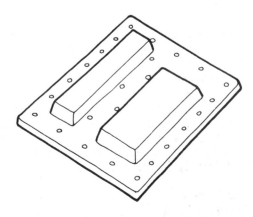
fig 1.53. Former for moulding acrylic

11

STAGE 8: TESTING

Testing the solution is an important part of designing. It will discover whether your solution works, and if so, how well. Testing may be functional, seeing how well your solution works by trying it out, or it may involve repeated tests, checking your solution's reliability. This can be done by carefully setting up an experiment to discover whether the solution meets the requirements in the brief. Testing should place the solution in its intended environment, and observe how it works.

However, if the test could cause an accident, it may be wise to carry out a simulation. This involves testing in an artificial way which is similar to the real situation.

Testing can also concern the appearance of your solution. Here good testing will involve getting opinions. You might find it helpful to draw up a list of questions on a response sheet.

When you have completed your testing, your results may include the need to start designing again, to improve the solution further still.

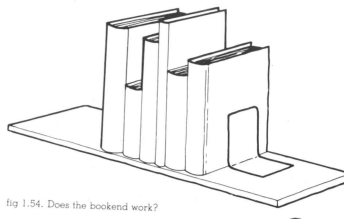

fig 1.54. Does the bookend work?

STAGE 9: EVALUATION

The final stage is concerned with assessing the whole process, from deciding upon the task, creating ideas, and leading to a fully realised design which has been tested. The evaluation should be critical in identifying faults in the process, lessons you have learnt for the future, and possible improvement to your design. Throughout an evaluation, it is wise to be constructive. The following questions may be helpful:

1. Did I use my time effectively?
2. What are the strengths and weaknesses in my design?
3. How can I improve my design?
4. Did I overcome the problems which arose during the project?
5. Where the planning and working drawings adequate?
6. What are the views of others about the solutions?
7. How would I tackle it again doing the same or similar projects?

On completing the project it is clear that you are now ready to begin again, because there is no doubt the solution could be improved. This shows clearly that designing is a fully integrated process.

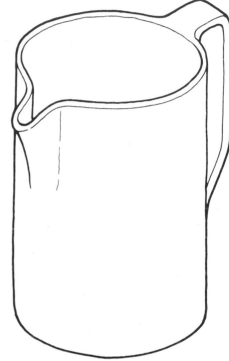

fig 1.55. How would you evaluate and improve this product?

DESIGN FOLDER LAYOUT

Examination boards are likely to suggest a layout for design folders and this should be followed. If no structure is provided, the layout opposite may help you organise your work so it can form a piece of effective communication.

Throughout the design folder, all pages should be named and numbered, with different sections clearly identified.

The presentation is important, but rough sketches should be included to show your thoughts. Do not put research booklets or leaflets in without explaining their value to your design work. Do put letters written and received in the folder. If possible use photographs to explain stages of modelling and making which may be lost in a final solution.

1. Title page – your name, title of project, school and year.
2. Contents page.
3. Design brief.
4. Investigation – analysis, research data and specification.
5. Ideas and their evaluation.
6. Development.
7. Planning.
8. Working drawings.
9. Making – may be shown with sketches or photographs.
10. Testing.
11. Evaluation – including report diary if used.

DESIGN AND COMMUNICATION IN SOCIETY

Examples of communication can be seen almost anywhere in society today. In this chapter we will be concerned mainly with the area of **visual** communication, that which we can see, rather than the communication that takes place through other senses, such as touch and smell. Every day we receive messages from our environment through books, signs, illustrations, television, photographs, magazines, advertising and the like.

All of these rely heavily on factors such as colour, shape, form, size, position and style to pass on their messages. Many have been cleverly designed so that they attract or even demand your attention. Others are more subtle in their approach, but effective nevertheless. However, not all methods of communication are good; we clearly take in some messages and not others.

In fact, examples of the passing on of messages, ideas and information in society are endless. However, in order to give a broad flavour of the type of work that can be found in this area, a number of situations have been selected and explored briefly for examples of design and communication. In Design and Communication courses you may be able to take other situations and explore them more thoroughly. The situations chosen are:

HOME

WORK

SCHOOL

SHOPPING

DRESS

THE ROAD

SPORT

TELEVISION

fig 2.1. A crowded railway station

First, let us look at fig 2.1, which shows a railway station during rush hour. It is crowded with people trying to find their way. Some are waiting for trains, but others may be searching for a restaurant, a timetable, a taxi, a toilet, a ticket machine or even the way out!

Whatever they are looking for, there should be good examples of communication to help them. How many can you find in the picture, and do you think they are communicating effectively?

HOME

The home has many good examples of design and communication on display. This section will concentrate on two main areas, but you will certainly be able to think of others that you find interesting.

First, we shall look at products that are purchased regularly for the home such as food, drink and cleaning materials. Second, we shall look at the communication found on household appliances such as cookers, vacuum cleaners, refrigerators and washing machines.

Fig 2.2 shows a great number of examples of communication that can be found on products bought for the home. We need to ask ourselves why these particular products have been selected from the huge range available in the supermarket. If all were of equal quality and price, then part of the answer has to be found in the **packaging**.

Packaging must not only appeal to the purchaser, it must also reflect the type of product it contains. It must be factually correct in the way in which it describes the product, or the manufacturer may be liable (it could also be very dangerous if instructions are not clear and precise). This does not mean that it cannot emphasise a particular point and play down another. However, the design that influences you to buy a packet of Oxo cubes (fig 2.3) may not sell many bottles of wine (fig 2.4).

Some of the factors that determine whether a packaging is successful or not are the colour, product name, lettering and illustrations used. All are important individually, but in the final design they come together to create the correct **image** to sell the product.

The right colour, or combination of colours, is very important to the product's image. There are certain traditions concerning the use of colour. Pastel colours are often used for baby products, whereas a combination of primary and secondary colours (red, yellow, blue, green, purple and orange) are attractive for young children's toys. Blue is seldom used in food packaging, probably because there are not many blue foods. White is often used in the packaging of dairy foods, suggesting cleanliness, freshness and purity. You must be very careful when selecting colours for packages because it can make a vast difference to the appearance of the end product.

The name gives the product its identity. It may be simple so that it can be easily remembered (as in fig 2.3). It

fig 2.2. Products bought for the home

is unlikely that there is anyone who has not heard of Oxo. However, the style in which the letters are written is also important because it can vary greatly from simple to elaborate, funny to aggressive or traditional to futuristic.

The choice of lettering is important because it can relate to the product. This is shown in fig 2.4, where the lettering is well suited for the label of a high-quality bottle of wine. The style shown in fig 2.3 would simply not have created the right image.

Fig 2.6 shows the main control panel found on a washing machine. It is used to select the required programme from the wide range available. This is essential if the clothes are to be washed correctly. A large amount of information has to be given in this small space and it is vital that it is given clearly. This is achieved by symbols and numbers that can be recognised easily.

fig 2.3.

fig 2.4.

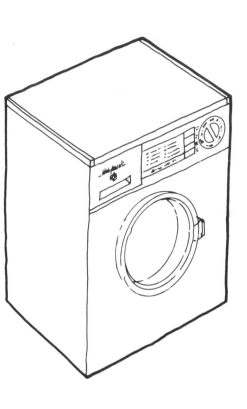

fig 2.5. Washing machine

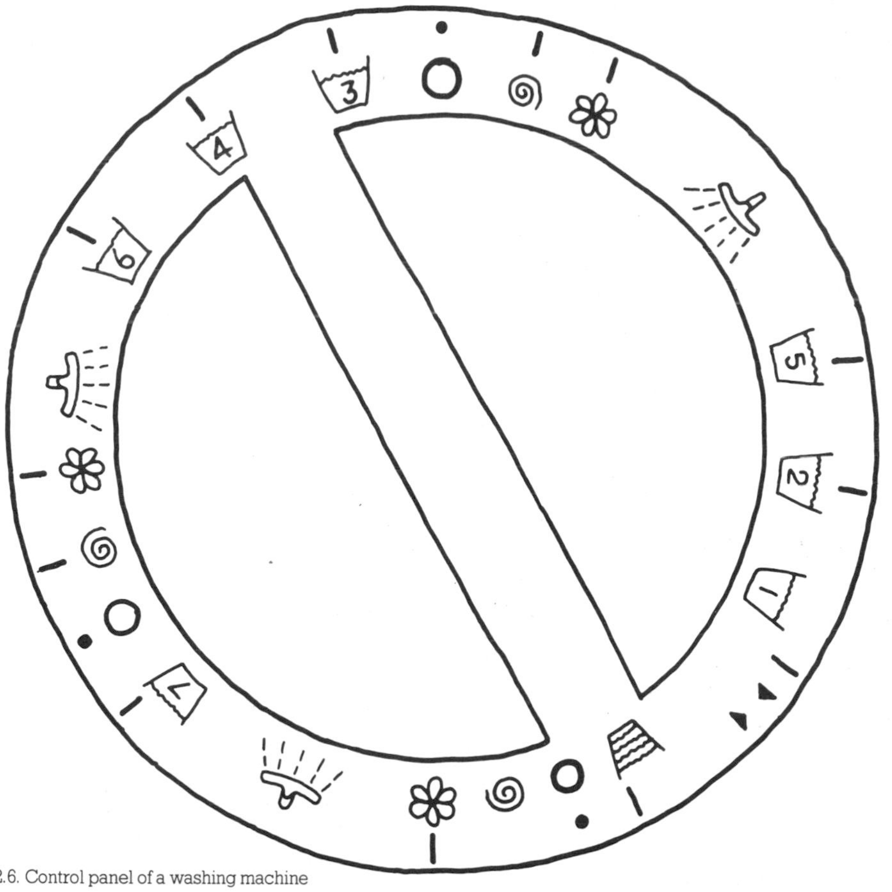

fig 2.6. Control panel of a washing machine

You will find examples of this kind of communication on many household appliances such as cookers, food processors, refrigerators, vacuum cleaners and of course washing machines. There is rarely sufficient room to write the information out in full, and, even if there were, it is doubtful if we would find the time to read it. What is required is something that can be recognised instantly and acted upon.

A clear symbol is important, so unnecessary detail must be excluded, and attention drawn to the facts essential to the message. Colour can play an important role in focusing one's attention onto a particular point. Everyone knows that when an electrical switch has the red part showing it is in the 'on' position. This colour suggests danger, and almost demands to be turned 'off' if not in use.

Four of the symbols from the washing machine control panel have been enlarged and shown in figs 2.7 to 2.10. These are used to show the operator what task the machine is performing. Fig 2.7 shows that the machine is rinsing and the symbol for this is, in effect, a shower head with water passing through it. Fig 2.8 shows the temperature wash that the machine is undertaking. Figs 2.9 and 2.10 are spirals and show that the machine is spinning. The broken spiral shows a slower spin speed very effectively.

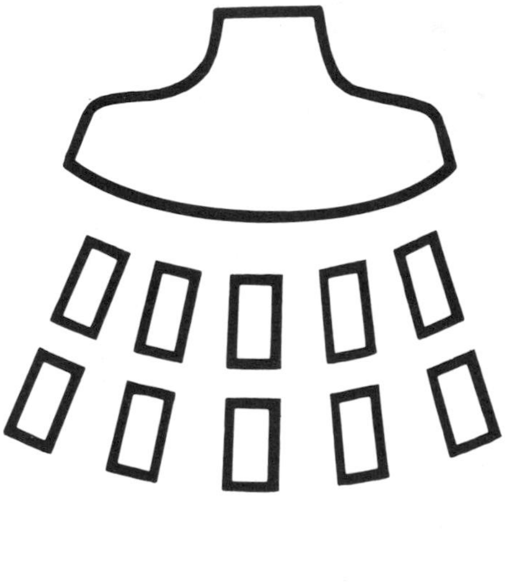

fig 2.7. Rinse symbol

fig 2.8. Temperature symbol

fig 2.9. Slow spin symbol

fig 2.10. Fast spin symbol

WORK

There are many good examples of communication to be found in any working environment. A number are shown in the chapter which deals with Environmental Drawing. Work situations vary tremendously and it is usual for the type of communication to be specific to a particular situation. However, most forms of communication are aimed at improving safety, efficiency or the quality of the **working environment**. This section will look at communication in three very different work situations. All will show different types of communication, but should give you some idea of the range of communication that can be found in work situations.

In a factory there may be hundreds of employees and it is essential that good communication is maintained at all times. Fig 2.11 shows scenes from a factory where you will find many examples of communication, including 'no smoking' signs, operating instructions, walkway and firefighting equipment signs. With so many employees in one place and noise levels that may be very high, it is essential that people can understand clearly any information that is relevant to them. A form of communication is also achieved through the uniforms that people wear. This gives a corporate identity, but also serves as a way of distinguishing between types of workers – trainees, supervisors and so on.

There are many examples of communication to be found in agriculture. If you look inside a tractor cab, as shown in fig 2.13, you can see that it is an excellent example of design by the manufacturer communicating with the operator. Other areas of communication that you

fig 2.11.

could look at in agriculture are logos and colour schemes found on farm machinery and the communication that is found in the packaging of sprays, chemicals and drugs. Some of these are highly dangerous and, therefore, communication concerning their use must be effective.

Perhaps the simplest form of communication is that which is found in identifying animals. You may have seen sheep with a coloured mark upon their backs, cows with a metal tag through their ears and chickens with a ring around their legs. These are effective ways of communicating

information concerning the breeding, age, weight and of course the owner of the animal.

Banks and building societies have many good examples of communication on display. From the moment you enter one you are directed towards a service point by the way in which the interior of the building is designed. Advertising is also very important because it is designed to attract customers to the various loan and investment plans. An example of the symbol used by one of the large high street banks is shown in fig 2.14.

fig 2.12. No smoking sign

fig 2.13. Interior of a tractor cab

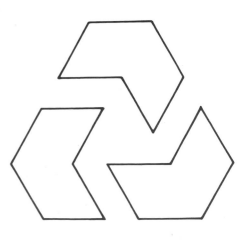

fig 2.14. Nat-West sign

fig 2.15. Modern vending machine

A common feature in many work situations is the refreshment break. Here it is essential to have a range of products that are readily available and can be dispensed quickly. The type of machine shown in fig 2.15 is becoming increasingly popular because it is very easy to operate and can offer a wide range of products. A drinks machine can be sited in any suitable space providing both water and electricity supplies are available. Other types of machine that dispense chocolate bars and similiar snacks can also be found.

The fascia of any drinks machine needs to show clearly what is available and its price. It must also tell the customer exactly how these items can be obtained. In order to achieve this a very precise layout has to be designed. Fig 2.16 shows an example of this. Details of the design are shown in figs 2.17 and 2.18.

The design of these machines has to take into account the necessary flexibility that is required to provide different products at varying prices. For instance, there are several combinations of drinks that must be catered for when offering tea and coffee: tea with sugar, tea without sugar, coffee with sugar, coffee without sugar and black coffee. This can become even more complicated when such things as hot chocolate, a variety of soups and a whole range of cold drinks are also available.

These machines are also designed to take a range of coins such as one, two, five, ten, twenty and fifty pence pieces. This allows the drinks to be individually priced and paid for in a number of ways.

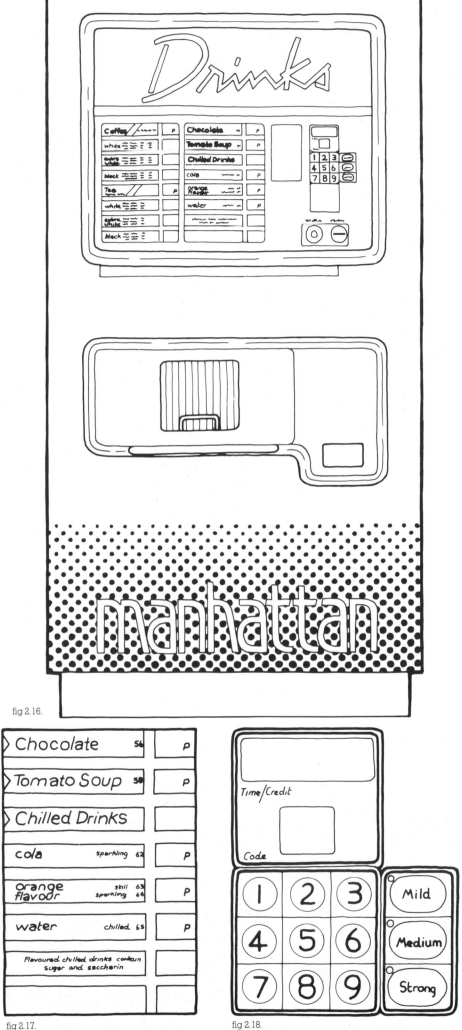

fig 2.16.

fig 2.17.

fig 2.18.

SCHOOL

Communication in schools has to be good, as it does in any highly organised establishment used by many people. Without it, at the very best we would find ourselves to be less effective and at the worst it could result in absolute chaos. It is beneficial to pupils, teachers and parents that good lines of communication are established.

There are many examples of communication within the school, but perhaps the one that should have the highest initial impact is the school entrance. In fact, these are often poor examples of communication, leaving visitors unsure of which door to use and whom to contact.

One of the first things you will be given when you go to a new school is a **timetable** (fig 2.20). This tells you what subjects you will be taking, with which teachers and in which rooms. Most will be laid out so that you can see clearly what subjects you have on the different days of the week. Although the style of timetables may vary from school to school, it is basically a very effective piece of communication because it gives a lot of information in a very concise form, while remaining very understandable.

Reports are another important line of communication because they inform parents of just how well their child is performing in a particular subject. The traditional system of giving these marks in grades is still used in many schools.

If you look around your school you will find **firefighting apparatus**. This may be an alarm system, fire extinguishers or fire blankets. A considerable amount of thought goes into the design and positioning of this apparatus. You will notice that the colour red is used extensively as it is in many other places where it is necessary to bring the article to one's attention. You will also see that any instructions for apparatus are written clearly in a sequential fashion so that they can be followed easily in the case of an emergency.

fig 2.19. Communication in school

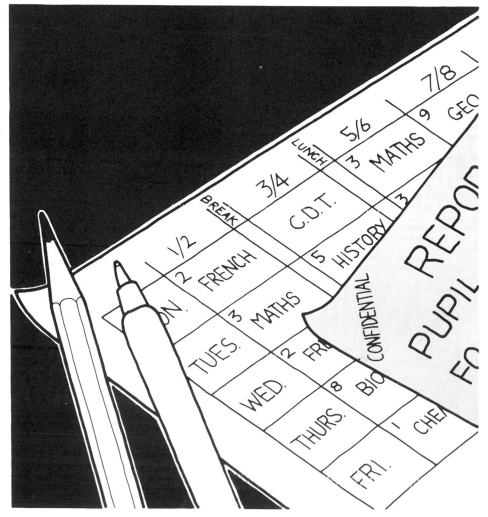

fig 2.20. School timetable and report

The **school badge** is perhaps one of the most easily recognisable and widely used forms of communication that a school has. It helps to give the school, and the pupils that wear it, an identity.

The example given in fig 2.21 shows a typical school badge and how it can be constructed from four arcs. The difficulty is in finding the centres of these arcs. These can be found by using a centre line and, in the case of arc A, drawing two 110 mm arcs with their centres at points B and C. Where these two intersect will be the centre on which your compass must be placed to draw arc A. This process can then be repeated for the remaining three arcs that make up the shield.

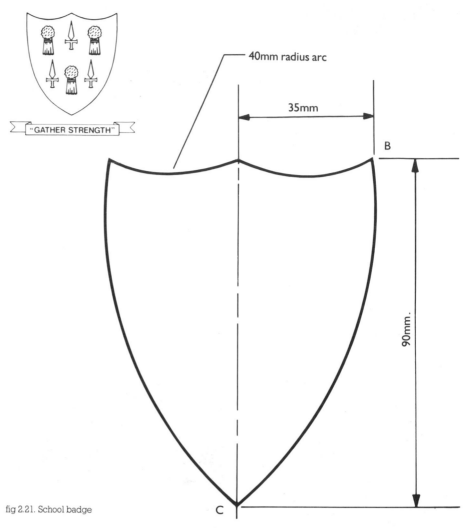

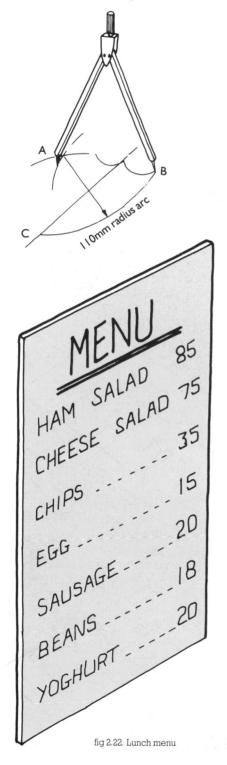

fig 2.21. School badge

fig 2.22. Lunch menu

Any school canteen relies heavily upon good communication. The canteen staff do not have sufficient time to tell each pupil the price of the items on offer. The easiest way of communicating this information is to place a menu, similar to the one shown in fig 2.22, in a suitable position. Exactly what is the best position will vary, but clearly it needs to be where it can be seen while people are waiting, giving them time to decide what they wish to purchase. The menu must be designed so that it is easy to read and can be changed when new dishes are on offer or the price alters.

You will also find a very simple, but nevertheless necessary, form of communication on classroom doors. Timetables usually refer to room numbers and it is essential that these numbers are displayed on the outside so that you can decide which room to enter.

fig 2.23. A school door

SHOPPING

There are many good examples of communication to be seen in the retail trade. We can find examples across the whole spectrum of retail outlets. This can vary from the large supermarket (fig 2.24) to the small village shop and from market stalls (fig 2.25) to vans that travel around the countryside selling their goods. The forms of communication on display will vary enormously.

We must also consider the very wide range of **products** that is being offered for sale. These include electrical goods, do-it-yourself materials, food and clothes, to name but a few. It is important to realise that the communication that is effective and appropriate in one situation may not be in another. For example, the very simple form of communication that we may see on a market stall (pieces of card with the name and price written on) would not be very successful in selling high-quality clothes. A much more refined **marketing strategy** is required in this situation.

The real area of interest in design and communication in the retail trade is the communication that confronts you when you walk into any retail outlet, i.e. the colour, the lighting, the displays, the cash tills, the uniforms worn by assistants, the shop layout.

The main aim of this communication is to make it easier for the potential buyer to buy. Therefore, it must make it easier for him to find the goods he wants, easier to see if the goods are what he wants, what price it is, what size it is, what colour it is and so on. If

fig 2.24. Interior of a modern supermarket

these things are not communicated effectively, then the retail outlet may be selling fewer goods than it might otherwise have done. Some customers may ask an assistant for help, but many will not. They prefer the answers to their questions to be obvious so that they can make a decision without being pressurised by a sales assistant.

From the moment you walk into a shop you will be receiving messages. Sometimes you will already have an idea of what you wish to buy and the first thing you need to know is where to find it. This may be fairly straightforward in a small shop, but in larger shops you may have to refer to a display or map. These signs may be

suspended from the ceiling or the goods arranged in such a way as to point you in the right direction. Colour and lighting can play an important role in this. Just how well you are led to the appropriate area is a most important feature of modern shop design.

Fig 2.26 shows a selection of **shopping bags** that are given away, or sometimes sold, at supermarkets. This is obviously most helpful to the customer because it gives him a way of taking his shopping home. It is also beneficial to the supermarket because it is a form of advertising for them. Note the way in which their name, logo or colour scheme are always clearly printed on the side.

fig 2.25. Market stalls

fig 2.26.

Direction signs and **price tags** are another important feature of modern shop design. Sometimes signs are suspended from the ceiling of supermarkets, showing what is on sale directly below that sign. This is a good position to put a sign because it is not possible to see all the goods that are on offer due to shelving that may block one's view. By looking up at the signs you can immediately go to the area that is of interest. It is important that the lettering on these signs is clear and large as they usually have to be read from a distance.

Often a display shows what goods are available on each floor of a supermarket. This is vital because it avoids customers having to walk about unnecessarily. It is usual to group products in a logical order. For instance, all the food may be in one area and the household goods and clothes in a separate area.

Sometimes this information is put into a map form. These are often used in shopping precincts where many shops are housed in one large building. A map should make it very clear to the customer exactly what is available and where. You could try to draw up a similiar map for your local shopping precinct.

Fig 2.27 shows a selection of **labels** found on products in supermarkets. You will find many other different types of labels in supermarkets. They vary enormously in their design depending on what particular job they have to do.

Fig 2.28 shows a typical **sales uniform** worn by a shop assistant. This helps to inform the customers of who is working in the shop and who is shopping. It also gives a smarter image if all the workers are wearing the same type of clothes.

Communication in the retail trade is highly varied and visually exciting. This page should have given you some areas to consider when looking for examples of design and communication in the retail trade.

fig 2.27.

fig 2.28. Sales uniform

21

DRESS

You will find that in most of your clothes the manufacturer has left you some information about the product. This is necessary because long after the original packaging has been thrown away you may want to know what materials the article is made from and how it should be washed. Fig 2.29 shows a typical label that you may find fastened into a garment. It gives washing instructions (with a symbol relating to those found on washing machines), the size and country of origin.

Figs 2.30, 2.31 and 2.32 show other symbols found in clothes. They are very bold symbols and should be instantly recognisable when sorting through washing. There are many similar symbols that are effectively passing on a message from the manufacturer to you.

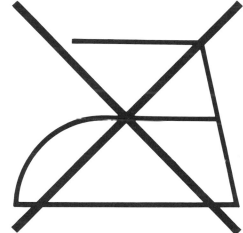

	MACHINE	HAND WASH
4 50°	HAND HOT MEDIUM WASH	HAND HOT
	COLD RINSE SHORT SPIN / DRIP DRY	

MADE IN ENGLAND SIZE M

fig 2.29. Wash label

fig 2.30. Dry clean symbol

fig 2.31. Pure new wool symbol

fig 2.32. Do not iron

fig 2.33.

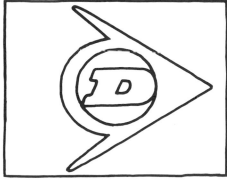

fig 2.34.

Manufacturers are content to leave these types of messages hidden away inside garments. However, they are keen to incorporate their **trademark** or name in prominent positions. This is very useful for the manufacturer because he is getting a certain amount of free advertising whenever he sells a product.

The **symbols** and **logos** shown in figs 2.33 and 2,34 should be familiar and are associated with good-quality sports equipment. It has become highly desirable to be seen wearing garments bearing these kinds of logos and they have, therefore, become a strong selling feature for the product.

Footwear may seem to be rather a strange area in which to look for examples of communication. However, there are many examples of communication in footwear, though we shall only look at three.

First, the shoe itself has a message to pass on. Its colour, style and the materials it is made from all have something to say. The kind of message that a pair of sports shoes gives to a potential buyer is different from that given by a pair of fashion shoes. Shoes can appear comfortable, light, colourful or practical.

Second, most shoes are boxed and stacked in a shop so that only the ends of the boxes are visible. The label from a shoe box must pass on a very clear message to the shop assistant. It must indicate the size and fitting of the shoe. It must also show the style, colour and material the shoe is made from. The label of a shoe box is shown in Fig 2.36 and you can see that it gives all the necessary information. All these markings are essential to the shop assistant so that the correct pair of shoes can be selected without opening many boxes. A **bar code** allows the sale to be registered quickly at the till, thus allowing reordering of stock to be carried out quickly and efficiently.

Third, once the shoes have been taken out of the box it is essential that they can be recognised and returned to the correct box. Pairs of shoes must also be kept together. This information is usually given either inside the shoe, or underneath it, as in fig 2.37.

There are other areas of design and communication concerned with footwear that can be studied. Perhaps you could look at the ways in which shoes are displayed in shops, advertising of shoes on television or patterns on the soles of shoes.

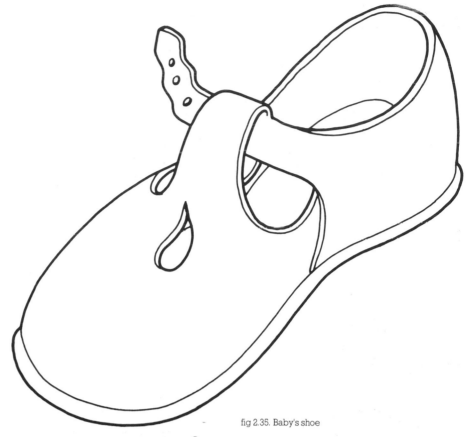

fig 2.35. Baby's shoe

001   8829   55   065

09

8829 55C   FIT   SIZE   6½

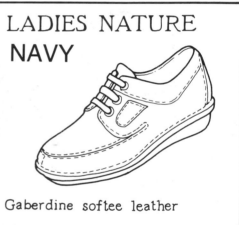

LADIES NATURE NAVY

Gaberdine softee leather

fig 2.36. Shoe box label

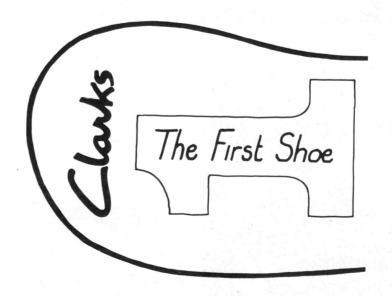

Clarks   The First Shoe

fig 2.37. Shoe information

THE ROAD

Britain's roads are subjected to a tremendous volume of traffic and huge numbers of people every day. In order to make sure this all moves as smoothly as possible, certain rules have to be made, and obeyed by all users. These rules are outlined in the current highway code. They are communicated by means of **signs**, positioned at the side of the road, and **markings** on the road surface itself. They are purely visual.

It is vital that the information, or messages being sent, are understood immediately so that accidents can be avoided. Many vehicles will be travelling at speed and the information must be presented in such a way that it can be picked out easily from other features of the environment. Colour, shape and positioning have an important role to play in this. Figs 2.39, 2.40 and 2.41 show examples of communication that can be found on the street. They must be constructed to

fig 2.38.

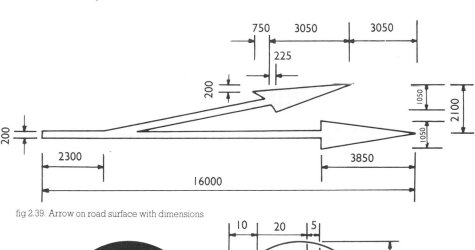

fig 2.39. Arrow on road surface with dimensions

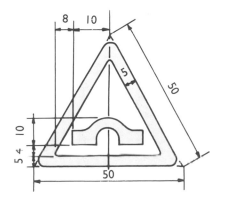

fig 2.40. No left turn sign with dimensions

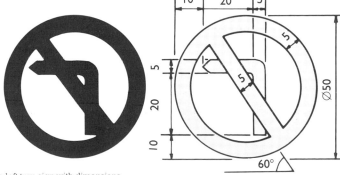

fig 2.41. Hump back bridge sign with dimensions

certain sizes, as fig 2.39 shows, so that they can be seen by the passing motorist.

The traffic lights in fig 2.38 are an example of a sign that changes. It is interesting to note that red is again associated with danger – you must stop – and green associated with go. On several occasions in this chapter we have referred to the use of red and green as colours which are instantly recognisable as opposites. In fact they are on opposite sides of the colour circle and are therefore known as contrasting colours.

Signs have been divided into five main groups according to the type of instructions they give. All rely heavily upon positioning, shape and colour to get their message across. For example, nearly all round signs with a red border are **prohibitive**: they prevent you from doing something. Round, blue signs give **compulsory orders** such as 'turn left ahead'; triangular signs with a red border are **warning signs**, such as 'crossroads ahead'. Signs that give **directions** are mostly rectangular, but the colours vary. On primary routes they have a green background, they have a white background on other routes and signs are blue-bordered in local places. **Information** signs are again mainly rectangular, but rely on a variety of colours, with blue perhaps being most dominant.

You will no doubt have seen many examples of communication on the outsides of lorries, vans and buses, but do not forget aeroplanes, trains, boats and hovercraft. This is a very important area of communication because it can provide moving advertising. Much of it is painted in bright and distinctive colours. Fig 2.42 shows the trademark of a well-known car manufacturer. It is a very distinctive and instantly recognisable symbol.

Many examples of design and communication can be seen in the interiors of modern vehicles. Fig 2.43 shows a typical instrumentation panel that is designed to provide the driver with all the information required during a journey. It is laid out in such a manner as to make everything visible to the driver from the comfortable driving position. This is most useful in terms of safety and convenience.

We can generally divide the information given into two types. First, there are the things one needs to know in order to operate the vehicle, such as the position of switches for lights, windscreen wipers and heater.

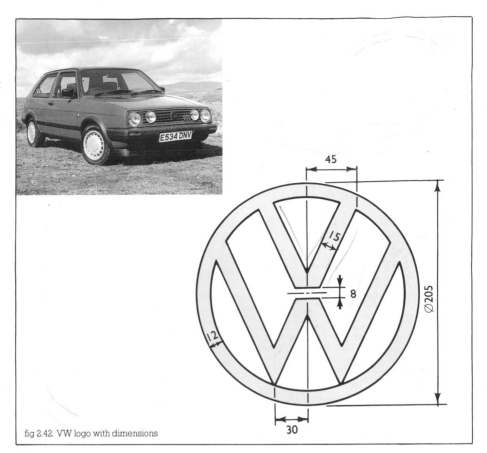

fig 2.42. VW logo with dimensions

fig 2.43. Interior of a modern car

Second, there are warning displays for such things as oil level, engine temperature and worn brake shoes.

This information is communicated by means of very easily recognisable symbols, as shown in figs 2.44 to 2.47, which are often illuminated to show the 'on' and 'off' states. It is important that the information is given in a simple form for two reasons. First, a driver will not have time to study the panel, but will need to know at a glance what is happening. Second, cars are now made and sold on worldwide markets and their operating instructions need to be universally understood. This has led many manufacturers to use drawings to communicate rather than words that may change from country to country.

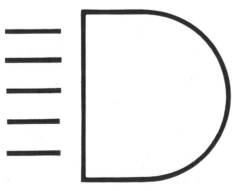

fig 2.44. Headlamp symbol

fig 2.45. Oil symbol

fig 2.46. Handbrake symbol

fig 2.47. Windscreen wiper symbol

SPORT

There are many examples of design and communication in sport. They include methods of defining **playing areas**, the **aims of the sport**, the **state of play**, the **teams** or **competitors** and **spectator facilities**. It is essential to all concerned that this information is given in a clear and precise manner. Imagine a game of rugby where the playing areas are not marked clearly or a horse race with all the jockeys wearing the same colour jerseys. Obviously great confusion would result and the sport would suffer.

Playing areas on grass are usually marked in white so that they stand out against the green background. On other types of outdoor surface, such as tarmacadam, the lines may be different colours, but they should always be a colour that can be seen clearly.

Indoor playing areas tend to have many different coloured lines marked on them. An indoor facility, such as a sports hall, has to be fully used and is therefore marked out with several different playing areas (fig 2.48). Figs 2.49, 2.50 and 2.51 show (in metres) the individual playing courts for badminton, basketball and tennis. To mark these onto a playing surface will require many of the skills that you have developed during design and communication lessons, such as measuring and constructing angles. In order that they can all be marked out in one sports hall, different coloured lines are used. It may be red for

fig 2.48. Sports centre hall

badminton, green for tennis and yellow for basketball. It is suprising just how quickly one can adjust to the particular set of lines that are relevant to the game being played.

In many sports it is necessary to inform the spectators, players and perhaps even the referee of exactly what the state of play is. This is

often achieved by means of a scoreboard that can be seen by everyone. The design and complexity of these scoreboards will depend on the sport concerned, but they can range from an electronic scoreboard to a chalkboard with the score written on it.

fig 2.49. Badminton court

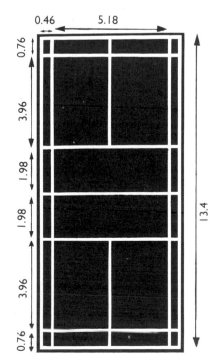

fig 2.50. Basketball court

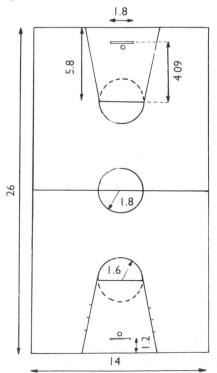

fig 2.51. Tennis court

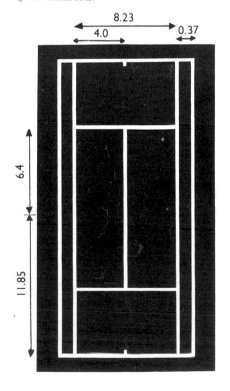

Having considered the way in which communication is used in sport in general, we will now take a look at three sports in greater depth. The sports selected are motor racing, horse racing and basketball. These have been chosen because they are very different types of sports and should give some idea of the very wide range of communication that can be found in this area.

In motor racing we can look at the ways in which the individual drivers and cars are identified. In some cases this is achieved by numbers alone, but more often than not a colour scheme, which incorporates the names and logos of **sponsors** (people who pay to have their name on a car) is used as well. Further examples of communication in motor racing can be seen in the way the track is marked out, advertising around the circuit, boards that are held out to show lap times and the flag system that marshalls use to communicate with drivers. It is universally understood that a black and white chequered flag signals a victory, but there is also a range of flags to cover such incidents as accidents and oil spillages. All must be identified while the driver is travelling at high speed.

In horse racing the main problem is in identifying the individual horses and riders. This may be impossible from a distance unless the jockeys wear distinctive jerseys and caps similiar to those shown in fig 2.53. These are in fact the colours of the horse owners, and are often very colourful and quite complicated in their design, with

fig 2.52.

fig 2.54.

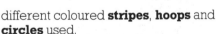

fig 2.53.

different coloured **stripes**, **hoops** and **circles** used.

In basketball, the main area of design and communication to be considered is the way in which the two teams are identified. This is achieved through coloured **playing kits** that are numbered and often include a sponsor's name or emblem. This is clearly shown in fig 2.54, where it is easy to see which players play for which team.

All sports have examples of design and communication that can be identified and studied. In some sports they may be obvious, while in others they may take a little more searching out, but it is essential that we realise that the quality of this benefits all concerned.

TELEVISION

Television is perhaps the most influential form of communication today. Although much of the information is given by the transmission of sound, there is still a large amount of purely visual communication. To find out exactly how much television relies upon visual communication turn down the volume and look at the picture. Notice the **colour**, the **lettering**, the **set layout**, the **costumes**, the **lighting** and the **computer graphics**. All of these are providing us with some of the most exciting examples of design and communication available today.

Many programmes begin with a short scene, perhaps involving computer graphics, that will give a flavour of what the programme is about. This is nearly always accompanied by music, which is usually catchy and easy to remember. The idea is to give the programme an identity. An example of a still from a computer graphics sequence can be seen in fig 2.56. This is part of an introduction to a sports programme.

At the end of a programme it is necessary to communicate clearly who has appeared in it, or helped in its making. This is usually achieved by showing a list of names and their particular role in the making of the programme. A programme without an effective beginning and ending would lose much of its identity.

The location in which programmes are filmed is important. If this is an outside location, a suitable site must be carefully selected and then used effectively. Programmes that are filmed in a studio owe much of their success to the set designer. The quiz programme shown in fig 2.57 features many examples of design and

fig 2.55. TV programme being made

communication. The score must be displayed, the names of the teams, the prizes that are on offer and so on. These must be communicated in an interesting manner so that some excitement can be created for the viewers and participants.

Advertising on television is big business, because the cost of showing an advertisement is high and the audience it reaches runs into millions. The advertisement must help to sell the product in the short time, perhaps less that 30 seconds, that is available. Communication in this situation has to create a quick impact and convince the viewer to buy. Some

advertisements have managed to do this very effectively and have almost become a part of television history, making their characters famous and synonymous with the product.

Television stations also operate their own **information services** such as Ceefax and Oracle. These carry a large number of pages giving information on a wide range of subjects. You can select the one that is of interest to you by punching in the correct number on the control unit. Each page is an excellent example of visual communication, which is essential, because there is no sound used.

fig 2.56. Computer graphics sequence

fig 2.57. Set of a quiz programme

fig 2.58. TV information screen

Having considered communication in television across a wide field, let us now look at one area in detail. The one chosen is the broadcasting of **weather information**. This is very important because many people rely upon this service. Farmers and fishermen are two examples, but all of us benefit from an accurate weather forecast.

Weather reports are usually short, perhaps two or three minutes, and in this time they have to give a picture of the weather that the whole country can expect over the following 24 hours. You may also see local weather reports from time to time dealing with the particular area in which you live. However, the general forecast must give a picture of what can be expected regardless of where you live.

This is achieved by having a large **map** of the country as shown in fig 2.59 onto which **symbols** are placed. It is important that viewers can recognise the messages that these symbols are giving because they may be changed several times during a broadcast. It may begin with the evening weather, then the expected overnight temperatures, followed by the daytime weather and finally the daytime temperatures. Although this sequence is explained, there is a tendency to look at what symbols fall on the particular area in which you live and draw your conclusions from them.

Some common weather symbols are shown in figs 2.60 to 2.63. Fig 2.60 shows the symbol for wind speed and direction. The number in the centre of the circle gives the wind speed in miles per hour. Fig 2.61 shows an example of the symbol that gives the temperature. This is now usually given in centigrade, though in the past fahrenheit was more commonly used. This symbol is yellow for temperatures above freezing and blue for those below. Fig 2.62 shows the symbol for rain showers. The cloud symbol is also used to show cloudy weather with sunny intervals, snow showers and hail showers. Fig 2.63 shows the symbol that we all like to see, sunshine! This is always coloured yellow for very obvious reasons.

fig 2.59. Weather forecast being read

fig 2.60. Wind speed symbol

fig 2.61. Temperature symbol

fig 2.62. Rain symbol

fig 2.63. Sun symbol

EXERCISES

1. A new packaging is to be designed for the chocolate bar shown in fig 2.64. Make sketches to show your ideas of how this bar could be packaged. The suggested name for the bar is 'Choco-Bar'.

2. You are required to design a new control panel for any existing household appliance. You may choose a stereo, a cooker, a microwave, a vacuum cleaner or similar appliance. Produce two drawings, one that shows the existing controls and the second to show your modifications. Include notes to explain the improvements you have made.

3. A vending machine is to be sited in a school common room to sell cold drinks. Make sketches to show your design for a new fascia panel. This must include a coin slot, a place for the drinks to be dispensed, a list of the drinks that are on offer, selection controls and operating instructions.

4. A great number of plastic shopping bags are given away or sold by supermarkets today. Look at some examples of these and consider the ways in which the designer has used them to promote the supermarket. Make a series of sketches to show a new bag for a chain of stores called 'Budget Bonanza'.

5. Many road signs and road markings can be seen on the highway. A new car park is to be opened and the shape of the tarmacadam area is shown in fig 2.65. The entrance and exit are marked, but you are required to design the markings for the tarmacadam surface and any signs that you think may be needed.

6. Produce a design sheet to show your ideas for an illustration of the interior of a new sports car. Draw out your chosen idea in the form in which it would appear in the promotional brochure. You must show all the traditional controls, but you can make this a futuristic car with digital displays and similiar high-technology equipment if you wish.

7. You are required to design a page for Ceefax or Oracle. The subjects you can choose from are sport, travel, cookery or weather. Make sketches to show the layout of your page and the colours that you would use. You may be able to put some of this onto a monitor if you have suitable computer equipment available.

8. Analyse a company logo and try to explain what the designer was trying to convey in the design. Choose a company and design a logo clearly stating what you intend to convey in your design.

9. Show three colour scheme designs for a new Formula One racing team. Trace the outline of the car shown in fig 2.66 and draw your ideas onto it. You may give the racing team any name you wish. Evaluate each of your ideas and state which one you would choose and why.

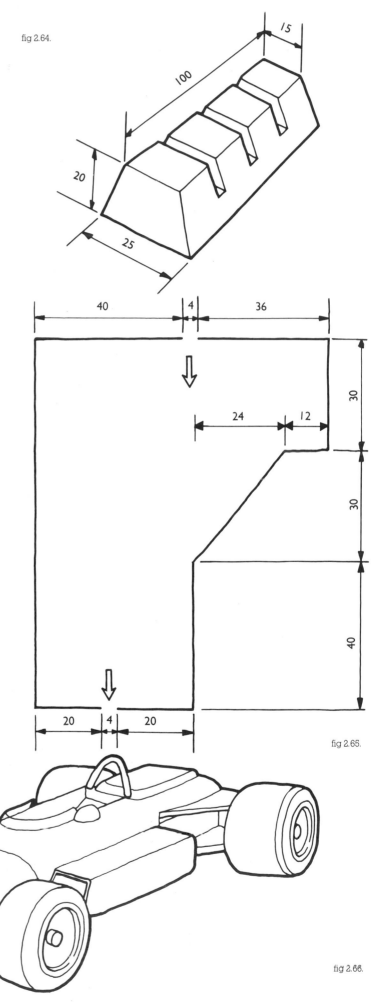

fig 2.64.

fig 2.65.

fig 2.66.

DRAWING AND GRAPHIC SKILLS

Drawing has many purposes, ranging from recording visual information to expressing ideas or feelings.

In CDT you are concerned with drawing as an essential means of **communication**. You may want to communicate with yourself in order to clarify your own thoughts or try to visualise an idea, or you may want to explain to someone else how something works or how it is made (fig 3.1).

In Design and Communication in particular, drawing and graphic skills are very important. You may need to display information or give instructions. This can be done graphically using drawings or diagrams. Design and Communication is concerned with the use of drawing and graphic skills to solve problems and communicate ideas and information.

We begin by using drawing as a means of communication when designing and solving problems. Other graphic skills are then used to help us to realise the chosen solution to the problem.

The importance of graphic skills can be seen by looking at the design

fig 3.1. Discussing a project

process framework in fig 3.2. Different graphic skills and techniques are used in the various stages of the design process.

Graphics are at the heart of both designing and Design and Communication itself. You are surrounded by examples of graphic

work in your everyday lives. Books, magazines, posters and instruction manuals are just some examples of the use of graphic skills, but you must not forget that graphic skills have also been used considerably in designing and producing most of the products around you.

fig 3.2. The design framework

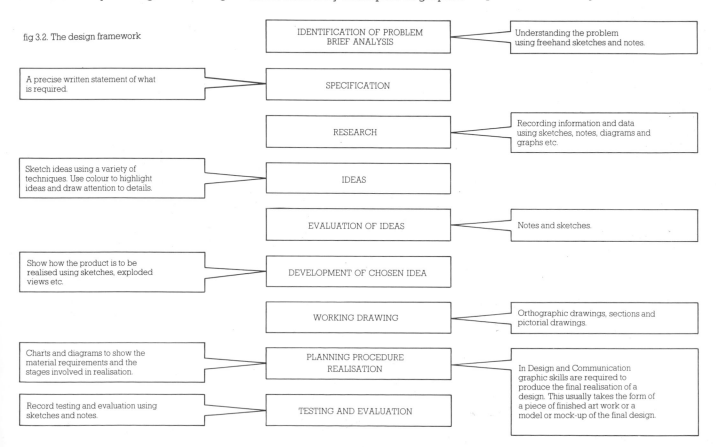

	IDENTIFICATION OF PROBLEM BRIEF ANALYSIS — Understanding the problem using freehand sketches and notes.
A precise written statement of what is required. —	SPECIFICATION
	RESEARCH — Recording information and data using sketches, notes, diagrams and graphs etc.
Sketch ideas using a variety of techniques. Use colour to highlight ideas and draw attention to details. —	IDEAS
	EVALUATION OF IDEAS — Notes and sketches.
Show how the product is to be realised using sketches, exploded views etc. —	DEVELOPMENT OF CHOSEN IDEA
	WORKING DRAWING — Orthographic drawings, sections and pictorial drawings.
Charts and diagrams to show the material requirements and the stages involved in realisation. —	PLANNING PROCEDURE REALISATION — In Design and Communication graphic skills are required to produce the final realisation of a design. This usually takes the form of a piece of finished art work or a model or mock-up of the final design.
Record testing and evaluation using sketches and notes. —	TESTING AND EVALUATION

MATERIALS AND EQUIPMENT

Most work in Design and Communication begins with drawing, and nearly all finished graphic work relies on accurate layout and constructional drawing. A very high standard of work can be achieved using simple and relatively inexpensive materials and equipment.

PAPER

Drawings can be made on a variety of surfaces, but normally paper and card are used in design work.

There are many different types of paper available, ranging from expensive hand or mould made papers to machine made papers. The two main types of paper you are likely to use in Design and Communication are **layout paper** and **cartridge paper**.

Layout paper is very thin, rather like white tracing paper. It is excellent for sketching ideas because it is thin enough to trace through when you need to redraw, yet it is white enough to draw on with pencil, ink or felt tipped pen.

It is rather fragile and therefore not suited to final drawing work or presentation drawing.

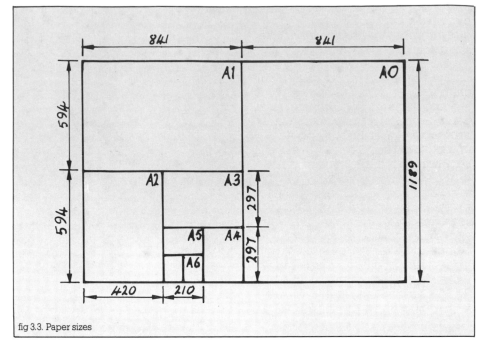
fig 3.3. Paper sizes

Most of our work is done on cartridge paper which is heavier and not as fragile as layout paper. Cartridge paper can be used with pencil, ink and a little colour wash, but if large amounts of water colour or other forms of 'wet' colour are to be applied then it may be necessary to use a much heavier, water colour paper.

Layout paper and cartridge paper are both available in the standard A sizes. You are likely to use A4 or A3 for most of your graphic work. Fig 3.3 shows the standard paper sizes. This system of sizing ranging from A6 to A0 is very easy to remember. A6 is the smallest, A5 is twice as big as A6, A4 twice as big as A5 and so on.

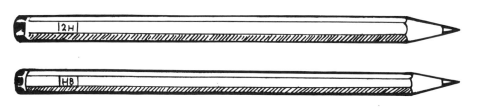
fig 3.4. Traditional pencils

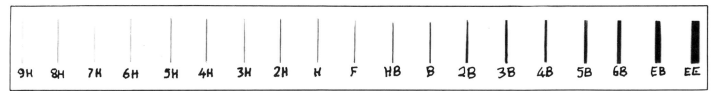
fig 3.5. Pencil grades

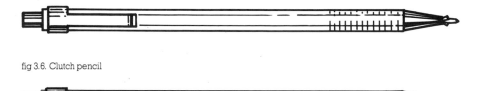
fig 3.6. Clutch pencil

fig 3.7. Automatic fine lead pencil

PENCILS

The most common piece of drawing equipment is the pencil. The traditional wood and graphite pencils are available in nineteen different grades ranging from the very hard **9H** to the extremely soft **EE**.

To begin with you will only need two pencils, a **2H** and an **HB**. Use the 2H for construction lines and layout and the HB for sketching and the final lining in of the drawing.

Some people prefer to use a **clutch pencil**. This has a plastic barrel rather like a biro, but there is a continuous length of graphite inside.

The **automatic fine lead** pencil is very similar to the clutch pencil except that it contains a polymer based 'lead' which may be less than half a millimetre in diameter in order to give a very fine, consistent line.

All pencils except the automatic line lead pencil need to be sharpened. There may be a desk mounted sharpener in your classroom or you may have a pocket sized sharpener of your own.

Clutch pencils usually have a detachable sharpener on the end of the barrel.

Some designers like to keep their pencils really sharp by occasionally rubbing the point on a piece of very fine glass paper. If you try this, be very careful not to get the graphite dust on to your drawing.

Many draughtsmen and designers prefer to sharpen their pencils with a sharp knife and then finish them off with a piece of fine glass paper. Using a knife allows them to sharpen the harder pencils to a chisel shaped point. This type of point, shown in fig 3.8, is used for all linework when high quality is required.

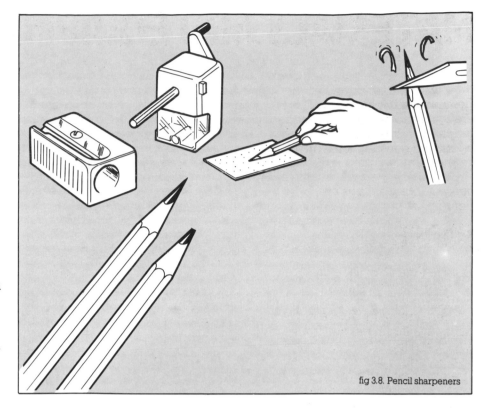

fig 3.8. Pencil sharpeners

PENS

Some designers prefer to use pens, especially if their work has to be copied or printed.

Some very fine line, **fibre tipped pens** are available, but they do wear out in time and cannot usually be refilled.

If you are doing a lot of drawing in ink it may be worth buying a **technical pen**. Technical pens have a very fine hollow nib which gives a consistent line. They are available in a variety of line widths. The most common sizes are 0.35mm, 0.5mm and 0.7mm.

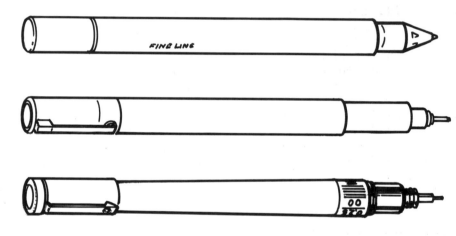

fig 3.9. Pens

fig 3.10. Technical pens

Technical pens can also be used with a wide range of **stencils** for either lettering or symbols.

At some time you are bound to make mistakes. Pencil lines can be rubbed out in the normal way with a rubber, but you may find it less messy to use a **plastic eraser** instead of the traditional rubber.

A **kneaded** or **putty rubber** is also useful for cleaning your paper after the drawing is finished. You may also find it useful for removing graphite

dust rubbed into your paper.

Mistakes in ink are much more difficult to remove. Sometimes an ink rubber can be used, but be careful not to damage the surface of the paper.

If a mistake cannot be removed with a rubber you may need to cover it with white ink or poster paint.

If you use correcting fluid to cover mistakes be extremely careful, and make sure you **read the instructions on the label carefully**.

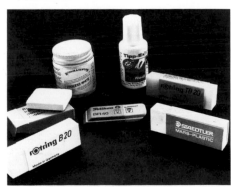

fig 3.11. Erasers

FREEHAND SKETCHING

Freehand sketching is a very important skill in Design and Communication. It is extremely useful when you are trying to explain your ideas or you are getting your thoughts down on paper quickly. Ideas can be explained far more easily with sketches than with words. Sketches can be used to communicate your ideas to other people, but they can also help you to see your ideas more clearly and allow you to develop them.

It is important not to use a ruler or straight edge such as a set square when sketching. Using a ruler will prevent you from working quickly and break up your flow of ideas. Ruler drawn sketches often appear dull and lifeless, while good freehand sketches are lively and interesting to look at.

fig 3.12. Freehand sketching

START SKETCHING

To start sketching you will need a piece of paper (layout paper will do for this) and a pencil such as an HB or softer. Pick up the pencil and hold it **lightly** between your thumb and first two fingers. Hold the pencil in a comfortable position and do not grip it tightly.

Begin by drawing a series of **horizontal lines**. Draw the lines about 75mm long and aim to keep them as straight as possible without using a ruler. Try to draw with your whole arm and not just by moving your wrist. Try not to rest your hand on the paper, use your little finger as a guide or support. Remember to work quickly and freely. When you have drawn about 20 horizontal lines you can try doing the same with **vertical lines**. (Do not cheat by turning the paper around!)

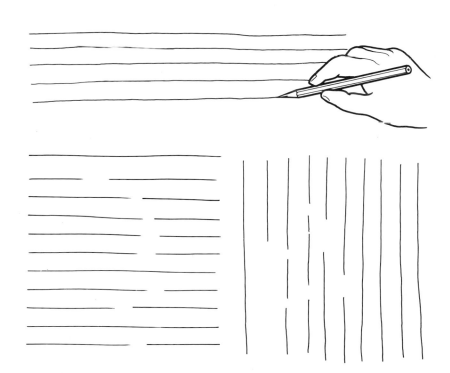

fig 3.13. Drawing horizontal and vertical lines

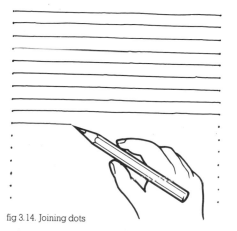

fig 3.14. Joining dots

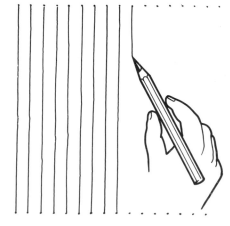

For the next exercise draw two dots about 100mm apart, as shown in fig 3.14 and, working from left to right, join up the dots with your pencil. Repeat this about 10 or 12 times. This simple exercise will help you to learn to control your pencil.

Don't forget!
Keep your pencil sharp and aim to work as freely and quickly as possible. Do not be tempted to use a ruler or straight edge.

Once you feel happy about pencil control and joining dots you can try drawing lines at right angles to each other like the ones shown in fig 3.15. Begin by drawing either a vertical or a horizontal line and then draw a line at right angles to it. Practise this, taking it in turns to draw either a vertical or a horizontal line first.

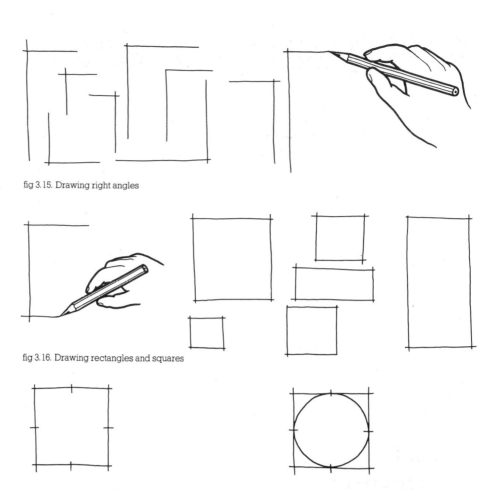

fig 3.15. Drawing right angles

After drawing right angles you will not find it too difficult to draw **squares** and **rectangles** like the ones shown in fig 3.16. Draw two lines at right angles to each other and then draw another pair of right angle lines crossing at 90° to the first pair. Practise this until you can draw freehand squares and rectangles quickly and easily.

fig 3.16. Drawing rectangles and squares

Drawing freehand circles is not difficult when you can draw a square. Draw a square with sides the same length as the diameter of the circle. Imagine that the circle is to fit inside the square and mark the centre points of each side of the square where the circle will touch, as shown in fig 3.17. Working on each quarter circle in turn, join the points to form the circle. Ellipses can be drawn in exactly the same way, using rectangles instead of squares.

If you have worked carefully through these exercises you should now be able to sketch squares, rectangles, circles and ellipses.

Look around you at everyday objects and you will notice that many of them can be drawn as simple shapes. Choose an object and make a freehand sketch of it. Begin by drawing the shape and then sketch in the object. The camera in fig 3.18 has been drawn using this technique.

fig 3.17. Drawing circles and ellipses

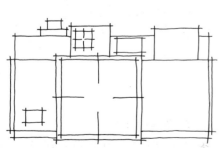
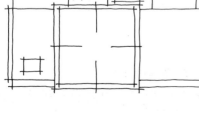

fig 3.18. Making a freehand sketch

3D DRAWING

The drawing you have done so far has been **two dimensional**. It shows the subject of the drawing as a flat shape. A two dimensional shape has only two dimensions or measurements; **height** and **length**. A three dimensional shape has three dimensions or measurements; **height**, **length** and **depth**. This is shown very simply in fig 3.19. A three dimensional drawing shows the **shape** and gives some idea of the **form** of the object.

The sketching technique shown on page 35 can really only be used if you wish to make a flat 'front view' of an object. It is a two dimensional drawing technique and needs modifying slightly if a side or plan view is to be included in the same drawing. This can be done quite simply, in fact, there are several traditional drawing techniques which are useful when working freehand. They will help you to produce a realistic, three dimensional drawing.

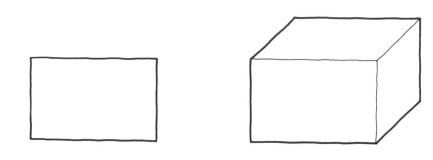

fig 3.19. Two dimensional and three dimensional drawing

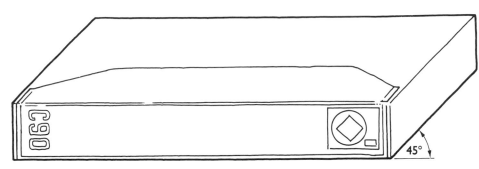

fig 3.20. Oblique drawing

OBLIQUE

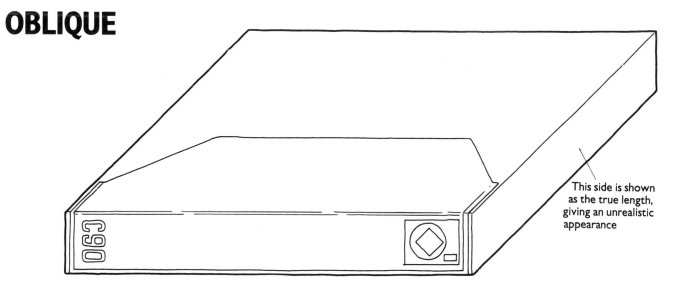

fig 3.21. Cavalier oblique

Oblique is a simple way of making three dimensional drawings. This method of drawing is used when it is important to show the **front view** of an object. The oblique lines are usually drawn at 45° to the horizontal.

Oblique drawing shows the front of the object as its true shape. The cassette box shown in fig 3.21 is an example of oblique drawing. If the sides are drawn to their length, then the effect is to make the drawing look unrealistic. To make it look more realistic the length of the sides are cut in half as in fig 3.22. This is known as **cabinet oblique** and drawings with full length sides are known as **cavalier oblique**.

AXONOMETRIC

Axonometric projection is another drawing system which gives a three dimensional view of an object. It is also known as **plan oblique**. If you look back to the oblique drawing on page 36 of this chapter you will see that the front view was drawn first. Axonometric drawing is very similar, except that the plan is drawn first. The true plan is drawn to an angle of 45° and the sides are then projected upwards from it. The top will also be the true size. Fig 3.23 shows an example of axonometric drawing. Because it can be drawn quite simply from a plan view, architects use this method to give a three dimensional view of buildings. The problems with this system in terms of CDT, are that it does not take into account perspective or foreshortening and to be accurate it really needs to be constructed using a drawing board and instruments.

ISOMETRIC

Isometric drawing is also useful when sketching freehand. It is best imagined as the object being turned until the horizontal lines appear to be at 30° to the horizontal. This method shows more of the top of the object.

These methods of drawing all distort the view of the object slightly. If a more realistic view is required, it is best to draw it in perspective.

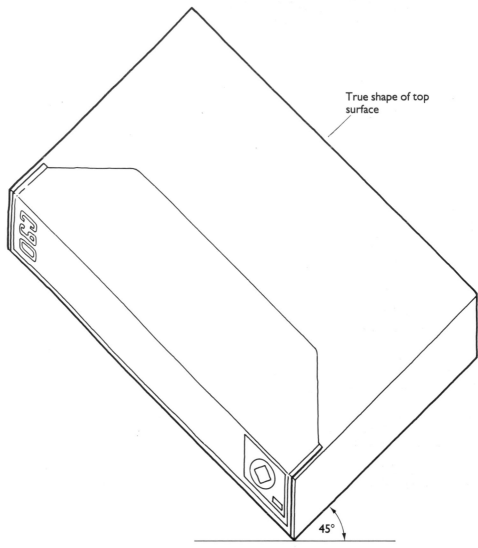

True shape of top surface

45°

fig 3.23. Axonometric view

fig 3.24. Isometric drawing

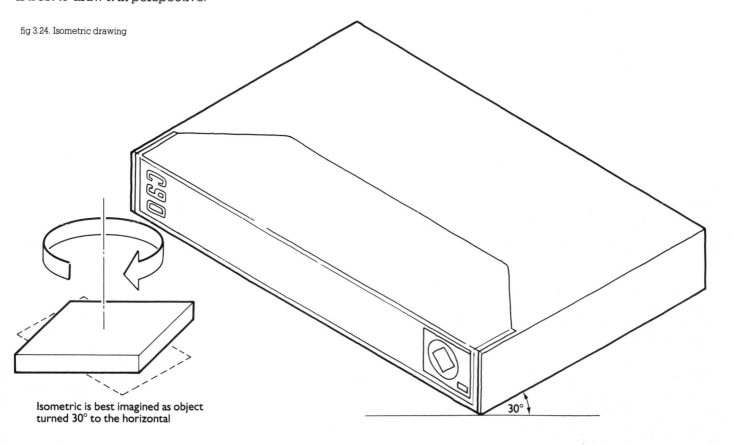

Isometric is best imagined as object turned 30° to the horizontal

30°

PERSPECTIVE DRAWING

Perspective drawing was first employed in the fifteenth century in Italy, and has been used to give the impression of depth and distance ever since.

Perspective drawing takes into account the fact that lines appear to converge and meet at a **vanishing point**. You have probably seen this visual effect when looking down a railway line or a very straight road.

There are two types used in CDT: **single point** and **two point perspective**.

fig 3.25. Vanishing point

SINGLE POINT

In single point perspective all horizontal lines converge and meet at one common vanishing point (fig 3.26). In this example, single point perspective shows the front, one side and the top of the object. If we want to make it look more lifelike then it is best to use two point perspective.

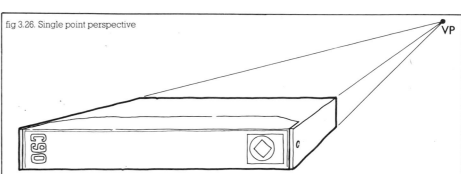

fig 3.26. Single point perspective

TWO POINT

This method, though a little more complicated, gives a more realistic view and allows us to draw objects at an angle. The horizontal lines of the object will recede in different directions and converge at two different vanishing points. Fig 3.27 shows the cassette box drawn using two point perspective and fig 3.28 shows the six simple stages of making the drawing.

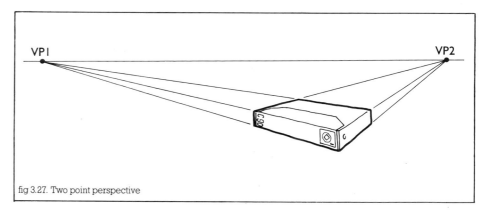

fig 3.27. Two point perspective

fig 3.28. Stages in perspective drawing

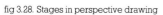

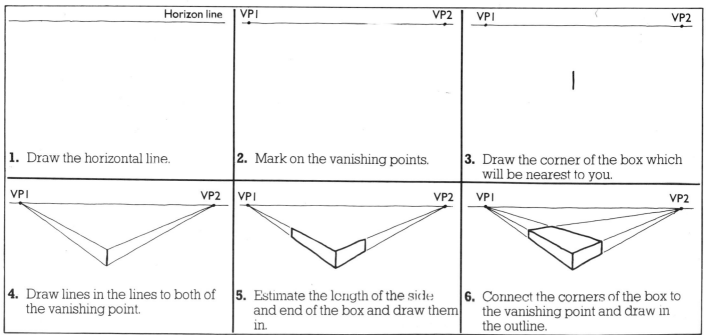

1. Draw the horizontal line.

2. Mark on the vanishing points.

3. Draw the corner of the box which will be nearest to you.

4. Draw lines in the lines to both of the vanishing point.

5. Estimate the length of the side and end of the box and draw them in.

6. Connect the corners of the box to the vanishing point and draw in the outline.

THREE POINT

When there is more than one object in a drawing, they do not have to share the same vanishing points. The cassette boxes in fig 3.29 are positioned at different angles to the viewer and so require their own separate vanishing points, but they must all be positioned on the same horizon/eye level line.

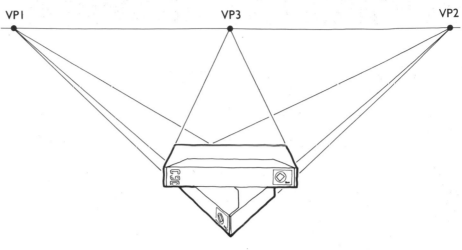

fig 3.29. Three vanishing points

VIEWPOINTS

The choice of eye level or viewpoint is also important. It is possible to show completely different perspective views of an object by moving the position of the eye level. Fig 3.30 shows a variety of different views which can be obtained by either raising or lowering the eye level. The view in fig 3.30a shows the bottom of the object clearly and is often known as a **worm's eye view**. The view in fig 3.30d shows the top of the object and is known as a **bird's eye view**. When making perspective drawings you must decide which viewpoint will show the information that you wish to convey most suitably. Having made that decision you can then decide where to position the horizon line and vanishing points in order to obtain the desired effect.

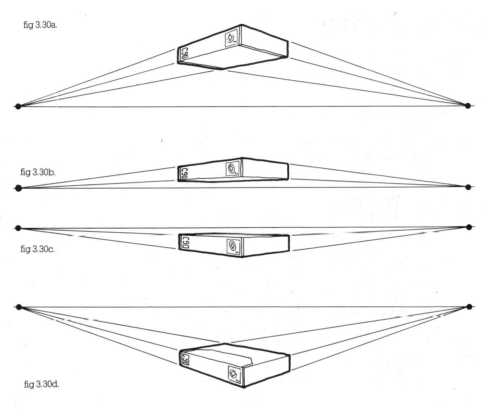

fig 3.30a.

fig 3.30b.

fig 3.30c.

fig 3.30d.

CIRCLES IN PERSPECTIVE

So far we have only looked at drawing rectangular shapes in perspective. It is also important to look at drawing circles and curves, as they form the basis of many perspective illustrations. Fig 3.31 shows a cylindrical shape drawn in perspective. Begin by drawing a rectangular shape which will contain the cylinder exactly. Then use diagonal lines to find where the cylinder will 'touch' the sides of the rectangle. The cylinder can then be sketched in freehand or drawn with an ellipse template (see page 41).

Perspective drawing is covered in more detail in the section on Technical Illustration on pages 111–131.

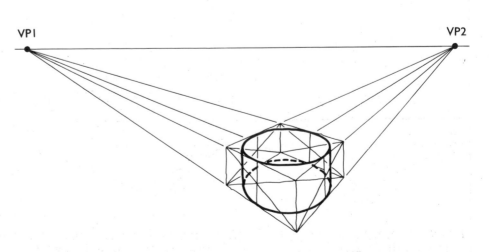

fig 3.31. Cylinder in perspective

MORE SKETCHING TECHNIQUES

Drawing is really about **looking**, and if you look closely at most objects you will see that they appear to be constructed from simple geometric shapes and solids such as cubes, rectangles, cylinders and spheres.

CRATING

Drawing objects can be made much simpler if they are reduced to their basic shapes. Once you have determined the shape, the object can be drawn within it. This technique is known as crating. Fig 3.32 shows objects which have been drawn in this way. The crate can be drawn using any of the 3D drawing techniques covered so far, oblique, isometric or perspective.

Begin by lightly drawing the crate using whichever 3D drawing technique you prefer (fig 3.33) and then draw in the object and add the details (fig 3.34).

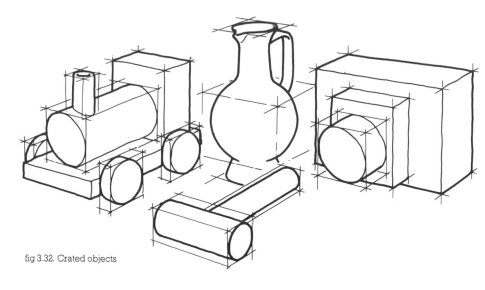

fig 3.32. Crated objects

fig 3.33.

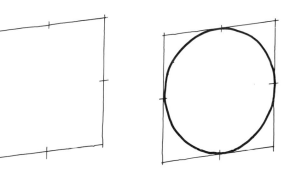

fig 3.34.

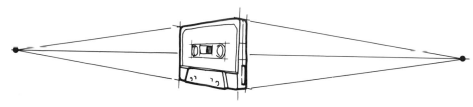

fig 3.35. Drawing ellipses

ELLIPSES

When circles are viewed at an angle they have to be drawn as ellipses. They no longer appear to be round, but oval or elliptical. Sketching ellipses is not difficult (fig 3.35).

This method of sketching ellipses will work whether you use oblique, isometric or perspective drawing methods.

SKETCHING CURVED SURFACES

Curved surfaces can also be drawn using this technique. Draw the crate and mark the points where the shape will touch it and then sketch in the shape. When you are happy with the shape, line it in with your **HB** pencil.

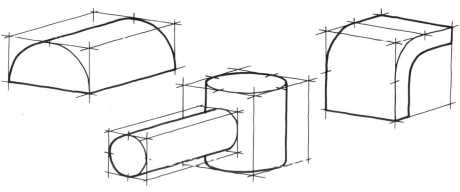

fig 3.36. Using crating to sketch curved surfaces

GRID PAPER

Special paper with feint guide lines printed on it is available to help you with your sketching. The drawing in fig 3.37 has been drawn on isometric grid paper. The lines on the paper are at 30° to the horizontal and it is quite simple to draw over the lines with HB pencil or fine fibre tip pen.

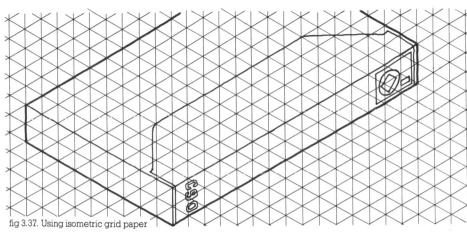

fig 3.37. Using isometric grid paper

BACKING SHEETS

Grids are sometimes used as backing sheets. They are placed **under** the drawing so that they can just be seen through the paper. It is then a simple matter to use the grid lines to guide your sketching. Backing sheets work particularly well with layout paper and can be seen through most medium weight cartridge paper. The advantage over grid paper is that once the backing sheet is removed, it appears as though the drawing has been sketched freehand on white paper. Backing sheets are available in a number of different grids including **bimetric** which is similar to isometric, but gives a more natural effect. A sheet containing horizontal lines is also useful for making sure that your lettering or handwriting is level and evenly spaced on your design sheets.

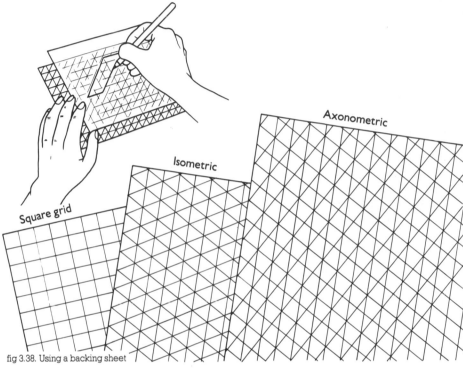

fig 3.38. Using a backing sheet

DRAWING AIDS

A considerable number of drawing aids are available to help the designer to achieve good results quickly when drawing. Fig 3.39 shows just a few items from the vast range available. **Stencils** and **templates** are used to draw things quickly without the need for technical construction. The ellipse template, for example, means that ellipses of certain common sizes can be drawn quickly without using a ruler and compasses. **French curves** act as line guides and provide a wide range of curves, while **flexi-curves** can be bent and re-bent to produce almost any curve you are likely to have to draw.

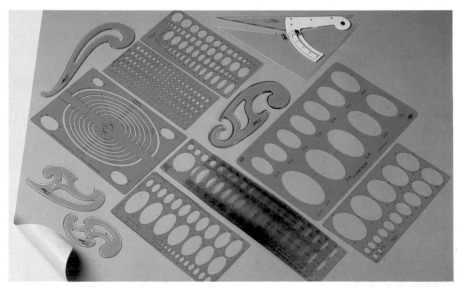

fig 3.39. Drawing aids

RENDERING

Drawings are usually rendered to make them look more realistic or lifelike. Designers often produce rendered drawings to show their clients what an idea or object will look like. Drawings can be rendered in a number of ways, but in CDT we tend to use tone produced with **pencil**, **ink** or **dry transfers**.

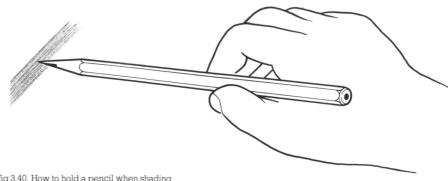

fig 3.40. How to hold a pencil when shading

PENCIL

A very simple method of making a drawing look more realistic is to shade it using a pencil. Shading uses tone to describe the nature of the surface and the form of the object. It is very simple to do and requires only the use of a soft pencil such as a grade B or softer. The angle at which the pencil is held to the paper needs to be much lower than for drawing or writing. This puts more 'lead' or graphite in contact with the paper. Fig 3.40 shows the usual method of holding the pencil for successful shading.

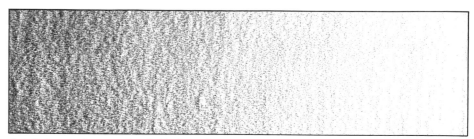

fig 3.41. A range of tones produced with a B pencil

fig 3.42. Hatched shading (left) and rubbed shading (right)

A soft pencil can produce a variety of tones, ranging from light grey to heavy black. Darker tones are achieved by pressing on harder with the pencil. Fig 3.41 shows an area of graduated tone which has been produced by gradually increasing the pressure on the pencil. Try this for yourself on a piece of scrap paper. The straight edge of a sheet of paper can be held against the outline of your drawing to act as a mask and give you a sharp, clean edge.

Shading can be left as hatched lines or it can be given a softer, more uniform effect by rubbing over it with your finger. Take care not to get your drawing dirty when doing this. Fig 3.42 shows the effect of both types of shading.

Careful consideration of how the light falls on an object can also help to describe its shape and form and add to the realism. The areas nearest to the light source will be lighter and those further away or in shadow will be darker in tone. **Highlights** can be produced by removing areas of tone with a rubber. This helps to create the effect of depth as the lighter areas appear to be nearer to us.

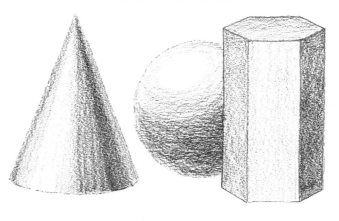

fig 3.43. Rendering used to describe the form of objects

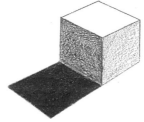 

fig 3.44. Highlights produced with a rubber

INK

Ink can also be used to render drawings in a number of ways. For example, **lines** can be drawn and, depending on their closeness, different tones can be created. **Hatching** and **cross hatching** can be used to produce a variety of different effects. **Dots** produced with a pen or spattered from a stiff brush can be particularly effective, especially when a textured object is being rendered. Ink can be diluted with distilled water and applied with a brush to produce a uniform area of tone. Tap water should not be used to dilute ink as the impurities often give the ink a spotty effect. Fig 3.45 shows these techniques and fig 3.46 shows their effectiveness when used together to render a drawing.

Technical illustrators often use ink to render drawings which are to be reproduced in technical books. Ink drawings provide them with an effective method of communicating technical information. A section covering pens and working with ink can be found on pages 111–115.

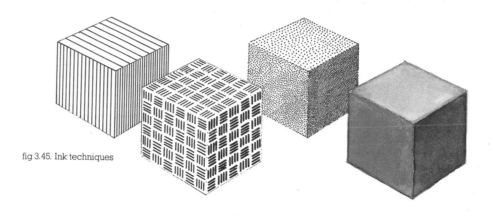

fig 3.45. Ink techniques

fig 3.46. Drawing rendered using ink techniques

DRY TRANSFERS

A wide range of tone and texture transfers are available from good art material shops. '**Letratone**' is available mainly in black, but white and some colours are also available. It consists of tones and patterns printed on a self adhesive plastic film. The tone is removed from its backing sheet, applied to the drawing and then trimmed to shape with a sharp knife or scalpel.

'**Instantex**' is available in 30 different textured effects, some of which are available in colour. This is applied by simply placing over the drawing and rubbing with a blunt pencil in the same way as instant lettering. Fig 3.47 shows the use of Instantex and fig 3.48 shows an illustration which has been rendered in Letratone.

fig 3.48. Illustration rendered using Letratone

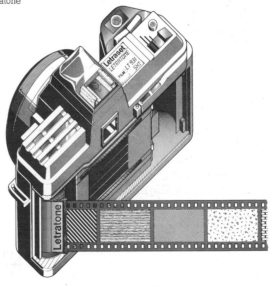

fig 3.47. Using Instantex

43

COLOUR

Colour is important in Design and Communication, both in terms of communicating ideas and presenting finished work. Colours and the way we see them can affect the finished design of a piece of work. Therefore, colour must be given careful consideration at the design and planning stage. The visual effects and the psychology of colour are covered in the Design Graphics section on pages 68–73.

Colour has fascinated artists since the time of cave paintings, but it was Sir Isaac Newton who first looked at colour scientifically. In the 1660s he discovered that white light could be split into seven different colours by using a prism. Over the following centuries many artists have developed various colour theories.

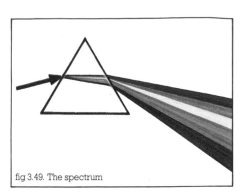
fig 3.49. The spectrum

A colour is specified by three features or elements: its **hue**, **chroma** and **tone**. Hue describes the colour it is. For example, red refers to the hue, while scarlet specifies the actual colour. Chroma describes the brightness or intensity of the colour and tone describes the amount of black or white found in it.

The tone of a colour can be altered by adding white or black to it. A colour with a lot of white in it will be pale and not very strong. Fig 3.51 shows the tonal range of a colour. The centre of the strip shows the original colour, while the right hand side shows the effect of adding white, and the left hand side shows the effect of adding black.

As far as we are concerned in Design and Communication, there are three important colours: **red**, **yellow** and **blue**. These are basic colours and cannot be made by mixing other colours together. They are known as **primary colours**. If two primary colours are mixed together, a **secondary colour** is produced. There are three secondary colours: green, orange and purple. If a primary and a secondary colour are mixed together, a **tertiary colour** is produced.

It sometimes helps to understand colours if you try to imagine that they are painted on a wheel, as in fig 3.54. The wheel helps us to understand why some colours look better together than others. Colours which are close to each other on the wheel go well together and create **harmony**. Those colours which are opposite contrast with each other and are known as **complimentary colours**.

fig 3.50. Colours of the same hue

fig 3.51. Tonal range

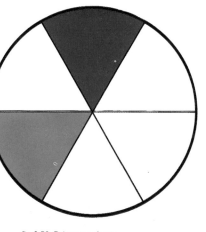
fig 3.52. Primary colours

fig 3.53. Primary and secondary colours

fig 3.54. The colour wheel

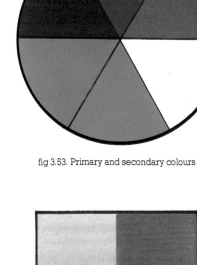
fig 3.55. Harmony

fig 3.56. Contrast – complimentary colours

COLOURED PENCILS

Coloured pencils are perhaps the easiest form of colour to apply and the one with which you are likely to be most familiar. There are several different types of coloured pencils, each with their own particular characteristics and uses. The normal coloured pencil has a fairly thick, soft lead which is waterproof and does not fade in bright light. Most makes of pencil have a range of between 60 and 70 shades.

The 'Veri-thin' range, as the name suggests has a thinner, non-crumbling lead and is used for work where fine detail is required. It is waterproof, but the range of colours is not as large as the normal coloured pencil.

Most types of coloured pencil are difficult to rub out with an eraser, but they can be removed by scraping with a sharp knife. Take care not to cut yourself when doing this. Colours can be mixed by either working the colours over each other, or by applying dots of colour close to each other so that it mixes 'visually'.

fig 3.57. Coloured pencils

fig 3.58. Coloured pencil background

Coloured pencils are a very useful and simple way to apply colour. The pencil is held in the same way as described for shading in fig 3.40 on page 42. Coloured pencil can be applied to make things easier to understand or to draw attention to it. The drawing in fig 3.58 has been highlighted to draw attention to it by adding a background or outline of coloured pencil.

In fig 3.59, coloured pencil has been used to help to describe the form of the object. The impression of form has been achieved by shading each surface with a different coloured pencil within the same hue. When deciding on the colours to use, you must take into account the position of the light source. The top surface will usually be the lightest and one area, which is in shadow, will always be darker. If objects close together cast shadows on each other, then the areas in shadow can be shown by shading with a darker tone of the same hue. Shadows cast on a white surface are usually shaded with a grey coloured pencil.

fig 3.59. Coloured pencil used to describe form

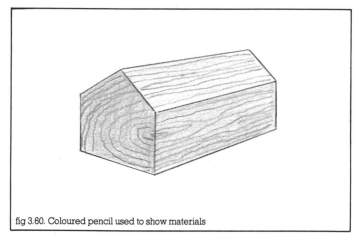

fig 3.60. Coloured pencil used to show materials

Objects can be rendered to show the material they are made from. Coloured pencil is particularly useful for rendering wood. Fig 3.60 shows an object which has been rendered in this way. Begin by filling in the overall colour of the block, taking care to give the impression of form and then, with a darker coloured pencil, draw in the detail of the grain. In this case the object has been rendered to give the impression that it is made from beech.

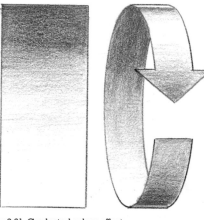

Like graphite pencils, coloured pencils can be used to achieve a graduated effect by varying the pressure applied to the pencil. This effect is useful when rendering cylindrical objects. The ribbon arrow in fig 3.61 makes good use of this effect. It is also useful when lettering or designing logos (see fig 3.62).

fig 3.62. Graduated colour used in lettering

fig 3.61. Graduated colour effect

WATERCOLOUR

Watercolour is used to render presentation drawings and to highlight ideas. Artist's quality watercolours are very expensive, but for most of the work in CDT, student's quality colours are perfectly acceptable. Watercolour brushes are usually made of sable and are also expensive. Good quality nylon brushes are a less expensive alternative.

A good quality, heavy paper is required for work in watercolour. Special papers are available, but cartridge paper should be suitable. Before starting work the paper must be stretched. This is done by soaking it in clean water until it is thoroughly wet. The excess is drained off, the paper placed on a clean drawing board and stuck down around the edges with gummed paper tape. Once dry, the paper can be used with watercolour and will not wrinkle or cockle when water is applied. When applying paint, try to work from the top of the drawing downwards. It helps to tilt the board slightly so that the paint runs down and forms a uniform wash. Watercolour is effective, but it takes time and skill to apply it properly.

fig 3.63. Watercolours

Watercolour is usually applied to the paper as thin, transparent washes of colour. The lightest colours are applied first, followed by successively darker ones. The advantage of watercolour over other forms of colour is that it can be used to give very pale and subtle tones of colour. It can also be used in conjunction with other materials such as coloured pencils or pens. When used with coloured pencil, it is very good for rendering and showing the materials used to make an object.

fig 3.65. Applying a wash

1. Mix up enough paint.

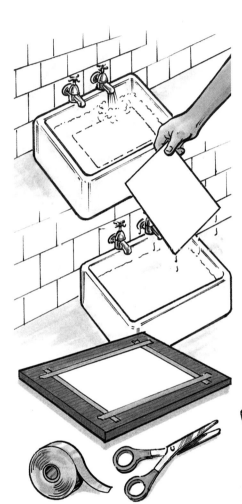

fig 3.64. Stretching the paper

1. Soak the paper thoroughly in clean water.
2. Drain off surplus water.
3. Lay the paper on a clean drawing board and stick down with gummed tape (not masking tape).

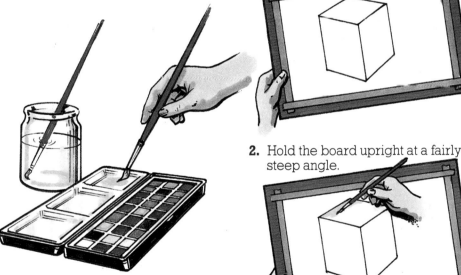

The procedure for applying a wash of colour is fairly simple but will need a little practice. First, make sure that the stretched paper is dry and then mix up sufficient colour to cover the drawing. The board should be held at a fairly steep angle so that the wash can run down the paper. Charge the brush and start work in the top left hand corner, working from left to right down the board. Take care not to stop or it is likely to leave a mark when the paint dries. Recharge your brush quickly if you need to. When you have covered the area with the wash, use a dry brush to remove the surplus paint. Remember not to apply any more washes until the last one has dried. Do not work in ink or pencil on wet paper as you are likely to damage the surface.

2. Hold the board upright at a fairly steep angle.

3. Begin to apply the wash at the top left hand side and work downwards.

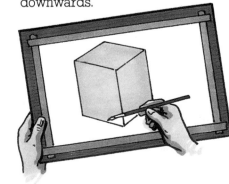

4. Remove surplus paint with a dry brush and allow to dry.

MARKERS

Marker pens are a fairly recent development in terms of colour materials. They are available in a wide range of colours and sizes from the fine fibre tips to the broad felt tips. Two types of ink are used in markers. Some are filled with **water soluble ink**, while others have a **spirit based type**. Markers are used extensively by graphic designers and illustrators and, when used carefully, can produce some striking effects. They allow the designer to work quickly and loosely without over-wetting the paper. Markers are expensive and unless special bleed proof paper is used the ink will 'creep' past outlines and soak through the paper, marking the surface beneath.

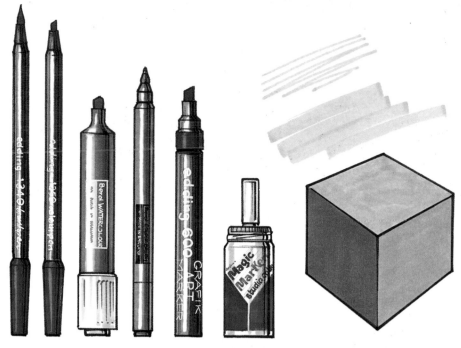

fig 3.66. Markers

Markers are often used as a convenient method of applying colour and are used to highlight ideas and text in the same way as a coloured pencil. However, when used in this way the full potential of the marker is not realised. Markers are very useful when making presentation drawings of a design idea or showing the materials used in the realisation of the design. Markers allow the designer to work very quickly compared to paint or airbrush techniques and still achieve very realistic effects.

Markers are not easy to use well and your first attempts might well be rather disappointing, but keep practising and your results will improve. When applying an area of even colour, work quickly and do not stop in one place with the tip resting on the paper or a 'pool' or colour will be left which will bleed outwards. Try not to overlap the strokes of the pen or the colour will darken. Apply the colour in single strokes next to each other and the colour will bleed slightly and blend together to form a uniform band of colour (see fig 3.67).

fig 3.67. Laying bands of colour to produce a uniform area

When making **presentation drawings** you will require a sharp, well defined outline. This can be achieved by cutting out the finished drawing and sticking it to a clean sheet of paper. A sharp outline can also be produced by using **masking film** or **tape** in the same way as air brushing. Masking techniques are covered fully on page 130 and most of them can be used when working with markers.

Details can be added to the drawing with coloured pencils. It is possible to obtain coloured pencils in shades which match the markers. This allows some useful blending and graduated effects to be achieved. Reflections can be produced by working over the drawing with a white pencil and highlights can be picked out with white poster paint. Careful use of reflections and highlights can produce a very realistic drawing. Study the reflections on objects very carefully and then apply them to your drawings. Remember that

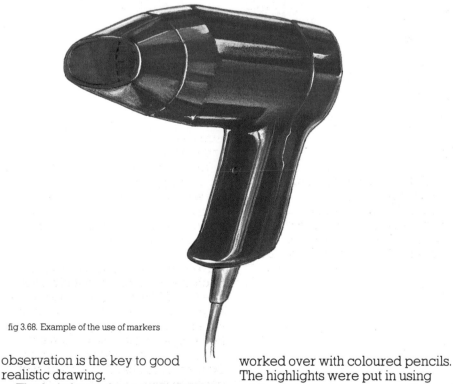

fig 3.68. Example of the use of markers

observation is the key to good realistic drawing.

The hairdryer shown in fig 3.68 was drawn using markers and worked over with coloured pencils. The highlights were put in using white poster colour or **gouache**, as it is sometimes known.

WORKING DRAWINGS

Working drawings contain the information needed to **produce** the object that you have designed. They need to convey details such as dimensions, materials to be used, construction details or assembly instructions.

EQUIPMENT

In order to make accurate working drawings you will need several simple items of equipment.

You will need a drawing board and a tee square or a draughting table fitted with a parallel motion.

In addition to your H and 2H pencils, you will also need two set squares; a 30/60 square and a 45 square. You will also need a pair of compasses and either clips or tape to hold your paper on the board.

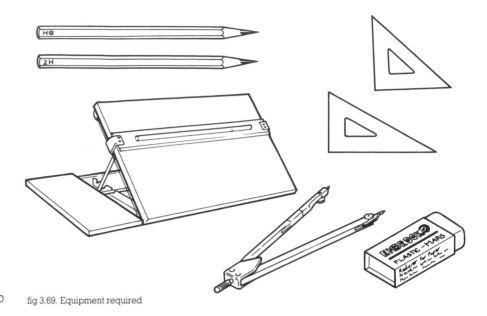

fig 3.69. Equipment required

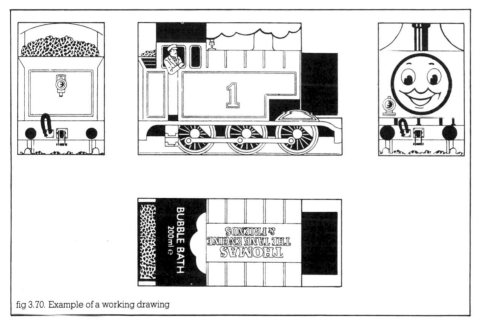

fig 3.70. Example of a working drawing

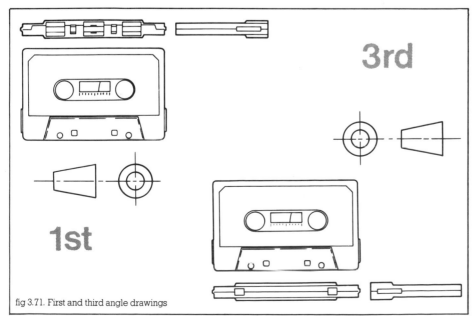

fig 3.71. First and third angle drawings

WORKING DRAWINGS FOR 3D WORK

Working drawings for three dimensional work usually use orthographic projection, but they often include pictorial views such as oblique or isometric and a variety of other drawings depending on the object to be made.

ORTHOGRAPHIC DRAWINGS

There are two types of orthographic drawings: **first angle projection and third angle projection**.

Both types are three view drawings consisting of front, end elevations and a plan. In first angle projection the views are projected through the object and drawn on the opposite side. In third angle the views are not projected through the object, but drawn next to it.

First angle is mainly used in Britain, but third angle, used in the USA and the continent, is becoming more popular. Third angle has the advantage that the adjoining views appear **next** to each other on the drawing.

Working drawings and orthographic drawing in particular are covered in more detail in the Engineering Drawing section of this book.

WORKING DRAWINGS FOR 2D WORK

Working drawings for two dimensional work such as posters, leaflets, books, book jackets and packaging take a different form. There is little point in showing three views of a two dimensional project.

LAYOUT

The designer needs to know how the work will be produced and needs to give the printer specific instructions regarding the layout of the work. If the work is extremely simple the printer can sometimes work from a written specification, but usually the designer will produce a detailed layout showing all the information the printer requires. Fig 3.72 shows an example of a marked-up layout for one of the pages in this book. It shows the size of headings, the type face to be used and the positioning of the artwork and the text.

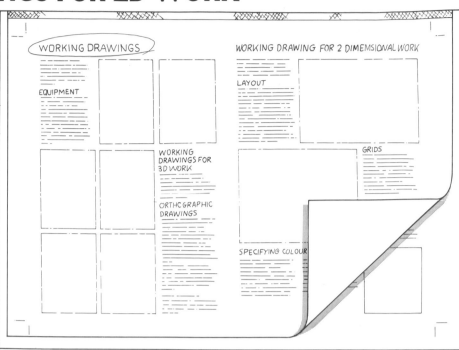

fig 3.72. A marked-up layout

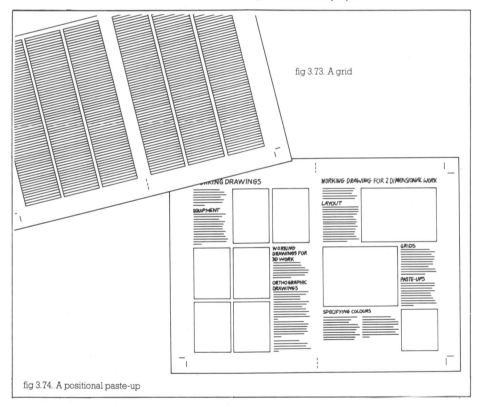

fig 3.74. A positional paste-up

GRIDS

The basic design of the page is worked out and a grid is made. The text and illustrations can then be positioned on the grid and the most suitable page layout chosen. Grids are used to ensure consistency of layout throughout the work. This is particularly important when designing books. Fig 3.73 shows one of the grids used in the initial design of the pages in this book.

fig 3.73. A grid

PASTE-UPS

Paste-ups are also useful in showing the design of two dimensional work. The **positional paste-up**, worked over a grid, shows the position of the text and illustrations. This allows alterations and adjustments to be made and gives a good indication of what the finished page will look like (see fig 3.74).

SPECIFYING COLOURS

It is also important that the designer specifies exactly the colours required in the layout and illustrations. An international colour referencing system is used. A range of products known as **Pantone** are available and allow designers to match and control colours throughout the design process. The range of products include marker pens, paper, overlay film and colour samples for use by printers. There are over 500 colours available in the range and each one has a reference number so that the designer can specify the exact colour of ink to be used by the printer. Fig 3.75 shows some of the products in the Pantone range.

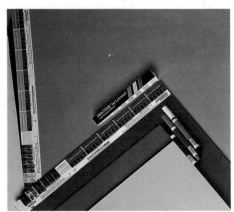

fig 3.75. The Pantone range of products

DIMENSIONING

As working drawings are used to provide information for making, they are usually drawn to scale and contain the necessary measurements or **dimensions**.

In order that everyone can understand our dimensioning, it is important that we all follow the same set of rules. These rules have been set out by the British Standards Institute (BSI) and are in a booklet known as **BS7308**. There should be a copy of BS7308 in your school for you to look at.

The main points to consider when dimensioning drawings are as follows:

1. Do not allow dimensions to confuse the drawing. The dimensions should be spaced well away from the drawing and the lines should be lighter than those of the outline.

2. Drawings should not be confused by too many dimensions. Each dimension should appear once only and it is not necessary to include

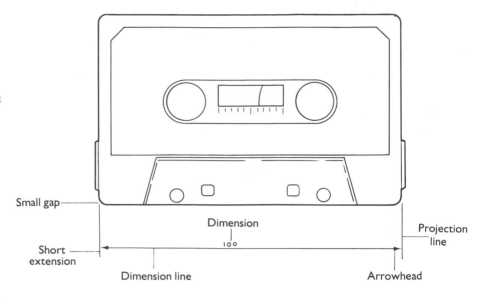

fig 3.76. Dimensioning

dimensions which can be worked out by adding or subtracting others.

3. Dimensions should be read from the bottom or right hand side of the sheet.

4. Arrowheads should be small, sharp and neat.

5. All dimensions should be shown in millimetres.

Dimensioning drawings is covered in more detail in the Engineering Drawing section of this book.

LETTERING

You may need to include some written information on your working drawing. This can be done in handwriting, stencils or dry transfer lettering.

It is not difficult to develop your own handwriting style for notes and instructions. Titles and dimensions need to be printed in block capitals. The size of the letters depends on how important the information is.

General information is usually about 6mm high, while titles are 8mm high. Main headings can be up to 10mm high.

Handwritten lettering
Develop your own handwriting style and use it to put information on the drawings.

e.g. handwritten information

Printed lettering
Rule a pair of parallel guidelines the correct distance apart and print carefully within them. Make sure that your letters touch both the top and bottom lines.

e.g.
PRINTED
INFORMATION

fig 3.77. Lettering

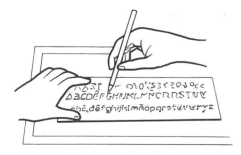

Lettering

fig 3.78. Lettering techniques

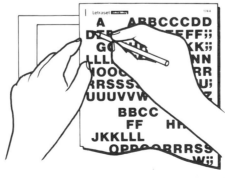

Dry Transfer Lettering

Plastic lettering stencils are available in a variety of different sizes and styles. Special stencils are available for use with draughting pens which correspond with the size of the nib.

When using stencils take care to ensure that the lettering is level. With some stencils it is possible to rest them on a tee square or a parallel motion straight edge.

Dry transfer lettering gives very professional results and is available in a wide range of lettering styles. The main disadvantage is cost. It can work out rather expensive if used on every drawing.

PRESENTING YOUR WORK

Presentation is an important part of Design and Communication. A badly presented piece of work will not communicate ideas or information as effectively as one which is well presented.

It may be necessary to display your work for other people to see. Drawings to be displayed usually need to be mounted. Good mounting help to draw people's attention to the work and also helps to protect it while it is on display. Two-dimensional work can be mounted on to card or mounting board. Items of work can be mounted individually or grouped together on the same mount. When mounting groups of drawings you must consider their layout very carefully, or the finished result may look messy and untidy. Work should be positioned carefully so that it forms an interesting, but balanced display (see fig 3.81).

It is a good idea to keep your work together. Designers often submit a folder of work to their clients and some examination boards may require you to hand in a folder of work at some time during the course. Individual design sheets and drawings can be held together with slide-on plastic binding strips. These are inexpensive and do not normally damage your work. There may be a binding machine in your school which will punch a series of holes down the edge of the sheet and allow you to fit a plastic comb binder like the one shown in fig 3.82. A cover or title page can then be added and if the work is to be used regularly, a clear acetate cover may also help to make it more durable.

Storing and transporting work can also be a problem. Ideally, work should be kept flat. Rolling work and sliding it into cardboard is unsatisfactory, especially if it is to be displayed at a later date. Artwork folders are available in a variety of sizes from most good art shops, but it is possible to make one for yourself like the one shown in fig 3.83.

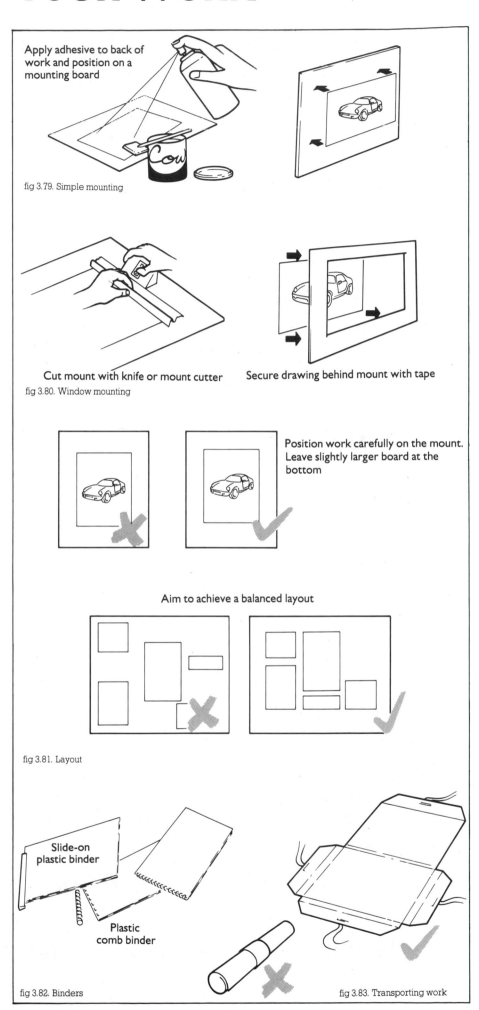

Apply adhesive to back of work and position on a mounting board

fig 3.79. Simple mounting

Cut mount with knife or mount cutter

fig 3.80. Window mounting

Secure drawing behind mount with tape

Position work carefully on the mount. Leave slightly larger board at the bottom

Aim to achieve a balanced layout

fig 3.81. Layout

Slide-on plastic binder

Plastic comb binder

fig 3.82. Binders

fig 3.83. Transporting work

EXERCISES

1. Work through the sketching exercises on pages 34 and 35 to 'warm up' before starting to draw.

2. Looking carefully at objects will help you to understand shape and form and improve your drawing techniques. Find a natural object and make a very detailed drawing of it.

3. Experiment with drawing material which is unfamiliar to you. Try drawing with fountain pens or 'biros' and compare the effects with pencil.

4. Choose a basically rectangular object, such as a camera or walkman, and draw it using each of the following methods: oblique, axonometric and isometric.

5. Trace the objects from fig 3.84 and apply tone to show the effects of light falling on them. Mark in the position of the light source.

6. Make a perspective drawing of the interior of a room in your house. Draw in the furniture and the positions of the doors and windows.

7. Draw a rectangle 150 x 25mm and within it paint the tonal range of a secondary colour of your choice.

8. Draw a circle 50mm in diameter and divide it into six equal spaces. Paint in each space with a different tertiary colour.

9. Make a perspective drawing of an everyday object of your choice and render it using markers and coloured pencils. Paint in the highlights using white poster paint.

10. Using ink, render the drawing of the camera shown in fig 3.85. Use rendering to achieve a contrast between the textured and the smooth areas of the camera.

11. Choose a simple object and make a first angle orthographic drawing of it. If the object is too large to draw full size, draw it to a suitable scale.

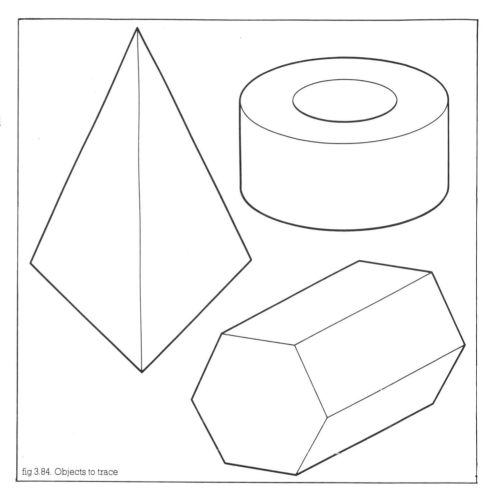

fig 3.84. Objects to trace

fig 3.85. Camera

MODELLING AND RELATED SKILLS

The making of models can be an exciting part of designing. It often presents the first opportunity of seeing a design come to life. It is the stage of changing from a two-dimensional drawing, or at best a three-dimensional drawing on paper, to a three-dimensional article. Some models can be made very quickly and easily by bending, cutting and glueing card, while others will take far longer to realise using a wide range of materials and techniques.

In this chapter we will look at some of the many different types of model that are produced and the working qualities of the materials that are used to make them. However, we must realise that the model has a dual role in the field of designing and communicating.

First, it can be an **exploratory stage** in the design process, allowing modifications that will improve the final article to be made. In such cases it would be usual to use materials that can be easily worked, and are perhaps cheaper than those to be used for the end product. The purpose of this type of model is to acquire knowledge before continuing with the design process.

Second, the model can be an **end product** in its own right (fig 4.3). This will generally put the model in one of two categories. It may be a **demonstration model** (fig 4.2) designed to show how a particular thing works, but not actually working itself, or a **working model** that may be a prototype for a production run.

A wide range of materials can be used in model making. It is often sensible to choose the most appropriate in terms of availability, ease of working and cost. Of course, a mixture of materials can be used in any one model.

In the example shown in fig 4.1, an architect has produced a model of a proposed building complex. The plans only show two dimensions, but the client requires a more realistic impression of what is to be produced. This is achieved through a cardboard model that is placed in a representation of the proposed setting. Naturally it would be inappropriate to use brick, glass and concrete for the model.

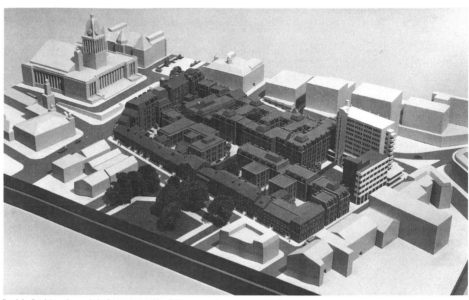

fig 4.1. Architect's model of a proposed building complex

fig 4.2. Demonstration model

fig 4.3. End product

53

STATIC MODELS

Static models are models that have no moving parts. Perhaps most of the models you have already made are of this type. This does not mean that they must be lifeless, as shape, colour, form and texture can make your models lively and interesting. Fig 4.4 shows a selection of static models that have been made as solutions to design problems. They show some of the wide range of materials and construction techniques that can be used in model making.

We will examine five ways of making static models from sheet material such as cardboard, thermoplastic sheet and balsa wood. These are making **a model stand up**, **product cut-outs**, **interlocking shapes**, **boxes** and **structures**.

fig 4.4. Static models

MAKING A MODEL STAND UP

fig 4.5.

fig 4.6.

fig 4.7

fig 4.8.

One of the first problems you will encounter when trying to make a model from a single sheet of thin material is that it is difficult to make it stand up. Solutions to this problem are shown in figs 4.5 to 4.8, where a variety of ways of displaying a cardboard clown are shown.

Fig 4.5 is the least effective solution because its **rigidity** depends entirely upon the thickness of the material used. However, figs 4.6, 4.7 and 4.8 have all gained a certain amount of **strength by folding**. The first has one fold, the second two and the third three. You may spend time experimenting with, and evaluating, other ways in which a single sheet of a flimsy material can be folded to produce a model with a certain amount of rigidity.

Having looked at several different ways of folding a single piece of material to produce a model we now need to consider how we can combine several individual pieces to produce a model. Fig 4.9 shows another solution to the problem of displaying the clown, by using two separate pieces of card which have been cut out, folded and glued together. One possible way of arranging these on a piece of card is shown in fig 4.10. Care should be taken when drawing the shapes onto the sheet to ensure that there is as little waste as possible. This will require a great deal of planning, as there are many different ways in which the shapes can be arranged on the material and some will be more economical than others.

fig 4.9. Cardboard clown with support

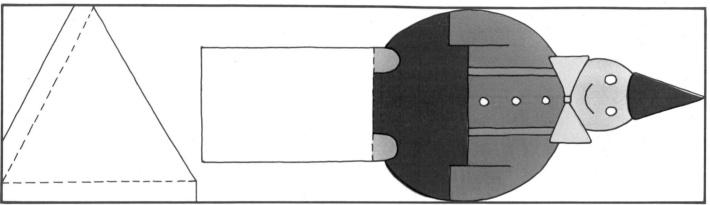

fig 4.10. Arrangement of clown and support on card

PRODUCT CUT-OUTS

fig 4.11. Card hat in flat form

Product cut-outs are models that have their parts already printed and only require cutting out (or pushing out if the lines have been perforated) and assembling. Sometimes there will be many parts involved, therefore assembly will be fairly difficult and time-consuming.

These types of models are often used to present promotional material. Their main advantage is that a **three-dimensional object can be stored in a flat form**. The example shown in fig 4.11 is a hat that is printed on a thin cardboard sheet. As it is cut in certain parts it can be fitted fit over the head, as shown in fig 4.12. Further examples can be found printed on some cereal and toy boxes.

fig 4.12. Card hat pushed into shape

INTERLOCKING SHAPES

A three-dimensional model can be made by **interlocking** pieces of sheet material at right angles (fig 4.13a). If the model is to be made from very thin materials, the cuts can simply be made with a pair of scissors and the shapes pushed together. With thicker materials, a slot from all pieces of the model that is equal in width to the thickness of the material must be removed. The depth of the slot should be half the height of the model. The slot is removed from the bottom half of the top pieces and the top half of the bottom pieces. This is illustrated in fig 4.13b. If this method of construction is used on wood, the resulting joint is called a **cross-halving** joint.

Where many of these joints are put together at one time, a complicated three-dimensional shape can be built up very rapidly. Fig 4.13a shows this very effectively; the six pieces that are required to make the model are drawn out in fig 4.14.

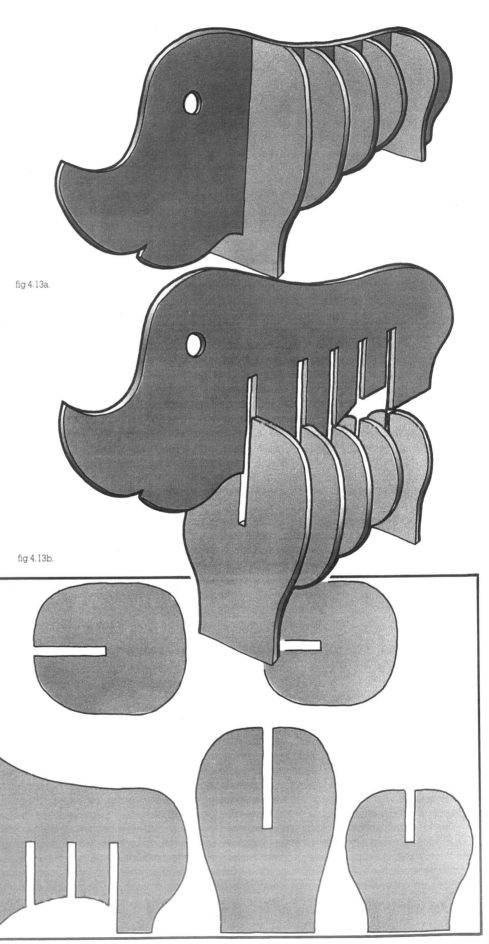

fig 4.13a.

fig 4.14.

fig 4.13b.

MAKING BOXES

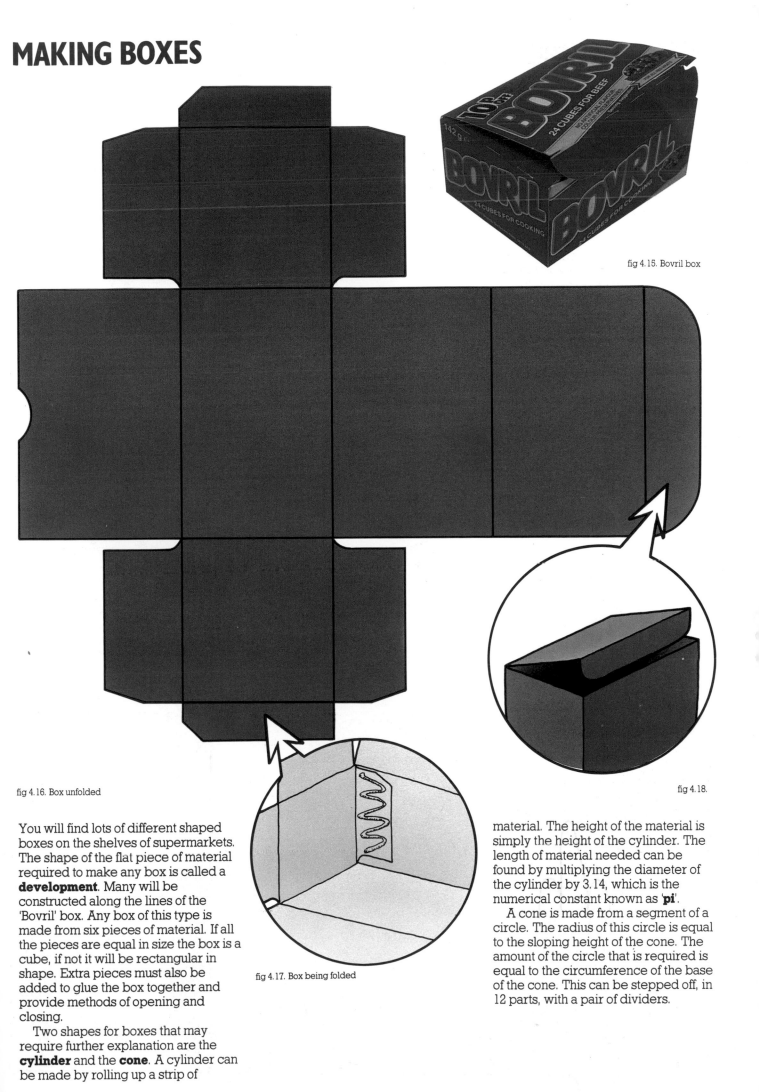

fig 4.15. Bovril box

fig 4.16. Box unfolded

fig 4.17. Box being folded

fig 4.18.

You will find lots of different shaped boxes on the shelves of supermarkets. The shape of the flat piece of material required to make any box is called a **development**. Many will be constructed along the lines of the 'Bovril' box. Any box of this type is made from six pieces of material. If all the pieces are equal in size the box is a cube, if not it will be rectangular in shape. Extra pieces must also be added to glue the box together and provide methods of opening and closing.

Two shapes for boxes that may require further explanation are the **cylinder** and the **cone**. A cylinder can be made by rolling up a strip of material. The height of the material is simply the height of the cylinder. The length of material needed can be found by multiplying the diameter of the cylinder by 3.14, which is the numerical constant known as '**pi**'.

A cone is made from a segment of a circle. The radius of this circle is equal to the sloping height of the cone. The amount of the circle that is required is equal to the circumference of the base of the cone. This can be stepped off, in 12 parts, with a pair of dividers.

MAKING STRUCTURES

It may be necessary to produce **structures** during Design and Communication lessons. Sometimes the structure will remain open (as in the case of a bridge) and at other times it will be covered to produce an enclosed shape (as in the case of a balsa wood aeroplane).

There are many different materials that can be used to make structures, ranging from drinking straws to steel rods. However, two of the materials that you will find most useful are balsa wood and construction kits, such as plawco.

Plawco is a range of rods and connectors (as shown in fig 4.19) that can be assembled to produce **frameworks**. The combination of steel rods (where strength is needed) and light plastic tube (for flexibility and ease of bending) makes this a very versatile construction kit. The steel rods may be cemented into the connections, making a permanent structure. The tubing, however, is a tight fit, so that structures can be built, then broken down, and used over and over again.

Balsa wood can be used to make structures by glueing together sections with balsa cement, a glue that is specifically designed for the purpose. Because it is nearly always thin sections of materials that are used, it is not practical to attempt to cut joints. Therefore, **butt joints** are commonly used.

The strength of any butt joint is largely dependent on the size of the area that comes into contact with the glue. It can be most frustrating attempting to glue small sections together to make frameworks, and it is also often unsuccessful. Figs 4.20 to 4.22 show three simple ways of overcoming this problem by using small pieces of card to strengthen the joint, thus increasing the chances of successful work.

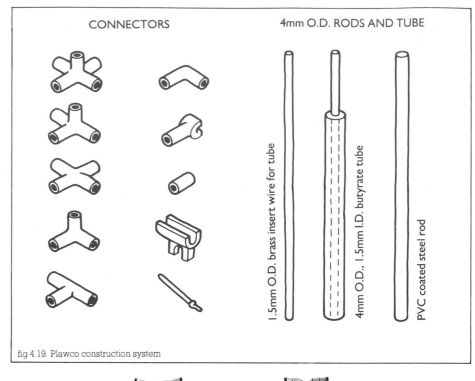

CONNECTORS   4mm O.D. RODS AND TUBE

1.5mm O.D. brass insert wire for tube

4mm O.D., 1.5mm I.D. butyrate tube

PVC coated steel rod

fig 4.19. Plawco construction system

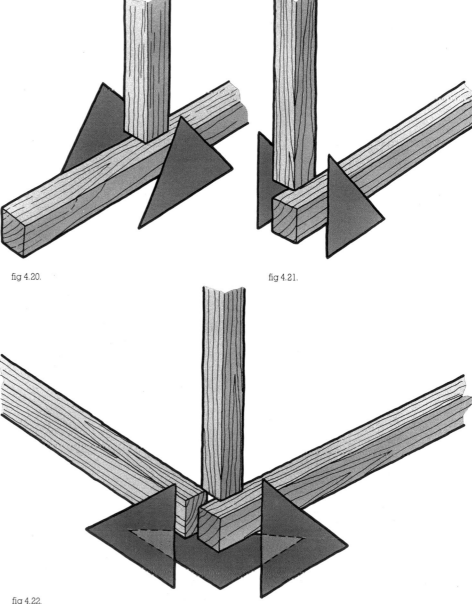

fig 4.20.

fig 4.21.

fig 4.22.

DYNAMIC MODELS

Dynamic models are models that have some moving parts. These could be similiar to those in the piece of model engineering shown in fig 4.23. However, in this section we will look at four different types of dynamic models.

The first are **mechanism** problems that can be explored with strips of cardboard and paper clips, as well as plastic gear wheels and axles. The second are examples of movement that can be found in **pop-up books**. The third are ways of making **pop-up boxes** that rely on rubber bands to pull them into shape; and the fourth are models that achieve movement through **thermal currents**. I am sure that you will be able to find many more ways of producing models with an element of movement in them.

MECHANISMS

One of the simplest forms of movement that can be applied to models is **rotation**.

fig 4.23. Moving model

fig 4.24. Creating links with cardboard and paper clips

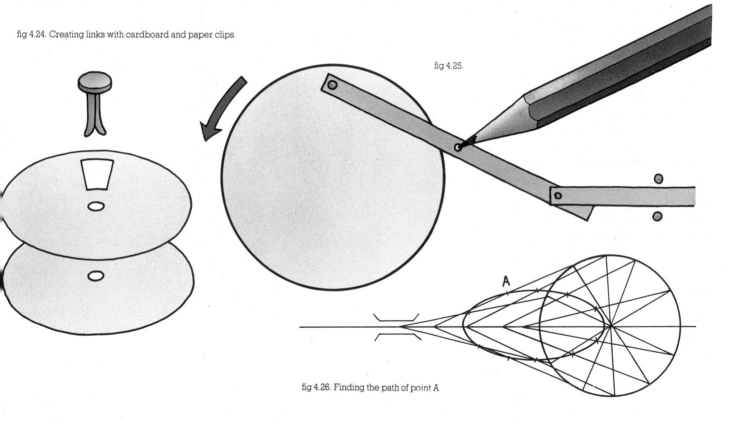

fig 4.25.

fig 4.26. Finding the path of point A

Fig 4.24 shows one way in which this can be achieved with two discs. They are held together with a paper clip so that as the top disc rotates information is revealed on the lower one. Of course, the complexity of the model can be increased by cutting two, three or more boxes in the top disc. It is also possible to increase the number and shape of the discs that are used. By cutting and interlocking them, a great deal of information can be presented. The design of these types of discs can be extremely interesting.

Links between moving parts can easily be created with cardboard and paper fasteners. Figs 4.25 and 4.26 show two ways of tackling the problem of finding the path of point A as the disc rotates. By constructing the simple model as shown and placing a pencil through the hole as the disc is rotated, the path of the point can be drawn. This is called the **locus** of a point.

The solution can also be found by drawing out the problem, as in fig 4.26. This involves finding the position of

point A when the disc has rotated 30 degrees. By repeating this 12 times, the positions of point A can be plotted. If these are joined the locus of the point is again drawn.

The production of the model is vital to the understanding of what happens to one part when another is moved. This can be invaluable when looking at more complicated mechanism problems involving several interlinking arms and pivots.

Dynamic models can easily be produced by purchasing a set of plastic **gear wheels** and **axles** similar to that shown in fig 4.27. By connecting these to electric motors, moving models can be assembled rapidly. Clearly the number of teeth on each gear wheel is vital to how quickly it turns in relation to another. By experimenting with the different components, speeds can be increased or decreased, directions of rotation changed and angles of rotation turned through 90 degrees.

Figs 4.29 and 4.30 illustrate an attempt to add movement to a model puppet. This model is made of thin card, but you could consider using other materials such as balsa wood and plastic sheet. The problem of producing a moveable joint is easily solved with thin sheet material by using paper clips. With thicker materials it may be necessary to use pop rivets or even nuts and bolts.

In fig 4.29 the task of adding movement to the arms has been dealt with. This has meant using three pieces of card, two for the arms

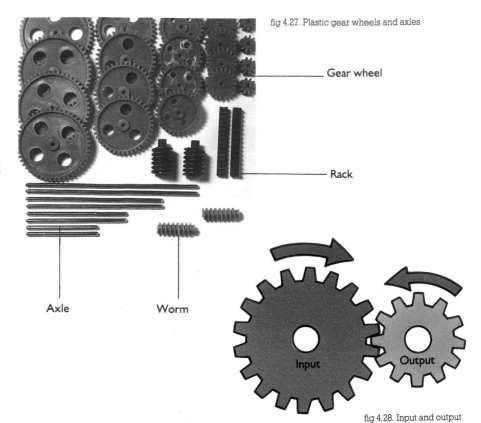

fig 4.27. Plastic gear wheels and axles

Gear wheel

Rack

Axle

Worm

Input

Output

fig 4.28. Input and output

themselves and a strip to operate them. The arms have a slot cut in them and are fastened through this onto the body. These are then connected to an operating strip which can slide up and down, thus moving the arms from side to side.

In fig 4.30 the problem of providing moving legs is examined. The solution shown uses three pieces of card, one for the lower leg, one for the upper leg and one as an operating strip. As the operating strip is moved, the upper leg moves up and down. The lower leg is free to swing and should, therefore, remain in a vertical position regardless of the position of the upper leg. The second leg would also be added and could be moved by the same operating strip.

There are many other ways in which movement can be added to a puppet using sheet material and a suitable method of linking the two together. For example, it could be achieved by using string and wire as an operating method.

fig 4.29. Movement to the arms

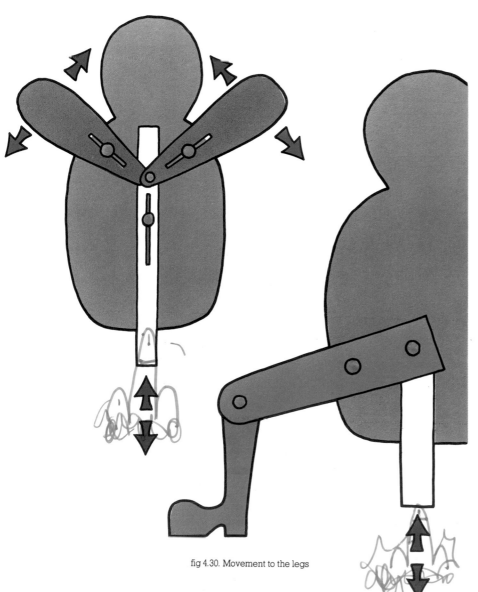

fig 4.30. Movement to the legs

POP-UP BOOKS

There are many **pop-up books** available on the market today. These are often aimed at the younger age group with their main advantage being that they bring the books to life. Even though the use of colour can make the pictures in traditional books interesting to look at, they are still only two-dimensional representations of three-dimensional objects. The book shown in fig 4.31 is a splendid example of a 'three-dimensional' book with each page really coming to life.

The first pop-up book was produced in the nineteenth century. It was called 'Little Red Riding Hood'. German designers and publishers developed the 'pop-up' and soon became experts in novelty book design.

Pop-ups use a variety of **mechanisms**. Some are very complicated but the three shown on this page are quite simple examples that you can develop during Design and Communication lessons.

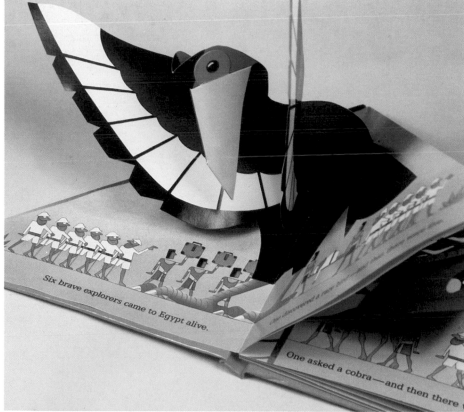

fig 4.31. A pop-up book

The simplest way to make a pop-up book is to use **multiple layers**. This method is based upon a parallelogram with all parts being parallel to one page or the other. This allows them to fold flat when the book is closed.

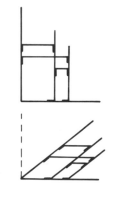

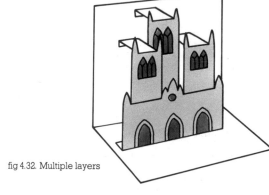

fig 4.32. Multiple layers

Floating layers are similar to multiple layers. The pages of the book are used to support a second layer to give an impression of depth.

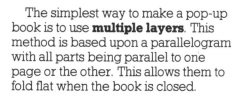

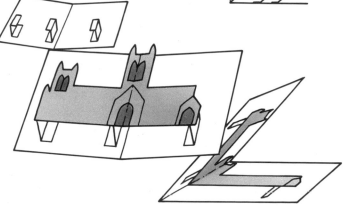

fig 4.33. Floating layers

The **V fold** is also a useful mechanism which can be adapted in several ways to produce surprising effects.

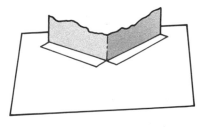

fig 4.34. V fold

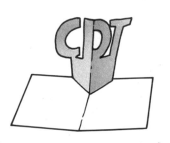

fig 4.35.

POP-UP BOX

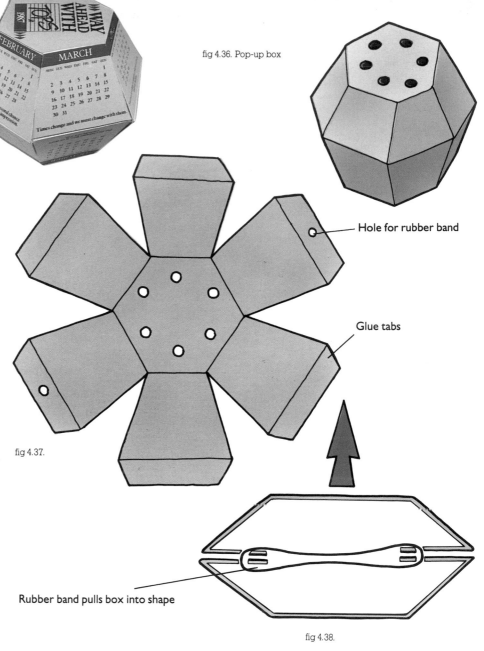

fig 4.36. Pop-up box

Hole for rubber band

Glue tabs

fig 4.37.

Rubber band pulls box into shape

fig 4.38.

You may consider making a simple **pop-up box** similar to the one shown in fig 4.36. This one is, in fact, a pencil holder and calendar which also displays a considerable amount of advertising. The advantage of this kind of box is that it can be put in an envelope and sent through the post to a customer.

This example is made from two pieces of card that are the same shape as the one shown in fig 4.37. It is a **regular hexagon** with a **trapezium** attached to each side. The two shapes are glued together with one pair of glueing tabs having a **rubber band** stretched between them. When the shape is in its flat form the rubber band is stretched and, if allowed to, it will pull the box into shape. A cross-section of this happening is shown in fig 4.38.

This is just one solution to producing a pop-up box from card and a single rubber band. You could make a similar box using a cube or tetrahedron. In either case you will be relying upon the property of the rubber band that allows it to be stretched and then spring back to its original length to pull the box into shape.

THERMAL CURRENTS

Dynamic models may be produced by using the natural movement of air, called **thermal currents**. Perhaps the most common form of this kind of model is a **mobile** that relies upon the gentle air movements in a room to rotate. This movement will add interest to the mobile, which much be carefully balanced in the first place.

In order to use different weight pieces in making mobiles, the basic **principles of balance** must be understood. This simply means that the piece that is largest in weight must be moved closest to the pivot in order to achieve balance. The opposite applies to pieces that are smaller in weight.

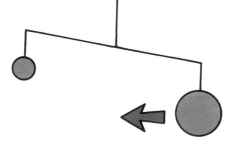

fig 4.39. Achieving balance with a larger object

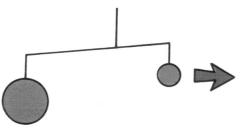

fig 4.40. Achieving balance with a smaller object

fig 4.41. A mobile

MODELLING MATERIALS

PAPER AND CARDBOARD

Many colours and thicknesses of paper and card are available. **Surface finishes** can vary greatly, from different colours to those printed to represent materials such as brick (fig 4.42). Depending on the thickness of the material, it can usually be cut with either scissors or a Stanley knife.

fig 4.42. Card printed to look like brickwork

BALSA WOOD

Balsa wood is available in a wide range of sizes, including **sheet** and **block**. Its main advantages are that it is light and fairly easy to work. It can be cut with a Stanley knife or simple woodworking tools and joined with balsa cement.

fig 4.43. Balsa wood sectons

STYROFOAM

Styrofoam is available in different densities for the model maker. It can be cut efficiently with an **electrically heated wire** to form any shape. Care must be taken to work in a well-ventilated room as the fumes released can be dangerous if inhaled. Pieces can be joined together with PVA adhesive and then painted with any water-based paints, but not cellulose, which dissolves styrofoam.

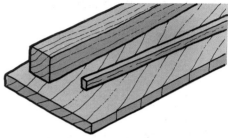

fig 4.44. A styrofoam cutter

PLASTIC SHEETS

Plastic sheet, **mouldings** (as in fig 4.45) and **vacuum-formed shapes** can be very useful for model making. Sheet material is available in a wide range of colours and materials. Most can be cut with a Stanley knife or abra file depending on the thickness and density.

fig 4.45. Plastic models

PLASTER OF PARIS

Plaster of Paris can be most useful for model making because it can be poured into a **mould** (as shown in fig 4.46), thus producing a replica of the shape. Once set it can easily be worked with simple tools, such as a **surform**, and then painted as required.

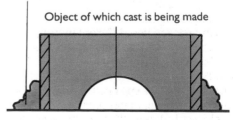

Plasticine

Object of which cast is being made

Softwood surround

fig 4.46. A plaster of Paris mould

EXERCISES

1. What types of people do you think use models at some time during their lives? Draw out a chart that is similar to the one shown in fig 4.47 and fill in the spaces. You should consider the term 'model' in its widest sense.

2. You are required to design a cut-out model that is to be printed on the reverse of a cereal packet similar to the one shown in fig 4.48. The model may be in several parts and instructions for assembly should be included. This model is to be one of a series based upon 'Transport through the Ages' and is for a child aged between 7 and 11.

3. Design and make a cardboard box to hold 24 sweets that are similiar to the one shown in fig 4.49. You must be able to open and close the box to remove individual sweets.

4. Complete the list shown in fig 4.50 for the main types of materials that can be used in modelling. This may help you when selecting materials for model making.

5. The three boxes drawn in fig 4.51 are to be made from thin card. Draw out the necessary shapes that would be required (developments) and remember to include glueing tabs as and where you think appropriate.

6. Design a mobile that is to be printed on the back of a toy box. The mobile is to be cut out and hung in a child's bedroom and should, therefore, be based on a theme such as animals or a nursery rhyme. The sizes of the toy box are shown in fig 4.52 and three pieces of wire 300 mm long and a length of string are supplied.

7. Design and build a model car made from balsa wood and powered by a single rubber band. The cars are to be judged by which is the quickest to travel along a 1 m horizontal track.

8. It has been decided to purchase a basic modelling kit for students studying Design and Communication to use at home. Compile a list of items that you think would be useful. The cost of the kit must not exceed £15.

MADE BY	MODELLED ITEM	REASON	MATERIALS USED
Architect	Office block	To show client 3D new of a possible solution.	Balsawood Plaster of Paris

fig 4.47.

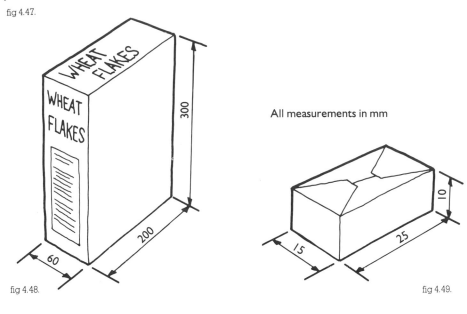

All measurements in mm

fig 4.48.

fig 4.49.

MATERIAL	ADVANTAGES	DISADVANTAGES
Paper	Fairly easy to cut and fold.	Very little strength unless folded into structures.

fig 4.50.

fig 4.51.

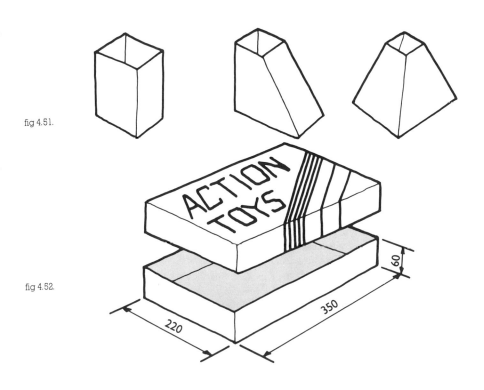

fig 4.52.

DESIGN GRAPHICS

In Design and Communication, design graphics refers to the conveying of information in graphic form. It is concerned with the designing of instructions and signs; instrument display design; logos and trademarks; display and exhibition design; advertising, sales promotion and package design.

Design graphics ranges from the straightforward conveying of information to the 'selling' of a product. Within this range the designer must consider the balance between the functional (does it work?) and aesthetic (is it visually appealing?) properties. In terms of packaging and advertising, he or she must consider the selling aspects, the persuasive properties of his or her design.

fig 5.1. Examples of design graphics

fig 5.2. Design sheets and sketches

The design sheets and sketches produced as part of a CDT project are themselves examples of design graphics, as are the designer's drawings of what an object will look like when produced. Perhaps you have seen the drawings of a new motor car or some other domestic product shown in a magazine or brochure.

The designer is also influenced by fashion and style, with the style of graphic work tending to reflect current fashions and trends. The graphics associated with records, tapes and compact discs often do this, as well as conveying information about the recording.

fig 5.3. Graphics for instruments and controls

When designing for machines, motor car instrument panels or controls and displays for radios, hi-fis and TVs, the technical implications of the design must be considered. The position of certain controls or components may be fixed and the designer will have to work within these constraints.

fig 5.4. Packaging and display

LINE, SHAPE AND FORM

Line, shape and form have characteristic qualities of their own which can be used with considerable effect in Design and Communication, particularly in design graphics.

LINE

Lines can be used to show direction and movement, express certain feelings, or create illusions, shapes and forms.

The lines in fig 5.5 indicate directions and those in fig 5.6 give an impression of movement.

Lines can be used to give a feeling of restfulness or anger (fig 5.7).

The lines shown in fig 5.8 give the impression of depth or distance and those in fig 5.9 give a climbing effect.

fig 5.8. Lines giving impression of depth

Horizontal parallel lines suggest lateral movement (fig 5.10), while vertical parallel lines increase the impression of height (fig 5.11).

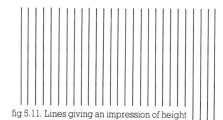

fig 5.11. Lines giving an impression of height

Lines are often used to create illusions. For example, which of the two lines in fig 5.12 is longer? Now look at the illustration in fig 5.13. Do you see two faces or a candlestick?

Many artists and designers have been fascinated by the illusions and effects which can be created by line. M C Escher created many fascinating illusions like the one shown in fig 5.14. The artist Bridget Riley used lines to create the effect of movement. Fig 5.15 shows an example of her work.

The way lines are used in graphic work can give some interesting effects. Graphics are used on the sides of cars to give an impression of speed and movement (fig 5.16). Horizontal and vertical lines can be used to make objects look wider or taller than they really are. This technique is sometimes used in interior design when a designer wishes to make a room look larger that it really is (fig 5.17).

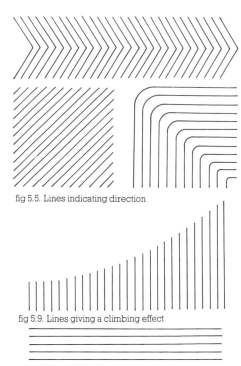

fig 5.5. Lines indicating direction

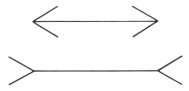

fig 5.9. Lines giving a climbing effect

fig 5.10. Lines suggesting lateral movement

fig 5.12. Lines creating an illusion

fig 5.14. Escher illustration

fig 5.16. Car with applied graphics

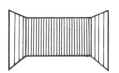

fig 5.6. Lines giving an impression of movement

fig 5.7. Lines giving feelings

fig 5.13. Lines creating an illusion

fig 5.15. Bridget Riley 'op-art' illustration

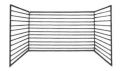

fig 5.17. Interiors using effects of vertical and horizontal panelling

SHAPE

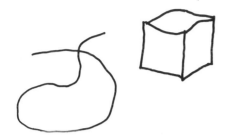

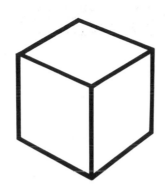

fig 5.18. Lines used to enclose space and create shapes

fig 5.19. Use of heavy and feint lines

Lines are used to enclose **space** and create **shapes** (fig 5.18). Heavy lines can make an object appear to be very solid while faint, thin lines can give an object the impression of being very light and fragile (fig 5.19).

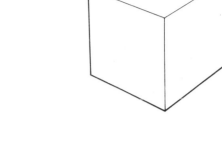

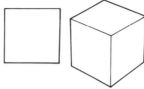

fig 5.20. Squares, cubes and rectangles

The square and cube, because of the repetition of their faces, appear to have a formal character. Rectangular shapes, on the other hand, can lie down or stand up. They are more interesting visually and appear to have more character (fig 5.20).

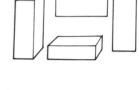

fig 5.21. Parallelograms

Shapes can also suggest movement. The parallelogram, for example, gives a strong impression of movement (fig 5.21).

Circles tend to attract the eye and draw it inside the circumference, which is why numbers on a drawing are sometimes enclosed in a circle (fig 5.22).

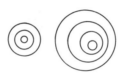

fig 5.22. Circles

FORM

Lines can be used to give form to an object by creating the impression of light and shade. Lines are drawn parallel to the edge of the object. Lines drawn close together create darker tones and those drawn wider apart give the impression of highlights (fig 5.23).

A circle, for example, can be given form in a variety of ways (fig 5.24).

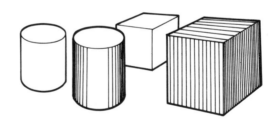

fig 5.23. Lines creating the impression of light and shade

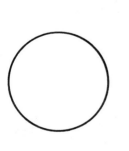

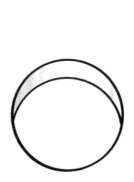
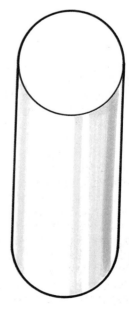

fig 5.24. Giving form to a circle as a disc, hole, sphere and cylinder

COLOUR

Colour is very important in design graphics. Much of the work carried out requires the use of colour in one form or another. It is used in advertising, packaging and exhibition design. The application and theory of colour have been dealt with in chapter 3. This section is concerned with the psychology and use of colour, rather than its application.

fig 5.25. Examples of the use of colour in design graphics

EFFECTS OF COLOUR

Colour can affect people in many different ways. Some colours can affect our moods, making us feel angry or calm. Red, for example, has an oppressive effect, orange can be aggressive and exciting, while green remains neutral and yellow gives a quieter, cheerful effect. Some colours appear to be nearer than others; they stand out while others recede into the distance. These are all important factors for the designer to consider when making decisions about the use of colour.

COLOUR TEMPERATURE

The colour circle (fig 5.26) can be divided into two halves according to the 'temperature' of the colours. The colours in the top half, ranging from blue-green to purple-red, give the effect of **coldness**, and the colours in the opposite half, ranging from yellow-green to red, give the impression of **warmth**.

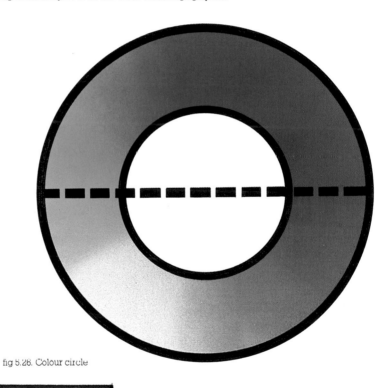

fig 5.26. Colour circle

APPROACHING AND RECEDING

The **warm** colours also appear to come forward towards the viewer, while the **cold** colours give the opposite effect and appear to recede into the distance. Reds appear to reduce space and blues make the space seem larger. Perhaps you have noticed how the same model of motor car appears slightly larger or smaller depending on its colour.

fig 5.27. Warm colours

fig 5.28. Cold colours

fig 5.29. Cars appear different sizes depending on their colour

COLOUR AND WEIGHT

In the same way that colours can make objects appear to be larger or smaller, they can also make them appear to be lighter or heavier. This is useful when a designer wants to give the visual impression that an object is lighter or heavier than it really is. Many domestic appliances are now made in light-coloured plastic instead of the traditional chromed metal. Kettles and teapots are a good example of this (fig 5.30).

fig 5.30.

fig 5.31. Dark/light colour comparison

Cycle design also illustrates this very well. At one time most cycles were produced in dark colours such as black, green, blue and maroon. Fashions have changed and cycles are now much more colourful. Modern racing cycles are designed to look lightweight and the colours used help to emphasise this. Fig 5.31 shows how a dark colour makes a cycle look much heavier than a lighter-coloured one.

COLOUR ASSOCIATION

Colours are associated with certain situations. Sometimes this is a deliberate or conscious association and at other times it is psychological or unconscious. Red is associated with potentially dangerous situations. People used to believe that bulls would charge at anyone wearing red until it was discovered that they are actually colour blind. However, the saying 'like a red rag to a bull' has survived. Fire engines and fire extinguishers are usually painted red, and so it is naturally associated with fire. Fig 5.32 shows examples of fire-fighting equipment painted red.

Red is also used as a warning. Red flags are used to warn people that it is unsafe to swim in the sea and red lights are used at traffic lights to warn drivers of danger and tell them to stop.

fig 5.32. Red: stop danger

fig 5.33. Green for go

fig 5.34.
Stop and start buttons

fig 5.35. Dashboard warning lights

Green is used to signify the opposite, that it is safe. A green man lights up at pedestrian crossings to show that it is safe to cross the road. At traffic lights, a green light indicates that it is safe to cross the road junction. At road works a green board with 'go' painted on it tells drivers that it is safe to proceed.

Most machines such as lathes, bandsaws and drills in workshops have coloured operating buttons. The start button is always green and the stop button is always red.

Motor cars use a system of colour-coded warning lights. Green usually indicates that something is switched on (e.g. a heated rear screen or an indicator). Orange or amber lights are used to give warnings that there is likely to be a problem, such as a low fuel or water level, and red lights are used to warn the driver of a more serious problem (e.g. a loss of oil pressure in the engine or a brake failure) and to tell him or her to stop immediately. Fig 5.35 shows the warning lights on a typical family car.

ABSORPTION AND REFLECTION

Isaac Newton discovered that white light or sunlight can be split up into seven different colours known as the **spectrum**. The spectrum does not actually consist of seven separate colours, but is a continuous band which gradually merges from one colour to the next.

When light falls on an object, most of the light is **absorbed** by it except for the light waves which are the same colour as the object. This light is **reflected** by the object; the lighter the colour of the object, the more light it will reflect. If we look at a blue object, for example, we actually see the blue light which is being reflected off it. The other colours which make up the white light are being absorbed and transformed into heat.

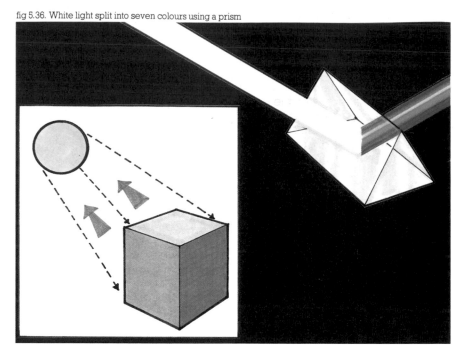

fig 5.36. White light split into seven colours using a prism

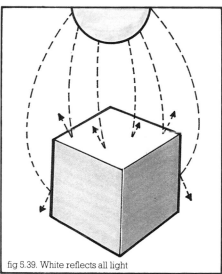

fig 5.37. Blue light reflected by a blue object

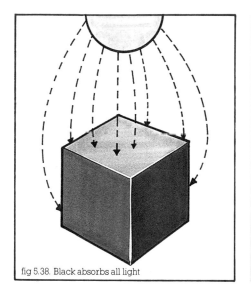

fig 5.38. Black absorbs all light

fig 5.39. White reflects all light

White objects will reflect all light and so keep fairly cool even on a hot summer's day. If you were to touch a white object that has been exposed to very bright sunlight it will not feel any hotter than the surrounding air. This is why white or light-coloured clothes are comfortable to wear on a hot day. Sportsmen and women have traditionally worn white clothes to play cricket and tennis for many years.

Black absorbs all light and so black objects can become too hot to touch when left in bright sunlight for any length of time. Perhaps you have felt some of the heat given off by a black motor car on a hot day?

Absorption and reflection are very important functions of colour which a designer must consider carefully. Some colours would be completely unsuitable for certain objects and products. Black would not be a suitable colour for a refrigerator, because it would absorb heat and the motor inside the appliance would have to work much harder to keep the food cool. Sometimes a non-reflective surface is required. This might be the area surrounding the screen on a TV set or the instrument panel on a motor car. Black does not reflect light and so is very suitable for this purpose. The choice of colour can be very important when designing packaging, especially if the package is to contain goods which are delicate or perishable. Pre-packed food could be damaged if the colour of the package is likely to absorb light and transform it into heat.

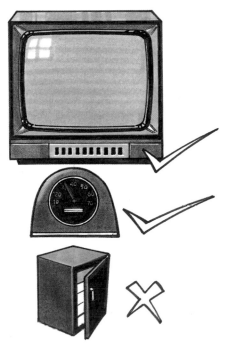

fig 5.40. Selecting suitable colours for objects

fig 5.41.

COLOUR INTERACTION

Colour interaction refers to the way colours appear to the eye. The human eye cannot see colours on their own, it always sees them in relation to at least one other colour.

The way colours are seen or 'perceived' can be affected by the background or even by adjacent colours. The circles in figs 5.42 and 5.43 are the same shade of grey, but they appear to be different shades when placed against different backgrounds.

fig 5.42.
fig 5.43. Colour interaction

Our perception of the grey circle in fig 5.44 is affected by the colours either side of it. If you lay your pencil vertically down the centre of the circle, the circle will appear as two different shades of grey. Take away your pencil and the circle appears as one shade of grey again. This shows clearly how colours are affected by other colours around them. This particular effect is known as '**simultaneous contrast**'.

fig 5.44. Simultaneous contrast

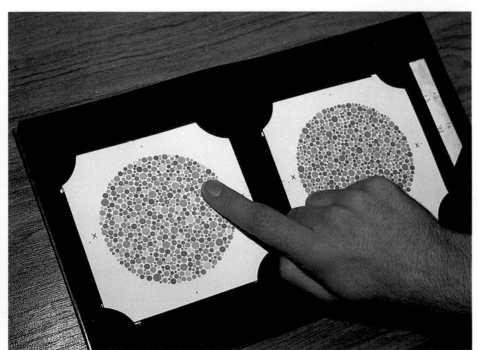

fig 5.45. Colour blindness test card

Doctors and opticians use charts and diagrams which make use of the interaction of colour to test eyesight. **Colour blindness** can be detected in this way.

Colour blindness is an eyesight condition which affects about 10 per cent of all men, but rarely affects women. It can range from a slight difficulty in identifying certain shades of red, to the point where red and green look the same. A person suffering from severe colour blindness would not be able to tell red from green or blue from brown.

Graphic designers sometimes need to consider this, especially when producing electrical wiring instructions and safety signs which rely heavily on the use of colour and colour association.

OPTICAL FUSION OF COLOUR

Methods of mixing colours to produce other tones and shades have been explained earlier, but colours do not always have to be mixed 'on the palette', they can be mixed '**in the eye**'.

Dots of colour can interact and produce a visual mixing effect. The example of fig 5.46 shows how orange can be produced by visually mixing dots of red and yellow.

A group of painters used a variation on this method, known as the **pointilliste technique**, in the nineteenth century. Fig 5.47 shows an example of pointillism by the painter Georges Seurat.

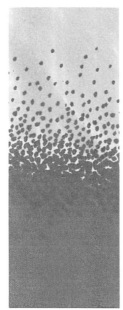

fig 5.46.

fig 5.47. Pointilliste painting by Georges Seurat

Colour printing makes use of the principle of optical fusion of colour. The range of colours is produced from dots of **three colours**, similar to the primary colours used in painting. They are known as the **process colours** and consist of a blue colour called **cyan**, a red colour called **magenta**, and **yellow**. Fig 5.48 shows the process colours.

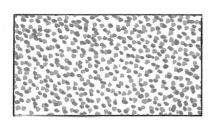

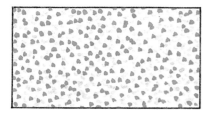

fig 5.48. The process colours

If you look closely at a large coloured advertisement or examine a coloured photograph in a magazine with a magnifing glass, you will see that it consists of thousands of tiny dots of these colours. The large numbers of tiny dots make it impossible for the human eye to identify them as individual colours and so it presents them as a '**mixed**' colour. The cyan and yellow dots combine and give the impression of green, while magenta and cyan appear to us to produce violet. Multicoloured effects can be created by overprinting several times using different colour combinations which will mix 'in the eye'.

fig 5.49. Colour photo seen through a magnifying glass

SHAPE AND COLOUR

The combination of shape and colour is useful to the designer when working on signs, posters and notices. Fig 5.20 on page 67 shows the formal nature of the square compared to the more interesting rectangle; other shapes have different effects. The triangle, for example, has a visually disturbing effect: it causes the eye to fly off at the corners. Triangles are not suitable for notices or posters which contain more than a few words, but they are suited to warning and road signs especially when they are combined with the colour red. Fig 5.50 shows the use of the triangle in road signs.

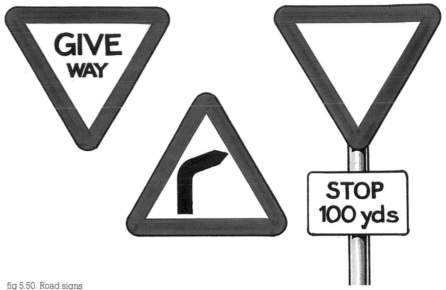

fig 5.50. Road signs

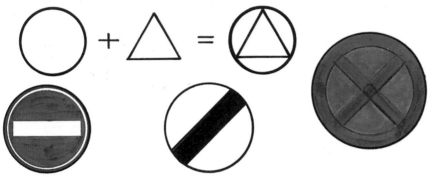

fig 5.51. Combined shapes

When two shapes which have little in common are combined, they create a disruptive effect and cause **visual tension**. This is also used in the design of road signs where the combination of both shape and colour are used to give commands, warnings and information.

Red is used to **warn** or give a **negative instruction** to road users, while blue is used to give a **positive instruction**.

fig 5.52. Pictograms

It is not only geometric shapes which are used. Simple symbols or **pictograms** are used to illustrate signs. A symbol which represents lightning is used to show that there is danger from high voltages. This symbol is often painted red, but it can be black on a bright yellow background. Diagonal lines and parallelograms create the impression of movement, and when they are combined with two contrasting colours, effective warning chevrons are produced (fig 5.54).

fig 5.53. Use of red (maximum speed) and blue (minimum speed) in road signs

fig 5.54. The use of diagonal lines, shapes and colour

ADVERTISING

Advertising can take a variety of forms including posters, magazine and newspaper adverts and features, TV commercials, product packaging and sponsorship, as in the case of sport. The main aims of advertising are to **inform** and **sell**. The advertiser makes people aware of a product or service and then attempts to sell it.

Advertising strategies vary considerably, from simply presenting the facts about a product and allowing the consumers to make up their own minds, to trying to convince people that they cannot live without a certain product.

fig 5.55. Advertising outlets

fig 5.56.

The psychology of advertising may try to exploit human weaknesses in order to sell. **Fashion** and **style** are used; many people would not want to be considered old-fashioned or out of date. An advert may suggest that you will be more attractive to the opposite sex if you wear a certain brand of jeans. They may also try to convince you that driving a particular make of motor car or using a certain type of after-shave or perfume will change your life.

POSTERS

One of the oldest graphic forms of advertising is the poster. Changing styles in art and design can be traced through examples of poster design. The styles and fashions of the day are reflected in posters and many have become works of art in themselves. Famous artists and designers have designed posters. The French painters Toulouse-Lautrec and Bonnard both designed posters during the latter half of the nineteenth century, producing work influenced by a fashionable style of the time known as **Art Nouveau**. They made use of flowing lines and flat areas of colour to create impact. Fig 5.57 shows an example of a poster by Toulouse-Lautrec.

fig 5.57.

TELEVISION AND RADIO

The second half of the twentieth century has seen the development of a very important form of advertising, television. Commercial television companies raise their revenue by selling advertising time between the programmes. Commercial radio stations have been operating in the USA for over half a century and, with the development of TV sets for the masses, the idea was quickly taken on by TV stations. Great Britain currently operates two commercial TV channels, ITV and Channel 4, and many new commercial radio stations are being opened.

fig 5.58. TV Advertising

Most manufacturers or service industries wishing to advertise on television engage the services of an **advertising company**. The company will normally carry out any necessary **market research**, design the commercial and arrange the production. Producing television advertisments will involve the use of **graphic designers** and **artists**, **computer graphics experts** and **musicians**. Often a television commercial may be only part of a specially designed advertising campaign. It may be used to coincide with the launch of a new product or to update the image of a successful existing one. Television and radio advertising provides valuable opportunities for designers to make use of computer technology and modern TV graphic techniques.

SPONSORSHIP

Another important form of advertising is sports sponsorship. Companies rent or buy advertising space at sports grounds and football stadiums. This type of advertising can be very successful, especially if a match or event is televised, as the advertisement will then be seen in thousands of homes all over the country. World cup or international events will obviously have greater effect. In recent years companies have begun to advertise on cars and boats. Company logos and colour schemes have become part of the livery and an important part of the graphic design of the vehicle. The football league relies heavily on advertising and sponsorship. The shirts worn by the players usually carry the name or logo of the sponsoring company.

fig 5.60. Sponsorship

Over the last 20 or 30 years, some products have had very successful advertising campaigns. The advertising for Coca-Cola, for example, a well-established product, has been constantly updated over the years. It uses an internationally recognised **logo**, a film which emphasises fun and enjoyment and a catchy tune or jingle. Coca-Cola theme tunes have gone on to become hit records in many parts of the world.

fig 5.59.

Advertising has become part of twentieth-century life and provides work for countless people ranging from graphic artists to business executives. Many TV adverts have captured public attention and some are eagerly followed by the viewing public. The theme tunes or jingles often become top ten hits and many famous television personalities can be seen endorsing a variety of products. However, there is a need for caution. Many advertising campaigns rely on human nature and the desire to conform or 'keep up with the Joneses'. In a society where adverts encourage people to borrow money, care must be taken to avoid debt and financial hardship made worse by over-enthusiastic advertisers.

LOGOS AND TRADEMARKS

LOGOS

The word 'logo', when used in CDT, is an abbreviation of the word 'logogram'. A logogram is a form of letter or symbol which forms or suggests a word. A logo will often take the form of a symbol or pictogram and will not rely on words. We have already seen the importance of pictograms when used as signs on page 73.

Logos are used to form the basis of many trademarks. Trademarks are distinctive marks or designs which companies and other organisations put on their products, signs, letter headings and vehicles. They are used to identify the company and make it easily recognisable. Many companies can be easily recognised from their logo alone. Look at the trademarks shown in fig 5.61. How many companies can you recognise?

A logo can be formed by using the **initial** letters of a company name rather than the whole name. Fig 5.62 is an example of this, while the logo in fig 5.63 is derived from the first letter of the company name.

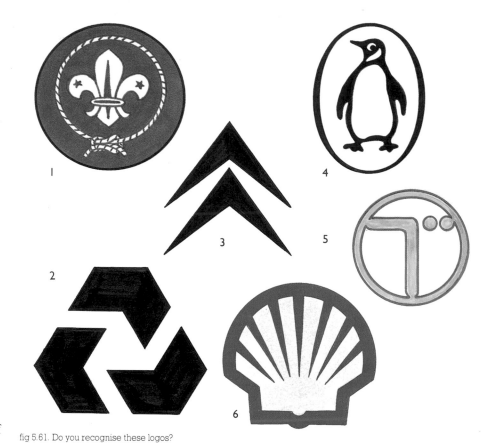

fig 5.61. Do you recognise these logos?

fig 5.63. Logo formed from the first letter of the company name

fig 5.62. Logo formed using initial letters of the company name

fig 5.64. Trademarks on backgrounds

TRADEMARKS

Trademarks do not always have to include a logo. The way in which a company name is written may form the basis of the trademark. It may be written in a certain style of lettering or be set against a particular shaped background. The colours used may be distinctive or perhaps associated with the company in some way. The 'Coca-Cola' trademark shown in fig 5.65 is a classic example of this. It relies on a certain style of lettering always being used.

fig 5.65. Trademarks based on names

Names of logos in fig 5.61

1.Scouts
2.National Westminster Bank
3.Citroen cars
4.Penguin Books
5.British Telecom
6.Shell

Logos often use symbols or simple pictures which relate to the function of the company or the product it produces. Look at the logos shown in fig 5.66. Can you guess what each company is involved in from its logo?

2

3

fig 5.66.

fig 5.67. Yamaha trademark

fig 5.68. RGT trademark

The Yamaha trademark shown in fig 5.67 can be found on motorcycles made by the company. Look closely at the logo used: it has no connection with motorcycles. It consists of three tuning forks, a reminder that the company began by making pianos in the latter part of the nineteenth century. When the company began making motorcycles in the early 1950s they used the same logo as a badge for their machines.

The trademark shown in fig 5.68 consists of the company's initials, RGT, and a symbol which relates to its products. Ruston Gas Turbines Ltd. is one of the country's leading producers of gas turbines and the symbol represents a turbine blade.

CORPORATE IDENTITY

Companies will often go to great lengths to create the right **impression** with their customers and the public. They may employ designers to create or update an image for them. This will include a **logo** or **trademark** and a **colour scheme**. This is known as corporate identity and is applied throughout the company from the colour of the vans and lorries, the buildings, employees' work clothes and office stationery to product brochures and in some cases even the products themselves. A to Z Couriers Ltd is an example of a company which has a corporate identity and the photographs in fig 5.69 give some idea of the extent to which it is used.

fig 5.69. Corporate identity

Logos and trademarks cut across language barriers. Many are used internationally and are easily recognised all over the world.

Logos are important in advertising and are normally a key point in most advertisements. They are also an important form of communication; for example, how many of the companies did you recognise from their logos in fig 5.61? Graphically speaking, logos are an important and accepted part of life, helping us to recognise and become aware of the existence of countless companies and organisations.

PACKAGING

Packaging is a very important part of design graphics, yet it is often thrown away without being given a second thought. Considerable work and effort goes into the important area of designing and making of packages.

Packaging has changed considerably over the years. In the past, many products were not packed until the time of sale, when they were simply put into a bag or wrapped in paper by the shopkeeper.

fig 5.70. Old fashioned shopkeeper

fig 5.71. A modern supermarket

Styles of shopping have changed over the years too and this has increased the need for packaging. Supermarket shopping means that most products need to be **pre-packed** before they go onto the shelves.

The pre-packing of food is not new. The idea of putting food into metal cans or tins was first patented in the early part of the nineteenth century by Peter Durand, a London merchant. Fig 5.72 shows some of the earliest types of cans used to contain food.

Canned food was taken on an Arctic expedition which ended in disaster in 1825. Some of the cans were found by another expedition in 1918, brought back and opened. After over 90 years the food inside was still in good condition.

Food is still preserved by canning and then heating. Processed peas are actually cooked for about 20 minutes in the can before they are cooled and the labels put on ready for sale. In some rural areas of this country, food canning provides work for many people. The canning factories are often situated near to where the food is grown so that it is packed while it is still fresh.

fig 5.72.

fig 5.73. Old and new Oxo containers

The materials used for packaging have changed too. Many items which were once packed in metal boxes or tins are now put into cardboard or paper boxes, due to the rising costs of materials. 'Oxo' cubes are a good example of this. They were once available in tins, but are now usually found in boxes. Fig 5.73 shows the two types of containers.

The introduction of **plastics** also brought about a change in package design. Many items are now attached to card with a thin skin of clear plastic film, while others are held onto card by a thin plastic bubble. Some jars and tins have been replaced by sealed plastic trays or containers. These are cheaper to produce, weigh less and can still be sealed to keep them airtight. Individual portions of food such as sugar, sauces, jam and marmalade are sometimes packed this way in restaurants and hotels.

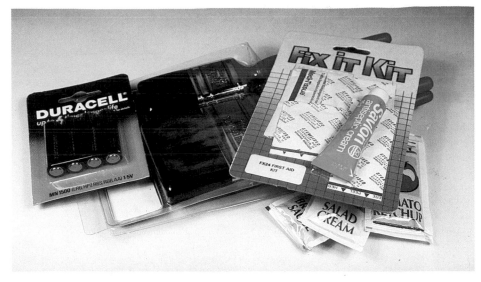

fig 5.74. Skin packing, bubble packing and sealed plastic containers

fig 5.75. Labels printed directly onto plastic containers

Developments in the field of plastics have greatly influenced package design. Washing-up liquid and similar containers have their designs printed directly onto the plastic. This eliminates the need for a stick-on paper label. Yoghurt and other dairy product containers are often manufactured in this way too.

The increasing use of technology has affected package design. Most items on sale in the shops now have a **bar code** printed on them. This looks like a series of thin black and white stripes with a row of numbers printed beneath it (fig 5.76). It is '**read**' by a **light pen** and the information is passed to a computer, where it is used in **stock control**. This is then used to work out how many items have been sold, how many are left in stock and when to re-order. In some cases even the re-ordering is done automatically.

fig 5.76. Bar codes and their uses

fig 5.77.

Packaging is big business. It is an industry in itself which employs its own specialist designers and manufacturers. Each year the packaging industry in Britain alone uses over 3 million tonnes of paper and card, 400,000 tonnes of plastic and 900,000 tonnes of tinplate. It has been estimated that packaging costs the average British family over £100 per year. Most of this is thrown into the dustbin, with only a relatively small amount **recycled** for future use.

Look carefully at the packages in fig 5.77. How many different materials have been used? Can you suggest why some of these materials were chosen?

FUNCTIONS OF PACKAGING

Packaging performs a variety of different functions. A well-designed package must **protect** the goods while they are being moved around, it must keep any separate parts together and yet still allow them to be taken out easily.

Some packages need to **communicate** a variety of technical information about the product ranging from how it is used to who made it. Other packages are designed to **advertise** or even **sell** the product they contain.

Package design differs according to the nature of the product it contains – and in some cases one function may be more important than another.

fig 5.78.

PROTECTING THE GOODS

fig 5.79. Examples of egg packing

Most goods need to be protected while they are in transit. This means protection on the way to the shops, as well as from the shop to our homes. Few things can be more annoying than receiving damaged goods. The packaging of eggs illustrates the need for protection. It is unsatisfactory to package eggs in a paper bag: it offers little or no protection and if just one egg is broken it will become wet and soggy.

Eggs are often transported in rigid trays made from papier-mâché and are often found on sale in shops in egg boxes made from moulded plastic sheet or rigid plastic foam. These boxes give the eggs some degree of protection, keep them together and allow a little space for displaying such information as the size of the eggs and the name of the company responsible for packing and distributing them (fig 5.79).

Televisions, hi-fi equipment and computers all need to be packed in such a way that they do not get damaged in transit. They are usually packed in some form of foam plastic, normally polystyrene, before being put into a strong cardboard box.

CONTAINING THE GOODS

Some packages need to keep separate parts of a product together and stop them being lost. Egg boxes keep six or 12 eggs together and hi-fi packing keeps the various component parts together. Imagine how you would feel if you bought a plastic construction kit, or some other DIY item, and found that some of the parts were missing. It is very important that the package contains the product, but it is also important that the user can get at the product when required for use. Paper tissues are packed in a box which automatically dispenses them. Each time one is used another is made ready for use. Some artificial sweeteners are packed in containers which automatically dispense one sweetener each time the top of the container is pressed (fig 5.80).

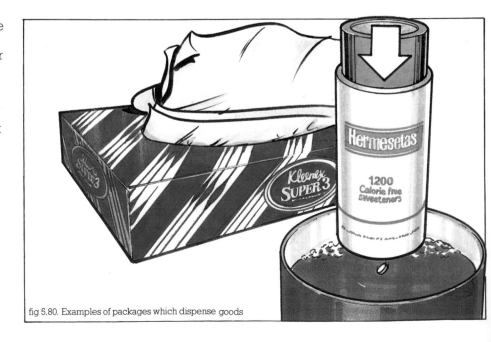

fig 5.80. Examples of packages which dispense goods

COMMUNICATION

Communication is very important in packaging. Vital information regarding the handling and stacking of the products is shown on the outside of the boxes. Symbols or pictograms are used to give a number of important instructions. The symbols in fig 5.81 show that the product is breakable and should be handled with care. One symbol shows that the product must be protected from moisture, while the others show which way up the boxes should be kept and how many boxes can be stacked on top of each other safely.

Other packages show technical information about the product itself. The film box in fig 5.82 conveys a variety of information including the type of film it is, the date by which is should be used and the number of photographs which can be taken.

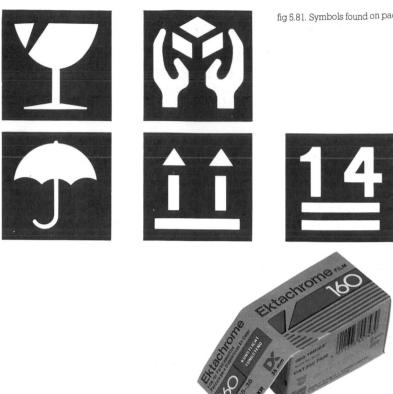

fig 5.81. Symbols found on packages

fig 5.82. Film box showing a variety of information

ADVERTISING AND SELLING THE GOODS

fig 5.83. Examples of packaging which advertises or displays goods

Many packages are actually designed to advertise and sell the product which they contain. They may show what the product can do or give detail of its special offer bargain price in order to make it look attractive to the customer. Fig 5.83 shows an example of this. The graphics on the can advertise what the product can do and offer a percentage extra at no extra cost.

Packages can help to sell the product if they can show what the product looks like. Many packages have a window in them which enables the contents to be displayed. The window is usually covered with a piece of thin, clear plastic. Other forms of packaging which allow the contents to be seen are blister packs and skin packs. Blister packs consist of a piece of clear plastic moulded to the shape of the product. The blister is placed over the product and then attached to a card backing piece. Skin packing is very similar except that a very thin clear plastic film is draped over the product and attached to the card by a method similar to vacuum forming. Both these types of package allow the product to be seen easily and the backing card provides an area which can be used to advertise, promote or communicate any other information required about the product. In situations where a window box or blister pack would not give enough protection, a photograph or illustration is used to show the product. This allows the use of strong, simple packaging and is often used to package large, bulky items.

EXAMPLES OF PACKAGING

The need for packaging changes as our lifestyles change. Methods of packaging goods in shops changed as the style of shopping changed. In the same way methods of serving and packing food changed as our eating habits have changed. Fast food and takeaway restaurants have very different needs in terms of packaging when compared to conventional restaurants. Many fast food restaurants do not use crockery, but instead serve the food in plastic and card containers. Fig 5.84 shows the way in which many restaurants and takeaways now serve hamburgers and similiar food.

fig 5.85. Chip container

fig 5.84. Fast food package

The illustration in fig 5.85 shows a chip container used by one of the major fast food restaurants. Traditionally, chips have been served in a greaseproof paper bag and wrapped in newspaper or newsprint paper. The paper keeps the food warm, but the grease from the chips tends to soak through the paper very quickly. Fast food restaurants aim to serve customers as quickly as possible and serving chips in the traditional way is expensive and time-consuming. Take a close look at the container in fig 5.85: it folds flat until required for use and so takes up very little space. It is bright and colourful and matches the company's colours. It is actually part of the company's corporate identity. The company's trademark, which includes a logo made up from the first letter of the company's name, is on the front of the container.

Fig 5.86 shows a container which has been carefully dismantled. It is made of one sheet of card or thin paper which is folded into shape with the tabs on either side glued down. Objects made from a flat material in this way are known as **developments**. Most boxes and containers used in packaging are developed in this way. This particular container uses only a small amount of material and so is **economical** to produce. The **two-colour printing**, red and yellow on white card, also helps to keep the production costs down. One of the disadvantages of packaging is the vast amount of litter and waste which is produced and the amount of material which is not reused. The paper used to make this container can be **recycled**, which further reduces the cost, does less harm to the environment and does not waste raw materials. There is also a logo printed on the container designed to encourage people to dispose of it carefully by putting it into a litter bin.

fig 5.86. Development of a chip container

The package in fig 5.87 is an example of **novelty** packaging. It has been designed to package a bottle of children's bubble bath. The cap on the bottle also serves as the face on the engine when it is in place inside the package. This type of packaging is often used for products intended for young children. Sweets and chocolate are sometimes packaged in this way and used as Christmas novelties, but one of the main uses is in the packaging of Easter eggs. The main design criterion, apart from containing and protecting the contents, is **visual appeal**. Characters popular with children are often used to generate interest and 'sell' the product.

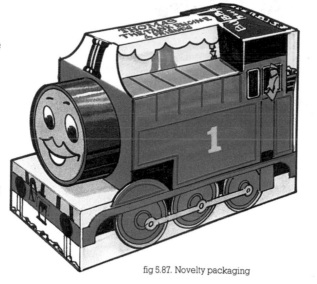

fig 5.87. Novelty packaging

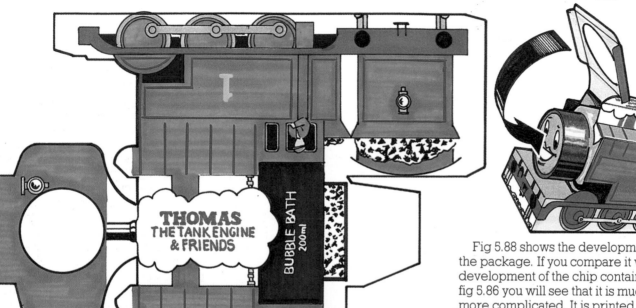

Fig 5.88 shows the development of the package. If you compare it with the development of the chip container in fig 5.86 you will see that it is much more complicated. It is printed in four colours as well as black on white card. It is made in such a way that the piece of card inside which supports the bottle is part of the development. The entire package, despite its complexity, is made from one piece of card. A package such as this has many folds and tabs and would require quite a lot of assembly work to put it together.

Which of the two packages do you think would be more expensive to produce?

The bottom of the package conveys a certain amount of information concerning the manufacturer and copyright details. It also contains the familiar tank engine logo and a bar code for stock control use.

fig 5.88. Development of the package

GRAPHICS FOR INSTRUMENTS AND CONTROLS

The design of graphics for instruments and controls is another important aspect of this area. Graphics are used here to communicate information in the form either of **data** from instruments, or of **instructions** concerning the use of equipment controls. Many examples of instrument and control graphics can be found around the home. Domestic appliances such as washing machines, microwave ovens, hi-fi equipment and electricity and gas meters all make use of graphics in some form or another. The motor car instrument panel provides many examples of the use of graphics. Machines in the school workshop or factory use graphics to convey important information. Graphics are also used in the form of nameplates, logos and trademarks and are displayed on machines and other equipment.

The main function of instrument and control graphics is to communicate information quickly and accurately. In some cases the information may be of vital importance and misreading it could have disastrous consequences. The control panel of an aircraft or high-speed train, for example, requires a very accurate display of information. So too does the modern motor car, which is also capable of transporting people at fairly high speeds. The designer must aim to reduce the possibility of **human error**. The graphics must be clear and well presented so that the operator does not misread the information displayed. The graphics used to convey control information on a machine or other piece of equipment must also be clear and accurate. Confusing graphics could lead to damage to the equipment or injury to the operator.

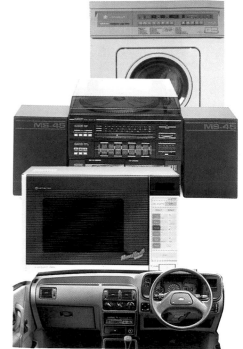

fig 5.89. Examples of instruments and control graphics

INSTRUMENTS

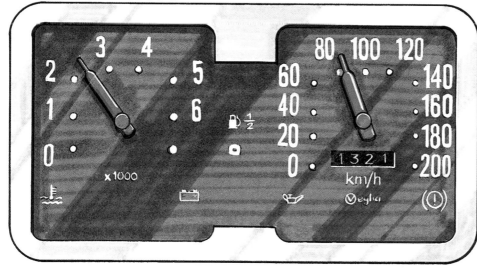

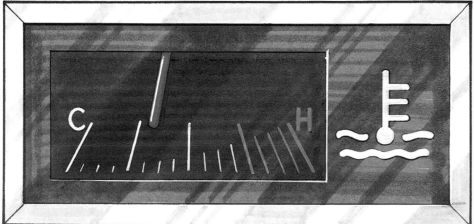

fig 5.90. Quantitative and non quantitative displays

The information from instruments has traditionally been displayed using a dial or gauge, but in recent years the developments made in technology have allowed digital electronic displays to be used.

Several factors must be taken into consideration when designing instrument graphics.

The nature and amount of information to be conveyed will affect the final design. For example, the driver of a motor car needs to know how hot the engine is, as overheating could cause serious mechanical damage. However, most drivers only need to know whether the engine is either operating at the normal temperature or beginning to overheat; they do not need to know how hot the engine is in terms of degrees centigrade. In this situation a **non-quantitative display** is required.

As far as the speed at which the vehicle is travelling is concerned, the driver needs constant, accurate information at all times. It is not enough to know whether the vehicle is travelling quickly or slowly, the driver needs to know exactly how fast the vehicle is travelling in terms of miles per hour, and so a **quantitative display** is required. Fig 5.90 shows the use of quantitative and non-quantitative displays in a motor car. The non-quantitative display allows designers to make greater use of colour and graphic symbols than the quantitative type which requires a straightforward, accurate presentation of the information.

The location of the instrument, the scale used and the size of the characters or figures will depend on their distance from the observer when the instrument is in use. In a motor car the graphics must be clearly visible from the driving seat. They must be neither too small, nor hidden by other controls such as the steering wheel. Any difficulty in reading the instruments may distract the driver and possibly cause an accident (fig 5.91).

fig 5.91. Location of instruments and controls

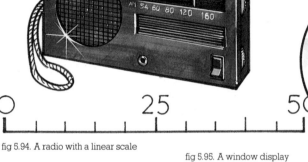

fig 5.92. The need for style

Style is important in any use of graphics, but in the case of instrument graphics the demand for style will vary according to the nature of the product involved. For example, the graphics on an electricity meter are less concerned with style than those on a radio dial or compact disc player. The style should be kept fairly simple; any ornate or over-elaborate styling could make the instrument very complicated and difficult to read (fig 5.92).

The instruments shown in fig 5.90 display the information by using a **rotating pointer** and are developments of the traditional dial. Fig 5.93 shows a speedometer which was fitted to motorcycles in the late 1930s and early 1940s. If you compare the two you will see that the later design relies more on the use of graphics and can be more easily read.

fig 5.93. An early speedometer

Not all dials and gauges use a rotating pointer and circular scale; linear scales are also used. Industrial measuring equipment sometimes uses **linear scales** and they are also often used on radio tuning displays. Fig 5.94 shows a typical transistor radio tuning display. In most linear instruments, the scale is fixed and the pointer moves, though in some cases the pointer is fixed and the scale moves in order to give a linear display. Sometimes the display takes the form of a window and the visible scale consists only of the numbers immediately before and after the pointer, as shown in fig 5.95. Some motor car manufacturers have used a window and rotating scale to display the speed at which the car is travelling. Fig 5.96 shows the type of speedometer used on the Citroen BX and CX models.

fig 5.94. A radio with a linear scale

fig 5.95. A window display

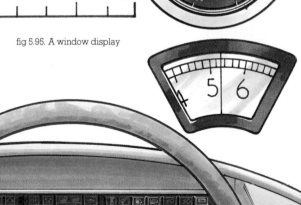

fig 5.96. Citroen speedometer, a rotating scale in a window display

Digital displays have been used more in recent years. Your gas or electricity meter at home may use a mechanically operated digital display rather like the mileage indicator on a motor car or motorcycle. Electronic digital displays are also becoming more commonly used. Fig 5.97 shows the **LCD** display on a modern stereo radio tuner. Compare it with the radio tuner shown in fig 5.94. The digital display conveys the information much more accurately and constantly updates it. Electronic digital displays can also be used to show different information at the press of a button. For example, the display on a video recorder can be made to act as a clock, a timer and a tape counter.

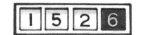

fig 5.97. Mechanical and electronic digital displays

CONTROLS

When graphics are used in the control of machines and equipment, **signs** and **symbols** are used to convey information. They are used to identify the various controls, show how the machine is operated or explain a sequence of actions or operations required to make it work. Important safety information can also be displayed graphically in the same way.

The control panel of the washing machine shown in fig 5.98 shows the user the program options available. In this example the program can be selected by matching the standard washing instruction symbol found inside the garment with the corresponding symbol on the machine. Once the required program has been identified the graphics enable the user to press the correct controls.

The microwave oven has a more complicated control panel. This particular machine is operated by touching the graphics themselves. They are actually a series of **touch-sensitive switches** which activate the machine.

The sewing machine illustrated allows the user to select the type of stitch required by simply moving the controls to correspond with the matching symbol. This particular machine is capable of producing 20 different types of stitch simply by following the graphic instructions.

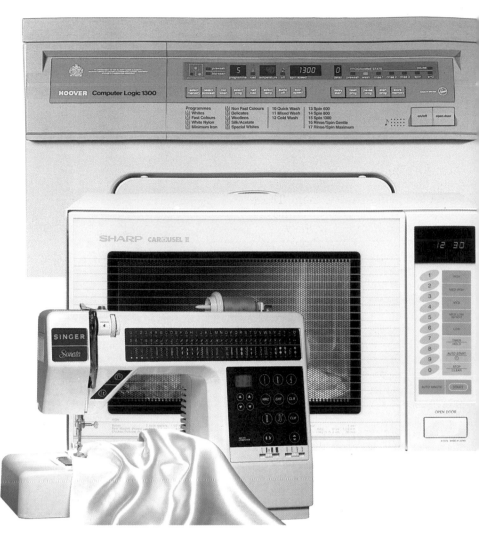

fig 5.98. Use of graphics in the control of machines

fig 5.100. Instruction plate from a milling machine

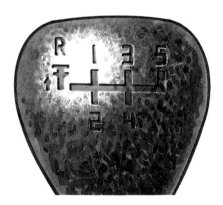

fig 5.99. Graphics on a motor car gear lever

When designing graphics for control, great care must be taken to keep them as simple as possible. On some machines, a simple misunderstanding could cause considerable damage. It must also be remembered that many manufacturers export their products all over the world and having to produce the graphics in different languages would add to the cost. As a designer, you should aim to use language only when absolutely necessary. The motor car gear lever shown in fig 5.99 shows the operation of the gear box very simply and without the use of language. It is clear from the graphics that the driver has to lift the lever to engage reverse gear.

Fig 5.100 shows an instruction plate found on the controls of a horizontal milling machine. This example uses the minimum language necessary to convey the message.

INSTRUCTIONS AND INFORMATION

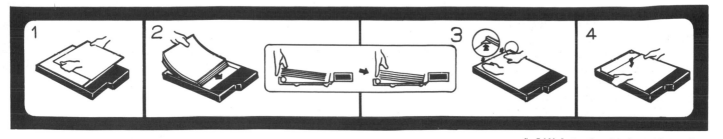

fig 5.101. Instruction plate from a photocopier

Many machines and other items of equipment have information or instruction plates fixed to them. These plates may simply display a company name or logo, or they may show detailed technical information or serial numbers and identification letters. The graphics shown in fig 5.101 were found on a photocopier. They explain very simply how to refill the machine with paper. The information plates in fig 5.102 were found on a grinding machine in a school workshop. They show the make and model of the machine, the maker's name and address and other technical information relating to the use of the machine.

When ordering spare parts, it is often necessary to know the name and exact model number of the machine. This is true when buying spare parts for motor cars. Fig 5.103 shows the type of identification plate which is fitted to motor cars. It clearly displays the model identification letters and numbers and shows code numbers which identify exactly the colour of the paint and interior trim of the car.

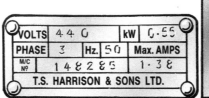

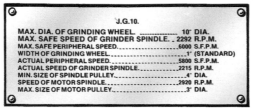

fig 5.102. Information plate from a machine in the school workshop

fig 5.103. Example of vehicle identification plate

fig 5.104. Dashboard warning light symbols

STANDARDISED SYMBOLS

When designing graphics for instruments and control, it is essential that simple, yet clear, symbols are used. Wherever possible try to make use of the current standardised symbols. These can be found in the British Standards booklet PD7307. If there is no suitable standard symbol available you will have to design your own. Fig 5.104 shows the symbols used on the dashboard warning lights of a modern motor car and fig 5.105 shows the symbols used to display the controls of a car heater. Motor car manufacturers have standardised the symbols used and most types of cars now use the same symbols.

Fig 5.106 shows the symbols found on the controls of a television set. Can you identify them from these symbols?

fig 5.105. Heater control symbols

fig 5.106. TV control symbols

DISPLAY AND EXHIBITION DESIGN

Display and exhibition design is another important aspect of design graphics. Good work can lose its visual impact and interest if it is poorly displayed. In some cases work of mediocre quality can be enhanced slightly by good display. The graphic techniques related to display such as lettering, mounting and presentation are covered in chapter 3. This section is concerned with the design and setting up of exhibitions and displays.

Companies specialising in exhibition design are often commissioned by manufacturers to display and promote their products. Some manufacturers employ artists and designers to work in their own publicity and exhibition departments.

The work of the display and exhibition designer can vary from designing a display stand at an international exhibition such as the Motor Show or a major trade exhibition, to producing a small counter display for a product in a shop. Whatever the scale of the exhibition or display, the aims remain the same. The basic aim is to show the subject or product to its best advantage and highlight its positive qualities. The display must catch the attention of the viewer; this is particularly important if it is part of a major exhibition where many other displays are present. Once the viewer's attention has been caught, the display must then attract their interest further and maintain attention while they absorb the information being displayed.

Display design brings together many aspects of Design and Communication, such as planning, drawing to scale, logos, corporate identity and model making.

fig 5.107. Major exhibition

fig 5.108. Counter display

An exhibition designer usually works from a **site plan** similiar to the one shown in fig 5.109. The permanent features of the building or exhibition hall are shown by heavy black lines. The site plans are always drawn to scale, so the designer can work out the size of space available for use. The designer can also consider the flow of spectators around the exhibition, the proximity of other stands and the visual impact his or her stand will create. He or she can work out sight lines from various points within the exhibition hall and then decide on the best position to place things such as logos and company trademarks.

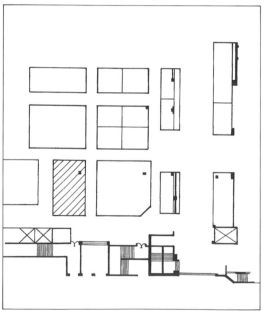

fig 5.109. Site plan

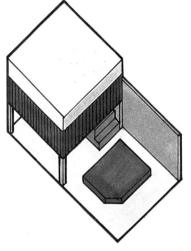

fig 5.110. Axonometric drawing

The designer will use a variety of graphic methods including **perspective** and **axonometric** drawings to show what the exhibition stand will look like. Axonometric drawings can be used to give a **'birds-eye' view** of the exhibition and can easily be developed from the site plan. Fig 5.110 shows an axonometric drawing of a possible exhibition stand. Once the designer has produced a satisfactory design, he or she will usually produce a scale model which can be used to show the customer what the finished exhibition stand will look like and provide the basis for discussing the construction methods. Once the details have been finalised a working drawing will be made and the exhibition stand constructed in a semi-permanent manner.

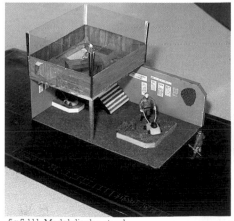

fig 5.111. Model display stand

Display areas can be created using one of the many display board systems that are currently available. Display systems like those shown in fig 5.112 are very suitable for this purpose because they can be put together in a variety of ways. They can be used to provide a linear type of display or they can be arranged so that they form display bays. This provides greater wall space and helps to create a more relaxed atmosphere by appearing to reduce the size of the display area.

Display areas must be suitably lit. Lighting can help to create the right atmosphere and be used to focus attention on the subject of the display. Lighting equipment is available for most of the display board systems. It is usually easy to fit and simply clips onto the boards or frames. The amount of light can be controlled by the use of dimmer controls. Display systems are very portable and usually fit into their own cases to protect them while they are being transported (fig 5.113).

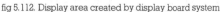

fig 5.112. Display area created by display board system

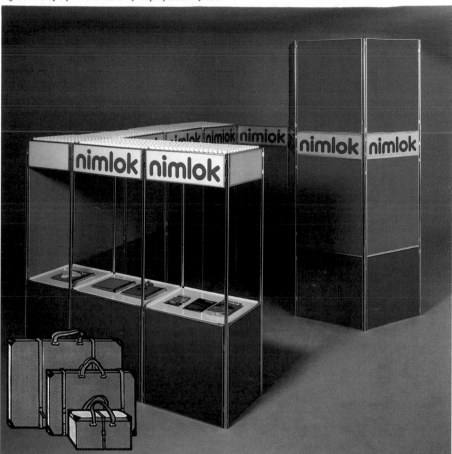

fig 5.113. Display boards packed into cases and boxes

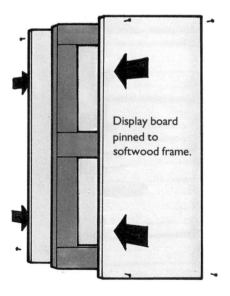

Display board pinned to softwood frame.

fig 5.114. Making display boards

Display board made from corrugated cardboard.

It is possible to construct your own display system using a variety of different materials. Boards can be made from plywood or chipboard as an alternative to the softer pin board material. However, chipboard is rather hard if you wish to use staples or pins. Boards can be constructed by covering a simple softwood frame with hardboard and then clamping a number of them together with one of the special display board clamps that are available. A very effective display surface can be produced by using a large roll of corrugated cardboard. The roll is simply stood upright and unrolled to form the required display space as shown in fig 5.114. Two-dimensional display material can then be pinned or stapled to the card.

fig 5.115. Decorative borders and colour schemes on display boards

The choice of colour is very important when designing display boards. A neutral colour with a matt finish is required. The background colour must be kept **neutral** so that it does not **clash** with the colours of the objects or the work being displayed against it. Dark green, grey, brown and beige are all suitable colours. A simple border design can be painted onto the boards to add interest. If the same style of border is used on each board, a unifying style can easily be developed. Lettering techniques are covered in chapter 3, but display designers should try to use the same style of lettering throughout the display so that it too has a unifying effect on the display as a whole. Using several different lettering styles will only serve to make the display look very untidy and unprofessional.

EXERCISES

1. Your favourite pop group are to release a compilation compact disc of their greatest hits. Choose the songs you would like to appear on the disc and design the graphics for the CD case.

2. Design a sign to draw attention to the emergency stop buttons in the school workshop. The sign should be no larger than 200 × 300 mm and must allow the stop buttons to be located quickly in the event of an accident. The function of the buttons should be shown by using simple symbols or pictograms.

3. A new after-shave and cologne for men known as 'Grand Prix' is to be produced by one of the country's leading companies. Design a display stand to be situated on the counter in major department stores and chemists. Design the accompanying graphics and make a model of the stand which should not exceed 300 mm in height.

4. The drawing in fig 5.116 shows a small, sporty hatchback car. Design a customizing pack which could be sold as an accessory. The pack should include luxury wheel trims, front and rear spoiler and self-adhesive plastic body graphics. The graphics must include the manufacturer's logo and some reference to the engine size.

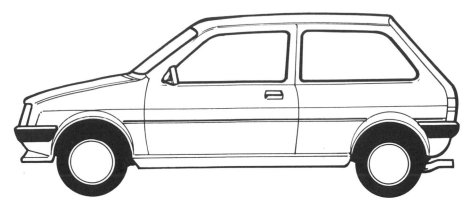

fig 5.116. Sporty, hatchback car

fig 5.117. Small pocket radio

5. The illustration in fig 5.117 shows a small pocket radio marketed under the name 'Trendsetter'. Design the colour scheme and the control graphics for the radio.

6. Fig 5.118 shows part of a site plan for a large indoor exhibition centre. You have been asked by the local radio station to design an exhibition stand to promote their services and programmes at the annual county show. You have been allocated stand W52 on the site plan. You must incorporate the radio station logo and colour scheme into your design. Make a model of the chosen design to a suitable scale.

7. A major cosmetic company is to launch a new range of cosmetic products intended to appeal to the younger generation of make-up buyers. The range is to be marketed under the name 'Images' and is to include lipstick, eye shadow and nail polish. Design the logo, colour scheme and packaging for the range.

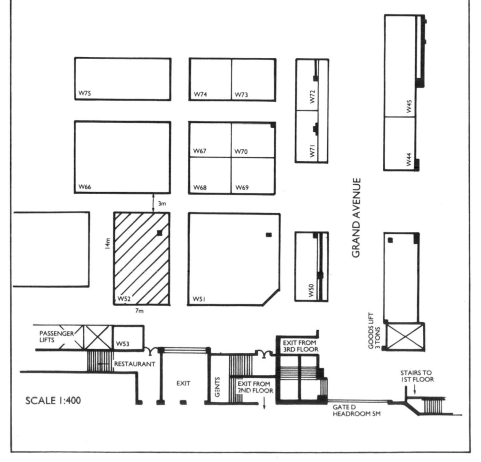

fig 5.118. Site plan

BASIC TECHNOLOGY AND RELATED SKILLS

CONTROL SYSTEMS

Most designing and making activities require some form of control. You need to control your hand to pick up a pencil or use a compass to draw a circle. You can control a television or model car by remote control. Computers can control drawing instruments, machines and robots to work with great accuracy and speed.

The way in which things are controlled can seem very complicated, but even complex control systems can be simple to understand if you use the right approach to them. This approach is called the **systems approach**. It involves looking at the building blocks that go to make up a system. It is rather like using building blocks to build a model house. Each block links to others to make up a whole house. In a control system each control block links to others to produce the required system. The basic building blocks that go to make up a control system are shown in this **block diagram**:

fig 6a. Block diagram

Here are some more examples of control systems shown as block diagrams:

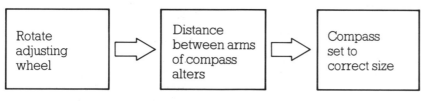

fig 6b. Controlling a compass

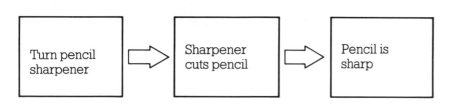

fig 6c. Controlling a pencil sharpener

As you can see from these examples, the systems approach can be used to explain any control situation without getting involved in the detail of how it is done. It makes no difference what kind of systems you are dealing with, each requires a control system of some sort. In industry the systems approach is used to identify the various parts of the problem before starting to work out the detail. You can use it in a similar way to design solutions to control problems.

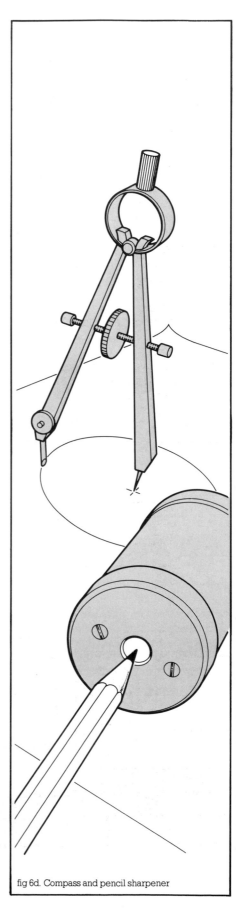

fig 6d. Compass and pencil sharpener

MECHANISMS

Most of the mechanisms you use are so familiar that you never think about them, for example, simple things like light switches, door handles and tin openers which you use every day. Each one has been designed to do a particular job. Most of the time they do it perfectly. It is probably only when they go wrong that you think about them. Although designed to do different jobs, all mechanisms have some things in common:

– they make a job **easier** to do

– they involve some kind of **movement**

– they involve some kind of **force**

– they need some kind of **input** to make them work

– they produce some kind of **output**.

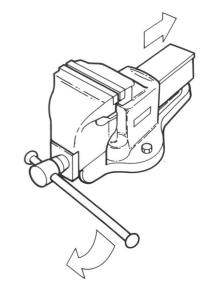

fig 6.1. Vice

For example, look at the vice shown in fig 6.1. It makes the task of holding your work very easy. The input movement is provided by the force you apply when turning the handle. The output movement is the vice jaws closing and applying a holding force to your work. The part that changes the rotary input motion into a linear output motion is a screw thread. The whole system can be shown in a block diagram similar to the one shown below:

A screw thread is one of the basic mechanisms. It can be used in many different ways. For example it can be used to provide powerful, accurate movements (e.g. car jacks) or to position and hold things in place (e.g. vices, cramps, screws and bolts).

Rotary and **linear** are just two of the four basic kinds of movement. The other two are **reciprocating** and **oscillating**, examples of which and the symbols used to represent them are shown in figs 6.2 and 6.3.

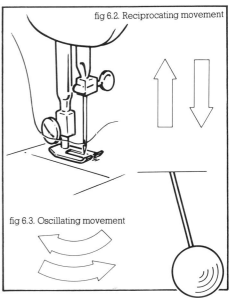

fig 6.2. Reciprocating movement

fig 6.3. Oscillating movement

LEVERS

Levers were probably the first kind of mechanism to be used, to help move large rocks or prise open shells. They were used in much the same way that we might use a crowbar to open a crate or a tyre lever to remove a tyre. These are very obvious levers, but there are many other less obvious levers you use every day, such as knives and forks, switches, door handles and cycle brakes. All levers are one of three basic kinds. These are shown in figs 6.4, 6.5 and 6.6. They can be used individually (e.g. a spanner), in pairs (e.g. pliers), or connected together to form a linkage (e.g. lazy tongs).

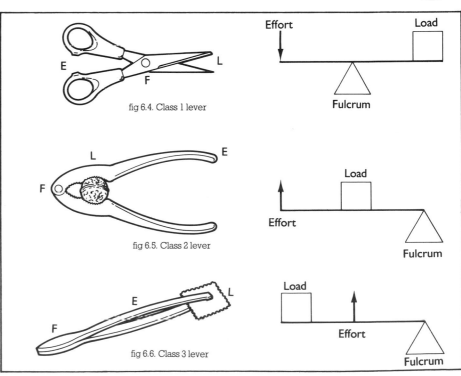

fig 6.4. Class 1 lever

fig 6.5. Class 2 lever

fig 6.6. Class 3 lever

MECHANICAL ADVANTAGE

Classes 1 and 2 are the most common types of lever because they give the user a **mechanical advantage**. That means that a large load can be moved using a small effort. The mechanical advantage of the Class 1 lever shown in fig 6.7 is given by comparing the weight of the load compared with the effort needed to move it.

$$MA = \frac{\textbf{Load}}{\textbf{Effort}} = \frac{50N}{10N} = \frac{5}{1} \text{ or } 5:1 \text{ or } 5$$

This means that it could be used to move a load five times greater than the effort applied to the lever. The MA of any mechanism can be calculated in the same way.

Class 3 levers are used less often because their mechanical advantage is less than 1. Thus the force needed to use them is greater than the force they can move. If being worked by hand, the use of Class 3 levers is limited to things like tweezers which only need small input forces.

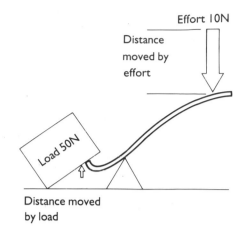

fig 6.7. Class 1 lever

VELOCITY RATIO

When calculating mechanical advantage it seems as if you are getting something for nothing: you are moving a large load using a small effort! However, if you look at the distance your effort is having to move, you will see it has to move much further than the load is moved. Comparing the two distances gives the **velocity ratio**. For example, using the Class 1 lever in fig 6.7;

$$VR = \frac{\text{distance moved by } \textbf{effort}}{\text{distance moved by } \textbf{load}} = \frac{50cm}{10cm} = \frac{5}{1} \text{ or } 5:1 \text{ or } 5$$

So, you are moving a load five times greater than your effort, but only by moving your effort five times as far as the load moves.

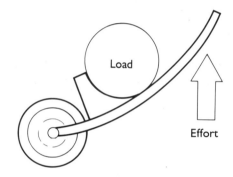

fig 6.8. Lever that bends

EFFICIENCY

All this assumes that a mechanism is 100 per cent efficient. It never is! In practice parts bend, twist and rub against each other, which makes them less efficient.

The **efficiency** of a mechanism can be calculated using the formula:

$$\textbf{Efficiency} = \frac{\textbf{MA}}{\textbf{VR}} \times 100\%$$

For example fig 6.8 shows a lever which, because it bends, has a MA of 4 and a VR of 5. Therefore,

$$\textbf{Efficiency} = \frac{4}{5} \times 100\% = 80\%$$

LINKAGES

Linkages are very important in mechanical control systems because they allow forces and motion to be transmitted where they are needed. They can change the direction of a movement, the size of a force, or make things move at the same time or parallel to each other. They usually do several of these things at once. **Bell cranks** or **reverse motion** linkages, as shown in fig 6.9, can be used to change the direction of motion. This is useful for taking motion round a corner or changing a push into a pull.

By changing the position of the fulcrum or lengthening one side of the lever, bell cranks can also be used to change the distances moved and the forces produced by the linkage. This is shown in fig 6.10.

Linkages based on a parallelogram can be used to make two or more parts move together or stay parallel to each other as the linkage moves. Fig 6.11 shows a scissor lift table which uses this principle. Many folding chairs, tables and pushchairs also use this idea.

One very useful linkage is the **toggle clamp**, which is used to lock things into position. It holds very firmly and is very quick to use. Mole grips and louvre window catches are examples you may have come across. Toggle clamps are used widely in industry to hold work in position while it is worked on. It works rather like your knee joint. If you have to stand on one leg for a while, you will lock your leg by pushing the knee back. Fig 6.13 shows how the toggle clamp works by forcing the middle of the three joints slightly over centre against a stop. Once in that position it is locked, and any force trying to open it only pushes it even further into the locked position.

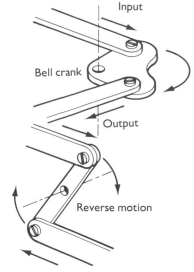

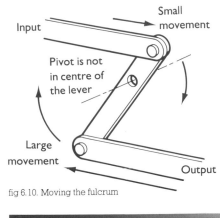

fig 6.10. Moving the fulcrum

fig 6.9. Bell crank and reverse motion

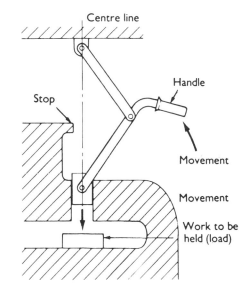

fig 6.11. Scissor lift table

fig 6.12. Folding pushchair

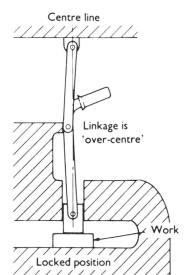

fig 6.13. Toggle clamp system

ROTARY SYSTEMS

The majority of machines use some kind of rotary movement. Some, like the cycle, are based totally on **rotating parts**. Others use a rotary input motion which they change into a different output motion. A graphic plotter is a good example of this (fig 6.14). The rotary motion of its stepper motors is turned into linear movement of the pen. A car engine does things the other way round: it changes the reciprocating motion of the pistons into a rotary motion of the wheels.

Many machines use electric motors to provide a rotary input movement. The speed of the motor is rarely the same as the speed needed for the machine, therefore a way has to be found of providing the desired output speed from the motor input speed. It may also be necessary to reverse the direction of rotation. These things can be done using one or a combination of the following systems.

fig 6.14. Plotter

Pulleys, chain and sprockets and gears

Pulleys use a belt to transmit motion from the driver shaft to the driven shaft. The **'vee' belt** is the one most often used. It fits tightly into the groove on the pulley wheels to stop them from slipping (fig 6.15). Most of the machines in your school workshops use pulley systems. The system is easiest to see on a drilling machine (fig 6.16). Most drilling machines have three or four sets of pulley wheels. By moving the belt from one set to the other the speed of the drill can be changed.

To reverse the direction of rotation using a pulley system, the belt must be crossed (fig 6.17). This will only work well if the belt is prevented from rubbing where it crosses.

Chain and sprocket systems use a chain to transmit rotary motion from the driver shaft to the driven shaft. Sprockets are the toothed wheels on which the chain runs. This means that, unlike pulley systems, the chain and sprocket system cannot slip. A bicycle is a good example of a machine that uses a chain and sprocket system (fig 6.18). In this case the driver shaft is turned by pedalling and the driven shaft is at the centre of the back wheel.

Gears are toothed wheels, fixed to the driver and driven shafts, which mesh together. Two gears, in mesh, will turn in opposite directions (fig 6.19). To get them to turn in the same direction a third gearwheel has to be fitted between them, as shown in fig 6.20. This **idler gear** has no effect on the speeds of the other two gears.

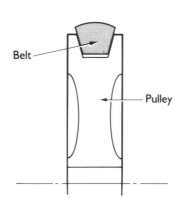

fig 6.15. Cross-section of a V-belt

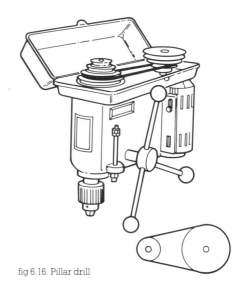

fig 6.16. Pillar drill

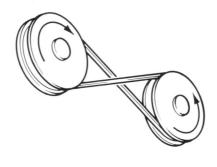

fig 6.17. Belt changes direction

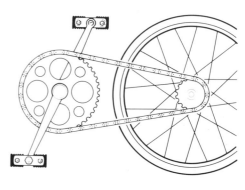

fig 6.18. Chain and sprocket system

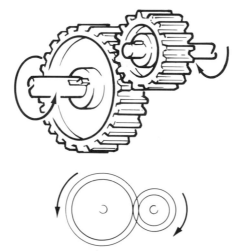

fig 6.19. Spur gears

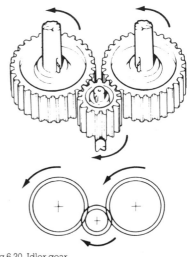

fig 6.20. Idler gear

Gears can also be used to change rotary motion through 90 degrees. This may be either by **bevel gears**, as in fig 6.21, or by a worm and wormwheel, as seen in fig 6.22.

Another change of motion, rotary to linear, can be achieved using a **rack and pinion**. A rack is a flat strip with teeth cut in it. The pinion is the gear which meshes with it. When the pinion turns it moves the rack along (fig 6.23). This is the system used on a drilling machine to bring the drill down into the work.

Speed changes

The speed (velocity) changes that take place in any of these systems can be calculated by comparing the sizes of pulleys or gears used:

$$\text{Velocity \textbf{ratio}} = \frac{\textbf{Driven}}{\textbf{Driver}}$$

With pulley systems the diameters of the pulleys are used.

With chain and sprocket systems and gear systems, use the number of teeth. For example, in fig 6.24:

Driven sprocket teeth = 20
Driver sprocket teeth = 120

$$\textbf{VR} = \frac{\textbf{Driven}}{\textbf{Driver}} = \frac{20}{120} = \frac{1}{6} \text{ or } 1{:}6$$

This means that one turn of the driver shaft will give six turns of the driven shaft. Another way of saying this is to say that the driven shaft is going six times faster than the driver shaft.

To calculate the output speed of any of these systems you need to know the input speed and the velocity ratio of the system. You can then use the formula:

$$\textbf{Output speed} = \frac{\textbf{Input speed}}{\textbf{Velocity ratio}}$$
$$\textbf{(OS)}$$

For example, if input speed = 2460 rpm and velocity ratio = 6:

$$\textbf{OS} = \frac{2460}{6} = 410 \text{ rpm}$$

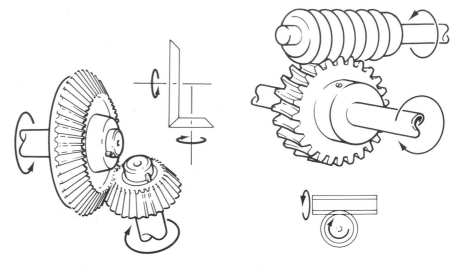

fig 6.21. Bevel gears   fig 6.22. Worm gear

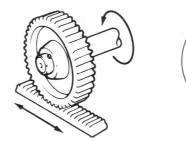

fig 6.23. Rack and pinion

fig 6.24. Chain and sprockets

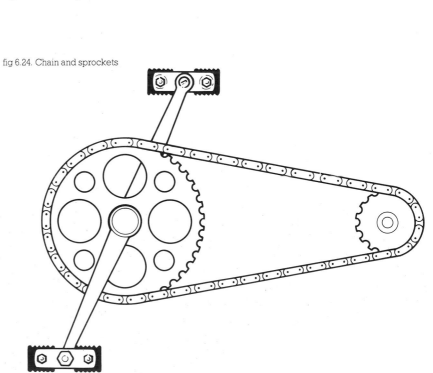

CRANK SLIDERS AND CAMS

Crank slider mechanisms can be used in two ways:

1. To change **rotary motion** into **reciprocating motion**, as in a power hacksaw (fig 6.25). An electric motor powers a crank which is connected to the saw frame. The saw frame is free to slide on the 'arm'. As the crank rotates it causes the frame to slide backwards and forwards on the arm. The longer the crank the further the saw frame will move.

2. To change **reciprocating motion** into **rotary motion**, as in a car engine. The reciprocating pistons are connected to the crankshaft by connecting rods. As the pistons move up and down the bottom end of the connecting rod pushes the crankshaft round (fig 6.26). Each piston in turn moves down, so keeping the crankshaft turning.

Cams

Cams are most often used to change rotary motion into either reciprocating or oscillating motion. They are shaped pieces of metal which are fixed to, or are part of, a shaft. A '**follower**' is held against the edge of the cam, usually by a spring (fig 6.27).

As the cam rotates, the follower moves. The way in which it moves and the distance it moves depend on the shape of the cam. Two cam shapes in common use are shown in fig 6.28. Each produces a different kind of motion in the follower. Figs 6.29 shows an overhead camshaft which, as it rotates, opens and closes the valves in an engine, using 'pear shaped' cams. Each valve reciprocates as its cam rotates.

Fig 6.30 shows a mechanical fuel pump. It too is operated by the rotary motion of a camshaft. Here the cam is a circular one, sometimes called an '**eccentric**'. As the cam rotates it causes an oscillating motion in the follower. This moves the diaphragm up and down, so pumping fuel to the engine.

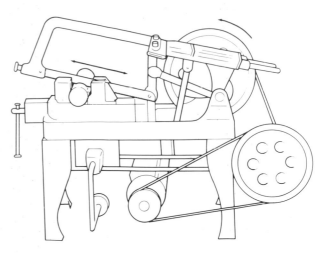

fig 6.25. Rotary motion into reciprocating

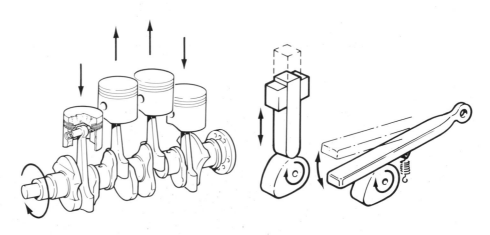

fig 6.26. Reciprocating motion into rotary   fig 6.27. Cam and follower

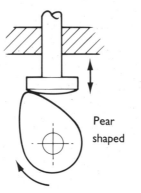

Pear shaped

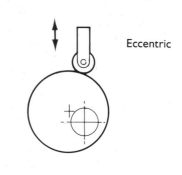

Eccentric

fig 6.28. Two cam shapes in common use

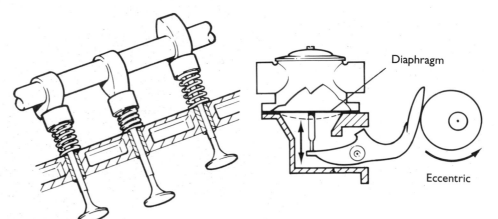

Diaphragm

Eccentric

fig 6.29. Overhead camshaft   fig 6.30. Fuel pump

STRUCTURES

When you think of structures you probably think of things like bridges, electricity pylons and tall buildings. These are very obvious structures, but there are other examples much closer to you, such as stools, benches, cupboards and even doors. With some structures, like the sledge in fig 6.31, it is very obvious how they support a load. Many **frame structures** are like this, but there are other frame structures which are not so obvious. They may have some kind of 'skin' over the framework, as with the door in fig 6.32.

The sledge shown in fig 6.33 does not have a frame; it relies on the shape it has been moulded into for its strength. It is an example of a **shell structure**. These are suprisingly strong, yet very light in weight compared to frame structures. That is why most car bodies are made this way. Sheet metal is pressed into the shapes of the various panels and welded together. The more curved or ridged a panel is, the stronger it will be. Large flat panels, such as the bonnet, are not very strong and often have to be supported by a framework (fig 6.34).

The frame and shell structures listed so far are manufactured, but they are all based on structures found in nature. Trees, leaves and spiders' webs are all examples of frame structures. An umbrella supports its load in a very similar way to the leaf in fig 6.35. Eggshells, honeycombs and the hollow stems of many plants are all examples of shell structures. The hollow stems support their load in exactly the same way that a metal tube supports a TV aerial.

fig 6.31. Traditional wooden toboggan

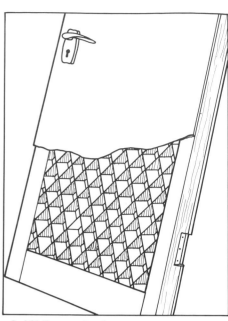

fig 6.32. Door construction

fig 6.33. Moulded plastic sledge

fig 6.34. Framework support

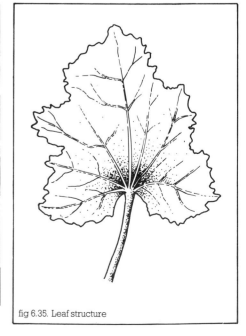

fig 6.35. Leaf structure

Structures are built to support a load, which may be **static** or **dynamic**. Static loads are those which do not move, like a book on a shelf. Dynamic loads are those which do move, like a diver on a springboard. Dynamic loads produce much greater forces than static loads. Many structures have to be built to withstand dynamic loads even though they spend most of their time supporting static loads; for example, bunk beds (fig 6.36) have to be strong enough to take the dynamic forces created by the children playing on them, even though their main purpose is to support a fairly static load.

fig 6.36.

There are five basic types of force that act on a structure.

Compression forces act to squash a structure. Axle stands are compressed by the weight of a car (fig 6.37).

fig 6.37. Car on axle stands

Tension forces act to stretch a structure. The wires supporting a suspension bridge (fig 6.39) are in tension.

Bending forces act to bend a structure. The bar in fig 6.38 is bending due to the weight of the gymnast. A closer look at the bar would show it is in compression on its upper surface and in tension on its lower surface.

fig 6.39. Suspension bridge

Torsion forces act to twist a structure. It was torsion forces which eventually caused the bridge in fig 6.40 to collapse.

fig 6.38.

Shear forces act to cut a structure in two. The forces acting in opposite directions on the bolt in fig 6.41 are trying to shear it.

Designers have to try and calculate the forces that will act on a structure in order to make it strong enough while not being too expensive. Getting this just right is a very tricky business. Even very skilled designers can never be absolutely sure they have planned for all the forces that might act on a structure. Who is to say that a 13-stone man will not sit on a swing designed for 5-year-olds, or that a jack designed to lift loads up to 500 kg won't be used to try to lift 1000 kg. To overcome problems like this, structures are designed with a **factor of safety**. This is arrived at by calculating the expected forces and then multiplying them by the required number, for example 4. So, if a swing frame is being designed to take loads of 120 N, using a safety factor of 4 it should in fact be capable of supporting loads of up to 480 N.

fig 6.40. Tacoma Narrows bridge

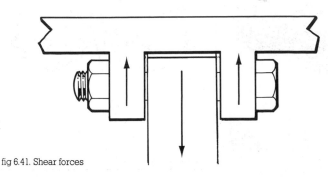

fig 6.41. Shear forces

BEAMS, BRIDGES AND STABILITY

Different members (parts) of a structure are often coping with different forces. For example, look at the swing in fig 6.42. The legs are being compressed. Members in compression are called **struts**. The chains are in tension. Members in tension are called **ties**. The top rail and seat are bending. The bolts supporting the chains are in shear. Each part has been designed to cope with the particular forces acting on it. The material chosen for a member, and its shape, are very important.

Beams of one sort or another are the most common kind of structural member. If designed and used correctly, they can cope with all types of forces. Originally, all beams were made of solid material, which made them very heavy and expensive (fig 6.43). Over the years many different beam shapes have been developed which are much lighter yet just as strong, or stronger (fig 6.44). For maximum strength, it is important that a beam is used the right way on, i.e. with the widest section taking the load (fig 6.45). You will see many of these beams in use around you every day; look at bridges, street lights, lorry chassis, bike frames and fence posts.

Some beams are only supported at one end. Fig 6.46 shows such a beam; it is called a **cantilever** beam. When loaded, it is in tension on the top surface and in compression on the lower surface. Cantilever beams are used either where it is only possible to support one end or where it is necessary to keep a large gap clear.

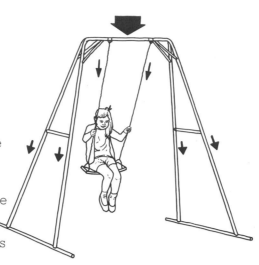
fig 6.42.

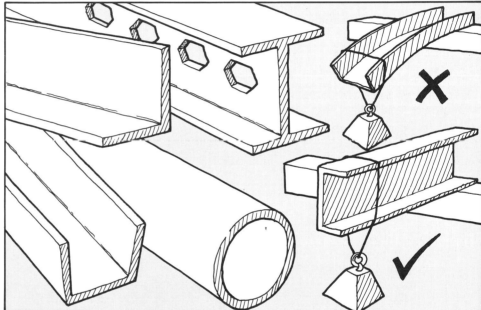

fig 6.43. Solid beams

fig 6.44. Beam shapes

fig 6.45. Beams bending

fig 6.46. Cantilever beam

fig 6.47.

Stability

Rectangular shapes can distort when loaded (fig 6.48). By adding one extra member, so creating two triangles, it can be stopped from distorting (fig 6.49). Many structures use triangular shapes to give them stability, for example pylons, cranes and bike frames.

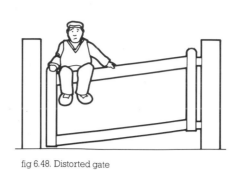

fig 6.48. Distorted gate   fig 6.49. Triangulation

Beam calculations – moments

Most structures are designed not to move under load. For this to happen the forces acting on the structure must be 'balanced'. If they are balanced the structure is said to be in **equilibrium**. Bridges and houses are examples of structures in equilibrium. In practice, however, small movements do occur due to how and where the loads are applied. Fig 6.50 shows a beam in equilibrium. The downward forces acting on it are balanced by the upward forces, called **reactions**, at its ends. Because the load is in the centre of the beam the reactions at X and Y are each half the value of the downward force. This can be proved by calculation:

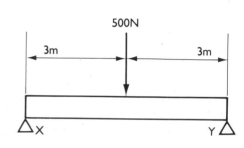

Given that **anticlockwise moments = clockwise moments**
and **upward forces** (Reaction X + Reaction Y) = **downward forces** (500 N)

Taking moments about end X,   Reaction Y × 6 = 500 × 3

$$\text{Reaction Y} = \frac{1500}{6}$$

$$\text{Reaction Y} = 250\text{N}$$

fig 6.50. Beam in equilibrium

If Reaction X + Reaction Y = 500 N then

$$\text{Reaction X} = 500 - \text{Reaction Y}$$
$$= 500 - 250$$
$$\text{Reaction X} = 250\text{ N}$$

If the load is not in the centre of the beam, the reactions will not be equal. Fig 6.51 shows such a situation. The reactions at X and Y can be calculated in the same way as before.

Given that **anticlockwise moments = clockwise moments**
and **upward forces** (Reaction X + Reaction Y) = **downward forces** (500 N)

Taking moments about end X, $Y × 6 = 500 × 2$

$$Y = \frac{1000}{6}$$

$$Y = 166.6 \text{ N}$$

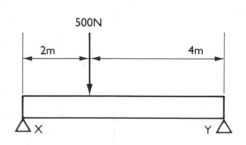

If Reaction X + Reaction Y = 500 N then

$$\text{Reaction X} = 500 - \text{Reaction Y}$$
$$= 500 - 166.6$$
$$\text{Reaction X} = 333.3 \text{ N}$$

fig 6.51. Uneven load on a beam

You can see that most of the load is taken by the support nearest to the load. The nearer the load gets to a support the more of the load that support is taking. So when a moving object, such as a car, goes over a bridge the load taken by each of the supports changes as it crosses the bridge.

ELECTRONICS

Electronics is an important part of your everyday life. Your calculator, television, radio and stereo system all use electronics. Although these are quite complex systems they rely on a few basic principles. All electronic circuits can be shown as block diagrams, having an **input**, **control** and **output** (fig 6.52). Most electronic components fall into one of these catagories, which makes the process of circuit design easier to understand. The more common ones are shown below.

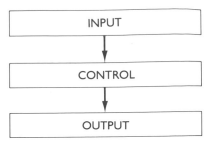

fig 6.52.

INPUTS

Batteries are used to provide the power for many electronic circuits, because they are small, portable and safe (fig 6.53).

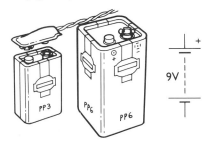

fig 6.53. Batteries

Switches come in many different styles, with different numbers of connections. They are used to 'make' or 'break' connections. Three manual and one magnetically operated switches are shown in fig 6.54.

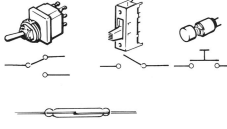

fig 6.54. Switches

Capacitors are used to store an electrical charge. Their value is measured in microfarads (μF). Two of the basic types are shown in fig 6.55.

Electrolytic capacitors must be connected the right way round. They have their value written on them, as shown in fig 6.55.

Polyester capacitors can be connected either way round. They have smaller values which can be worked out using the same colour code as for resistors.

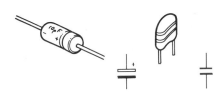

fig 6.55. Capacitors

Resistors are used to control and direct the flow of electricity. Resistance is measured in **ohms** (Ω). Fixed resistors have a fixed value which is indicated by the coloured bands (fig 6.56). For colour values see table below. The fourth band shows the tolerance.

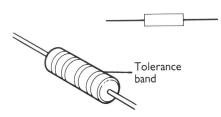

fig 6.56. Resistor

Colour	1st band	2nd band	3rd band
Black	0	0	–
Brown	1	1	0
Red	2	2	00
Orange	3	3	000
Yellow	4	4	0000
Green	5	5	00000
Blue	6	6	000000
Violet	7	7	0000000
Grey	8	8	00000000
White	9	9	000000000

fig 6.57. Resistor colour code

Variable resistors, also called potentiometers, can be adjusted to change their resistance. The two basic types are shown below.

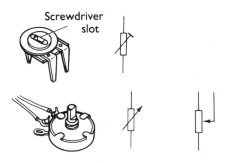

fig 6.58. Variable resistors

Thermistors sense temperature changes and convert them into voltage changes (fig 6.59).

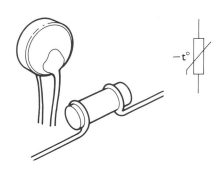

fig 6.59. Thermistor

The **light-dependent resistor** (LDR) and the phototransistor can both be used to sense changes in light intensity. They convert light changes into voltage changes (fig 6.60).

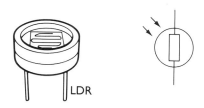

fig 6.60. Light dependent resistor

Moisture sensors convert changes in moisture content into voltage changes (fig 6.61).

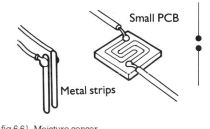

fig 6.61. Moisture sensor

CONTROLS

Transistors are useful because they allow circuits to work automatically. They act as a switch, reacting to voltage changes in the input. When the input voltage is below 0.6 V the transistor is switched off, which means that the output is off. When the input voltage rises above 0.6 V the transistor switches on, so the output is on. Street lights use a simple system based on this idea to switch on and off according to light conditions. The transistor shown in fig 6.62 is an NPN transistor. Its three legs must be connected the right way round.

Thyristors are similar to transistors, but have the advantage that once switched on, by a small input voltage, they stay on. This can be very useful in alarm circuits (fig 6.63).

The **555 timer** is an 'integrated circuit', or IC. It is used to give timed periods, from a fraction of a second up to several minutes. It can be used to control either lights or sounds. Its eight legs or pins are numbered as shown in fig 6.64.

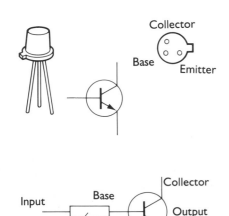

fig 6.62. NPN transistor

fig 6.63. Thyristor

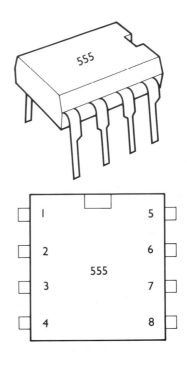

fig 6.64. 555 timer

OUTPUTS

Bulbs can be connected either way round. Their disadvantage is that they break quite easily (6.65).

fig 6.65. Bulb

Light-emitting diodes (LEDs) can be used instead of bulbs. They are much tougher and use much less power. They must be connected the right way round and protected by a resistor. They come in three colours: red, green and amber (fig 6.66).

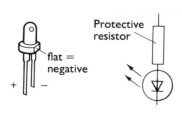

fig 6.66. Light emitting diode

Small dc **motors** can be used to create movement. They can be made to rotate in either direction simply by changing over the connections (fig 6.67).

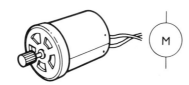

fig 6.67. Small dc motor

Relays are used as an interface between two electrical circuits. Although one circuit is controlled by the other, they are electrically isolated (fig 6.68).

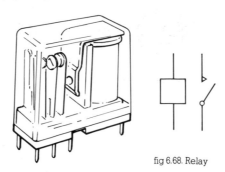

fig 6.68. Relay

Solenoids can be used to provide small linear movements. The core is pulled in when it is switched on and springs back out when it is switched off. They are sometimes used for door locks (fig 6.69).

fig 6.69. Solenoid

Buzzers give a continuous sound. The volume will depend on the supply voltage. They must be connected the right way round (fig 6.70).

Speakers change electrical pulses into sound. The pitch and volume of sound varies according to the pulses received (fig 6.71).

fig 6.70. Buzzer

fig 6.71. Speaker

103

SWITCHING CIRCUITS

Switching circuits are circuits which switch an output on or off according to the state of the input. Many different switching circuits can be built, some more sensitive than others. The best way to understand one of these circuits is to look at its three parts, input, control and output, before looking at the full circuit.

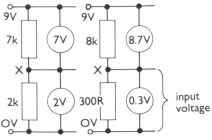

The **input** part of all these circuits is a **voltage divider**. Fig 6.72 shows two typical voltage dividers. In each case the total voltage available (9 V) is divided between the two resistors according to their resistance. The larger the resistance, the larger the voltage across it. It is the voltage measured between the ∅ V line and the point X that is important in these circuits. The input voltage is connected to the transistor from point X.

fig 6.72. Two typical voltage dividers

The **control** part of these circuits has to react to the voltage changes in the input, and so switch the output on or off. A single NPN transistor with a protective resistor can be used (fig 6.73). When its input voltage is below 0.6 V it is off and no current can flow through it. When it rises above 0.6 V the transistor switches on, allowing current to flow through (fig 6.74).

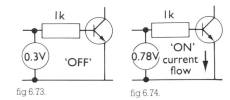

fig 6.73.   fig 6.74.

The **output** part simply switches on when there is current flowing through the transistor, and off when the transistor switches off.

The full circuit diagram (fig 6.75) shows all the parts connected together. By using a sensor whose resistance varies (e.g. the resistance of an LDR varies with light intensity) the input voltage to the transistor can be made to change. With the LDR in bright light its resistance is very low and the voltage across it is very low, below 0.6 V. With the LDR in shadow, its resistance increases and the voltage across also increases, to above 0.6 V. This switches on the transistor and so switches on the output. If the LDR goes into bright light again the input voltage will fall; the transistor will switch off and so the output will switch off.

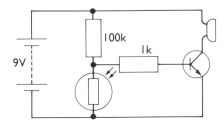

fig 6.75. Full circuit diagram

These circuits can be adjusted by using a variable resistor in the input part of the circuit (fig 6.76). In this circuit it allows you to adjust whether the buzzer is switched on when it first starts to go dark or when it is totally dark.

Although they are designed to do different things, each of the circuits shown in figs 6.77 to 6.80 is based upon the same principle. In fig 6.77 the output comes on when it is light; in fig 6.78 the output comes on when it is cold; in fig 6.79 the output comes on when it is hot; in fig 6.80 the output comes on when it is dry.

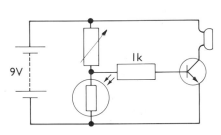

fig 6.76. Variable resistor in the input part of the circuit

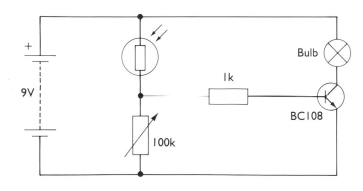

fig 6.77. Output on when light

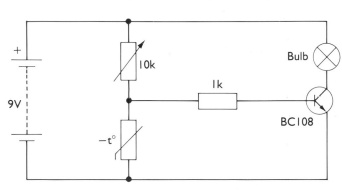

fig 6.78. Output on when cold

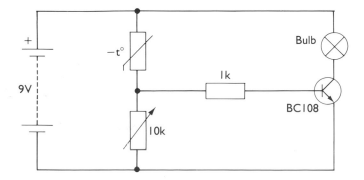

fig 6.79. Output on when hot

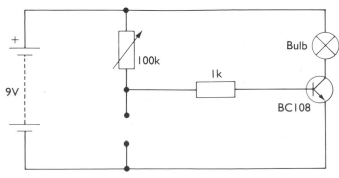

fig 6.80. Output on when dry

Any of these circuits can be made more sensitive by using two transistors connected together to form a **Darlington pair** (fig 6.81).

By using a **thyristor** in place of the transistor, the output can be made to **latch** on (fig 6.82). This means that once switched on it stays on, even if the input voltage falls. This is very useful in alarm circuits, because once triggered they keep going.

By using a relay (an **interface**), a low-voltage circuit can be used to control a high-voltage circuit (fig 6.83). They relay is simply the output of the transistor switching circuit. When it is swtiched on, contacts inside it move, switching on the other circuit. It must be emphasized that the two circuits are not connected electrically. The diode alongside the relay is to stop the transistor being damaged when the relay switches.

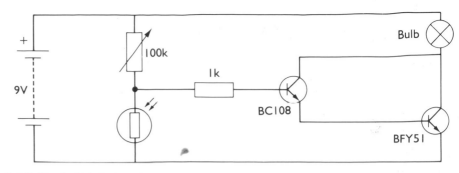

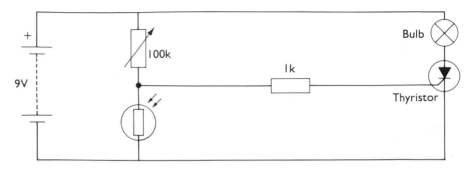

fig 6.81. Circuit with darlington pair

fig 6.82. Circuit with thyristor

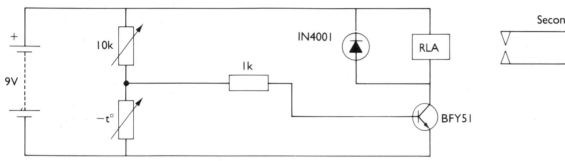

fig 6.83. Circuit with relay

Calculations can help you to understand and design circuits. Fig 6.84 shows a simple circuit and the three quantities involved:

1. Electrical potential is measured in **volts**.
2. The rate of flow (current) is measured in **amps**.
3. Resistance to that flow is measured in **ohms**.

If you know any two of these quantities you can work out the third by using the triangle shown in fig 6.85. For example, if a bulb has to have a resistance of 150 R, what current will flow through it? Current is measured in amps so cover up amps in the triangle and you are left with volts divided by ohms. Therefore:

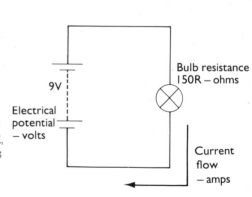

fig 6.84. Simple circuit

$$\text{Amps} = \frac{\text{Volts}}{\text{Ohms}} = \frac{9}{150} = 0.06 \text{ A or } 60 \text{ mA}$$

So, the current flowing in the circuit will be 60 mA.

You could arrange it so that the output was normally on and went off for the timed period. This would involve moving the output to the position shown by dotted lines in the circuit diagram in fig 6.88.

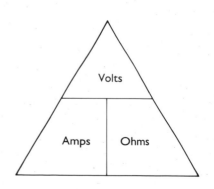

fig 6.85. Triangle used for calculation

105

TIMERS

A simple timer can be made using a transistor switching circuit (fig 6.86). It switches on an output after a time delay. The timing part of the circuit is made up of a resistor and an electrolytic capacitor. With the switch off, the voltage across the capacitor is ∅ V, so the transistor is off. When the circuit is switched on the capacitor begins to 'charge up' through the resistor. The voltage across the capacitor gradually rises. When it reaches 0.6 V the transistor switches on. The length of the time delay depends on the values of the resistor and capacitor. Fig 6.87 gives some idea of the times you can expect from different value components. However, because electrolytic capacitors cannot be made accurately, do not be surprised if the times come out differently when you try them.

The 555 timer IC can be used in two basic ways, either as a **monostable** or as an **astable**.

Monostable means stable in one state, in this case either 'on' or 'off'. The circuit will change its state for the timed period and then return to its stable state. In the circuit shown in fig 6.88 the output is normally off. When the input switch is pressed the output goes on for the timed period. At the end of that time it goes off again. As with the transistor timer circuit, the length of the timed period is decided by the values of the resistors and capacitors in the timer part of the circuit. The variable resistor allows the length of the timed period to be adjusted. You can use fig 6.89 to give you some idea of the times to expect.

You could arrange it so that the output was normally on and went off for the timed period. This would involve moving the output to the position shown by dotted lines in the circuit diagram.

Astable means not stable in any state, in other words it keeps changing from one state to the other, on/off, on/off, so it can be used to make lights flash or to make a continuous noise through a speaker.

At first sight, the astable circuit (fig 6.90) looks very much like the monostable circuit. However, closer examination will reveal some important differences. The timer part of the circuit works much as before, the variable resistor allowing you to vary the rate of flashing. By adding a second LED in the position shown by the dotted lines, they can be made to flash alternately.

By using a small-value capacitor in the timer part of the circuit the output can be used to power a speaker (fig 6.91). The note from the speaker can be varied by adjusting the variable resistor. This can be very useful as an output for an alarm circuit.

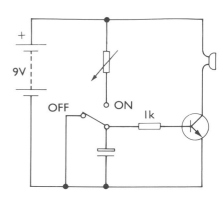

fig 6.86. Timer using a transistor as a switch

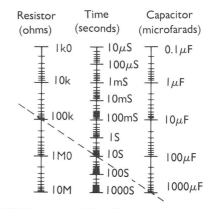

fig 6.87. Times expected from different value components

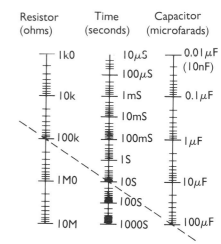

fig 6.89.

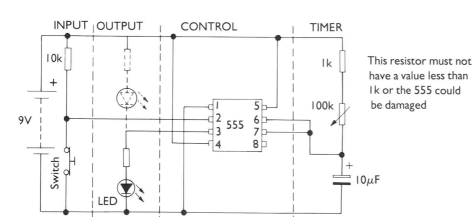

fig 6.88. Monostable circuit

This resistor must not have a value less than 1k or the 555 could be damaged

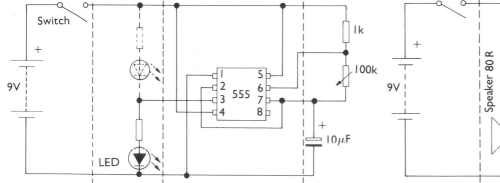

fig 6.90. Astable circuit

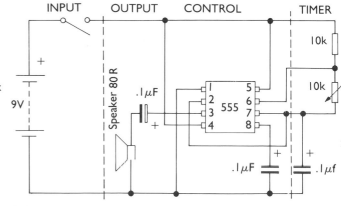

fig 6.91. Output powering a speaker

CIRCUIT BOARDS

A permanent circuit can be made by using either stripboard or a printed circuit board (PCB) (fig 6.93). Both types use a thin plastic board with a very thin layer of copper on one side. Stripboard can save time, but often leads to more mistakes than PCBs.

There are several ways to make a PCB; one is as follows:

1. Plan the layout on tracing paper, working from your circuit diagram. You must take account of the shape and size of each component (fig 6.94). Draw the lines clearly with a soft pencil, either HB or B.

2. Turn the tracing paper over and place it on the copper-clad board. Go over the lines of the circuit, pressing firmly (fig 6.95). This will transfer them onto the copper side of the board. It is vital that this stage is carried out correctly; if you do not turn the tracing paper over your PCB will be wrong!

3. Remove the tracing paper and go over the lines on the copper with an etch resist pen. Draw a circle for each connection, leaving a small patch of copper showing in the centre (fig 6.96).

4. Put your PCB in the etch tank to remove the unwanted copper areas (fig 6.97). This should take 10 or 15 minutes. When the etching is finished, wash the board and clean it with wire wool.

5. Drill holes in the circuit board ready to connect the components (fig 6.98).

SOLDERING THE COMPONENTS

1. Push the component 'legs' through the correct holes in the board and rest the board, copper track side up, on a flat surface (fig 6.99).

2. Place the tip of the soldering iron so that it heats the copper track and component at the same time. Hold it there for two or three seconds before touching the solder into the joint (fig 6.100). As the solder flows around the joint, remove the soldering iron and leave the joint to cool for a few seconds.

3. Cut off any bits of component 'legs' left sticking up using side cutters (fig 6.101).

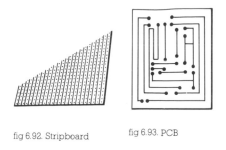

fig 6.92. Stripboard   fig 6.93. PCB

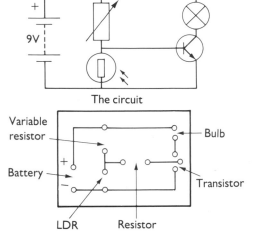

The circuit

Variable resistor

Bulb

Battery

Transistor

LDR   Resistor

fig 6.94. Layout for PCB

fig 6.95. Tracing the circuit

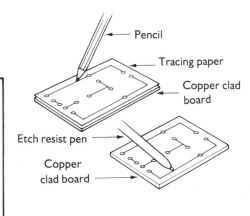

Pencil

Tracing paper

Copper clad board

Etch resist pen

Copper clad board

fig 6.96. Using an etch resist pen

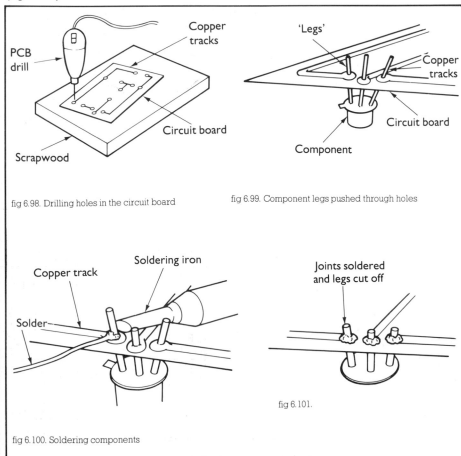

Copper tracks

'Legs'

PCB drill

Copper tracks

Circuit board

Circuit board

Scrapwood

Component

fig 6.98. Drilling holes in the circuit board

fig 6.99. Component legs pushed through holes

Copper track

Soldering iron

Joints soldered and legs cut off

Solder

fig 6.101.

fig 6.100. Soldering components

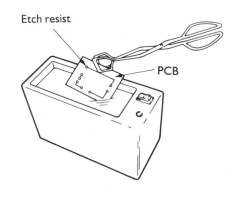

Etch resist

PCB

fig 6.97. Using an etch tank

PNEUMATICS AND HYDRAULICS

Both **pneumatic** and **hydraulic systems** are used to provide powerful linear movements. Pneumatic road drills and mechanical diggers are just two examples of the use of these systems you will have come across (fig 6.102). Pneumatic systems use compressed air as a power source, while hydraulic systems use pressurized oil. Industry uses these systems a great deal because they are powerful and reliable.

Both systems are based on the same principle. Fig 6.103 shows the basic idea. A piston can be forced along a cylinder, so creating linear movement, which can be used to do useful work. The force produced by the piston as it moves depends on two things:

1. The area of the face of the piston, in mm^2.
2. The pressure being used to push it, in N/mm^2.

For example, if a pressure of 0.5 N/mm^2 is being used to push a piston of 40 mm diameter, the force produced will be given by:

Force = Pressure × Area
$$= 0.5 \times \pi r^2$$
$$= 0.5 \times \pi \times 20 \times 20$$
$$= 0.5 \times 1256$$
$$= 628 \text{ N}$$

It can be seen from this that, by increasing either the pressure or the area, larger forces will be produced.

Fig 6.104 shows a pneumatic system for opening and closing a bus door. The movement of the piston is powered in both directions, the air being directed by the driver's control valve. Most buses use this type of system.

Fig 6.105 shows the hydraulic system used in car jacks. As the handle is moved up and down the oil is pumped into the large-diameter cylinder, through a one-way valve, so pushing up the piston and lifting the car.

Pneumatic systems have two disadvantages when compared to hydraulic systems.

1. They need a compressor to compress the air in the first place. These are not always readily available. Hydraulic systems can be powered by an electric pump, but simple systems only need muscle power. You can make a simple, yet quite powerful, hydraulic system using syringes and plastic tubing as shown in fig 6.106.

2. Air can be compressed, so there is a limit to the forces that can be produced. Hydraulic oil cannot be compressed, so much larger forces can be produced. You can use water in the system shown in fig 6.106.

fig 6.102. Pneumatics used in construction work

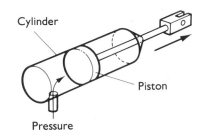

fig 6.103. Piston and cylinder

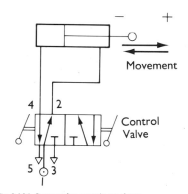

fig 6.104. System for opening a door

fig 6.105. Hydraulic car jack

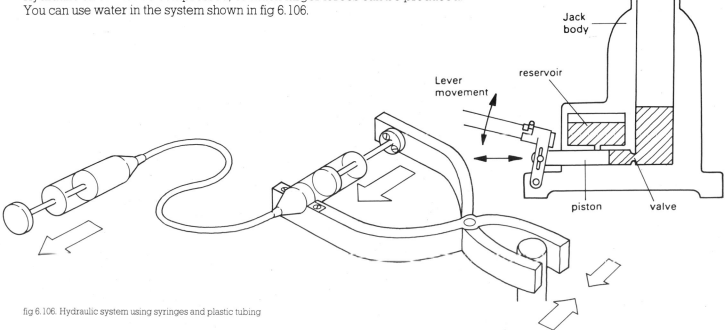

fig 6.106. Hydraulic system using syringes and plastic tubing

ENERGY

You need energy for everything you do. Even when asleep you are using energy to work your heart and lungs and to digest your food. That energy comes from the food you eat. Artificial devices also need energy to make them work. That energy may come from fossil fuels (e.g. oil, gas or coal), nuclear fuels, or renewable resources (e.g. sun, wind and waves).

Energy cannot be created or destroyed, **but it can change from one form to another**. It is usually when it changes form that you are able to make use of it. For example, when a light is switched on, electrical energy changes into light energy.

The three forms of energy you may find most useful are:

1. **Mechanical – movement energy.** For example, moving air powering a land yacht; a motor powering a model car; water turning a turbine.

2. **Stored energy.** For example, a twisted rubber band used to power a model aircraft or boat.

3. **Electrical energy.** Because it can be used in so many different ways and is easily available from batteries, you will probably find this the most useful form of energy. It can easily be changed into other forms of energy, the most common being light, sound, heat or movement. For example, lighting bulbs or LEDs; sounding buzzers or speakers; powering dc motors.

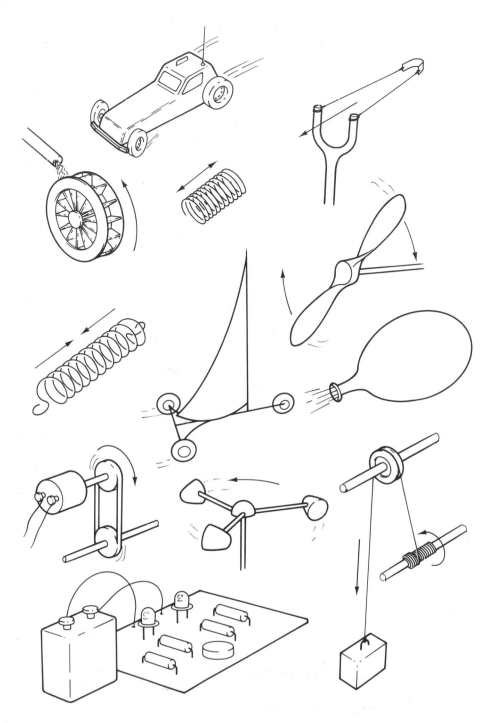

fig 6.107. Examples of energy

ENERGY EFFICIENCY

Energy efficiency means making the best use of available energy. The efficiency of any system can be calculated by comparing the energy input with the useful energy output using the following formula:

$$\textbf{Efficiency} = \frac{\textbf{Useful energy output}}{\textbf{Energy input}} \times 100\%$$

No system is 100 per cent efficient. Some of the energy input gets changed into forms you don't want, usually heat, sound or light. For example, an electric motor is meant to produce movement, but it also gets hot, makes a noise and creates sparks. You should design systems to be as energy efficient as possible. A few simple things will help:

1. Choose the right materials to rub or slide against each other. Lubricate them wherever possible.

2. Keep down the weight of moving parts and vehicles.

3. Choose electronic components which use less energy (e.g. bulbs use six times more energy than LEDs).

EXERCISES

1. Give two practical examples of Class 1 and Class 2 levers. What types of movement do they use?

2. Calculate the mechanical advantage and velocity ratio of the pulley system shown in fig 6.108. What is the efficiency of the system?

3. Give a practical example of the use of a parallel-motion linkage and sketch the important parts of the mechanism.

4. Give one advantage and one disadvantage of pulley systems compared to sprocket and chain systems.

5. Sketch a system that could be used to change the fast rotary motion of a small electric motor into the slow oscillating movement of windscreen wipers.

6. The gear system shown in fig 6.109 has 32 teeth (driver gear) and 16 teeth (driven gear). If it were connected to a motor running at 3240 rpm, what would the output speed of the system be?

7. Sketch a mechanism that could be used to change rotary motion into a reciprocating motion. Give one practical example of the use of this kind of mechanism.

8. Explain, using examples, the differences between frame and shell structures.

9. Explain, using an example, why structures have to be designed to take dynamic as well as static loads. How do designers build a factor of safety into the structures they design?

10. Frame structures are made up of two kinds of members: struts and ties. Sketch a simple frame structure and label each member to show which kind it is.

11. The beam shown in fig 6.110 is in equilibrium. Calculate the reactions at A and B.

12. Name and draw the symbol for an electronic sensor that can be used to detect changes in temperature. Show how it can be used in a simple switching circuit to sound a buzzer when the temperature falls to freezing point.

13. Design a low-voltage circuit which could be used to control a 110 V fan heater.

14. Show a circuit which could be used to give a 10-second delay before a bulb is switched on.

15. Design a circuit which would flash an LED at one second intervals.

16. Design a PCB for the circuit shown in fig 6.91 on page 106.

17. Describe two advantages of hydraulic systems over pneumatic systems and give three examples of the use of hydraulic systems.

18. Name four forms of energy and give a practical example of the use of each.

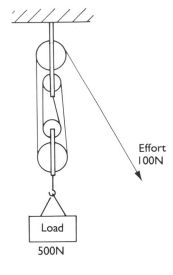

Effort
100N

Load

500N

fig 6.108.

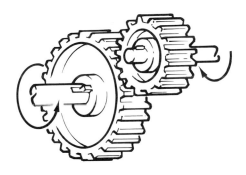

fig 6.109.

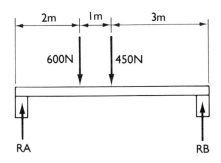

2m   1m   3m

600N   450N

RA   RB

fig 6.110.

TECHNICAL ILLUSTRATION

Technical illustation is the area of Design and Communication concerned with conveying technical information. It is best described as communicating technical information in a graphic form.

The technical illustrator is not concerned with drawing as part of the manufacturing process, but with conveying information about a product, operation or function.

Illustrators need to be familiar with the things for which they are designing the graphics: they must fully understand the information which is to be communicated. Therefore, many illustrators begin their careers with technical or engineering backgrounds.

This aspect of Design and Communication covers a wide area of graphic work ranging from technical illustration, technical graphics and graphic design through to commercial art. The illustrators themselves range from mechanical draughtsmen to fine artists.

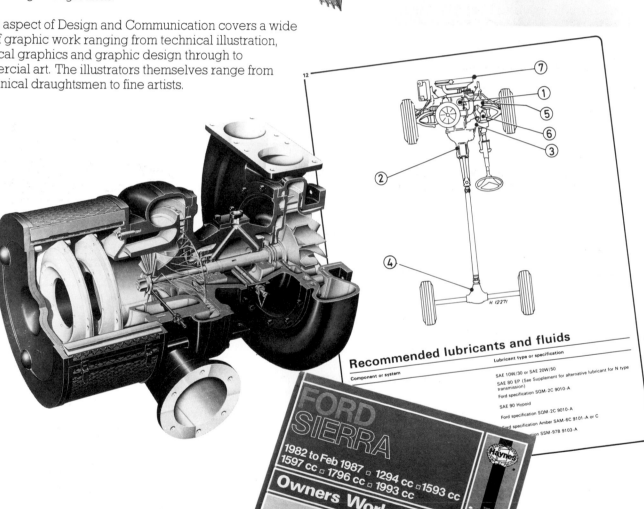

Illustrators may be required to produce a wide range of graphic material from simple operating instructions, maintenance details through to sales and promotional material. This work may take a variety of forms. It may be in the form of a workshop manual, a brochure, a poster or even graphic material to be included in a film or video.

The illustrations shown here are all examples of the work of technical illustrators and all communicate technical information.

fig 7.1. Examples of technical illustration

(© Haynes Publishing Group, 1983)

MATERIALS AND EQUIPMENT

Much of the finished work produced by the technical illustator will be required for publication. If it is to reproduce well, it will need to be of the highest quality possible. The work may be reproduced simply using a photocopier or a dyeline process, or by a more professional system, such as offset litho. The method of reproduction will depend largely on the nature of the work and the actual form it will take.

The need to reproduce the work will affect the way in which the illustrator works and the materials available. For example, if the work is to be reproduced in black and white, then the artwork will need to be drawn using ink rather than pencil. If tone is required on the work then it must be applied in the form of dots, lines or hatching in ink. Pencil shading will not reproduce well.

Most of the materials and equipment required for work in technical illustration have been described earlier, but it is necessary to look at methods of ink drawing in more detail. Pencils will be required for constructing and laying out in the normal way, then drawings are lined in and finished off using a variety of ink techniques.

fig 7.2. Basic materials

PENS

Ink can be applied with a variety of pens ranging from the traditional dip pen to the modern technical pen.

Dip pens are inexpensive, but tend to be messy to use. The line width will also vary if the pen is not always held in the same way.

Ruling pens are used to give precise lines which can be varied in width by turning a screw on the side. The disadvantage is that they need to be filled frequently and tend to blot if not used carefully.

Good-quality **fine line fibre-tip pens** are available in a wide range of line widths. They are inexpensive, but the tip is likely to wear in time.

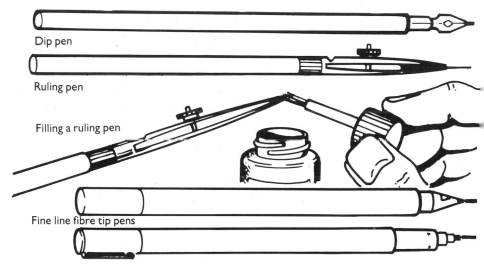

Dip pen

Ruling pen

Filling a ruling pen

Fine line fibre tip pens

fig 7.3. Pens

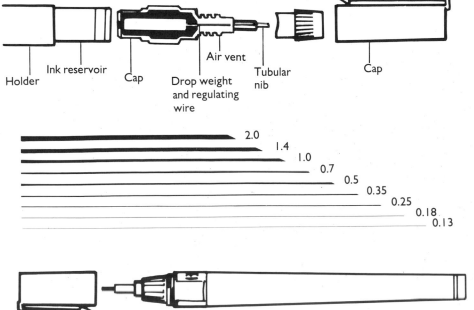

Holder — Ink reservoir — Cap — Drop weight and regulating wire — Air vent — Tubular nib — Cap

2.0
1.4
1.0
0.7
0.5
0.35
0.25
0.18
0.13

fig 7.4. Technical pens

The ideal pen to use is a **technical pen**. These are available in nine internationally recognized sizes and have a tubular nib through which the ink flows. Most types of technical pen have either a refillable or throwaway ink cartridge and so are easy and clean to use. Some pens have specially designed caps which prevent the ink from drying up when the pen is not used for a long time.

Technical pens are easy to use, but sometimes need a gentle shake to start the ink flowing. When drawing, the pen should be kept at between 80° and 90° to the paper. This ensures a constant line width, prevents the pen scratching the paper and reduces nib wear. Care should be taken with technical pens, especially when cleaning, as it is very easy to damage the delicate regulating wire which controls the ink flow.

CLEANING

Technical pens, especially the older types, tend to dry up and clog. It is good practice to replace the cap whenever the pen is not being used. This will also protect the pen in the event of it rolling off the table or board onto the floor. If the pen is not going to be used for any length of time, it is a good idea to remove the ink cartridge and wash the pen out in cold water. Special cleaning fluids are available from most pen manufacturers and badly clogged pens can be soaked in order to clean them.

Special pen stands which prevent them from drying out can be bought and expensive ultrasonic pen cleaners are also available.

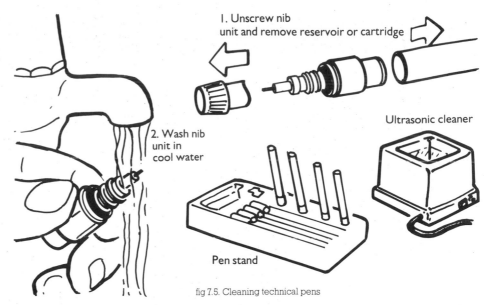

1. Unscrew nib unit and remove reservoir or cartridge

2. Wash nib unit in cool water

Ultrasonic cleaner

Pen stand

fig 7.5. Cleaning technical pens

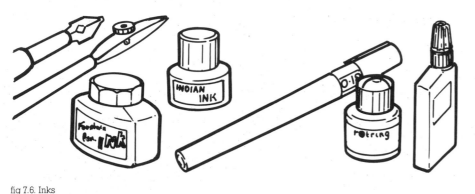

fig 7.6. Inks

When drawing with a dip pen or ruling pen, ordinary fountain pen ink can be used. If a dense black line is required it is best to use Indian ink, which is waterproof, and which also allows an ink or colour wash to be safely applied over it. Special non-clogging inks are available for technical pens. **Always use the correct ink** in them and on **no** account use them with Indian ink, as this will dry very quickly, clog the pen and will not wash out.

REMOVING MISTAKES

Mistakes are simple to rub out when using pencil, but mistakes made in ink can be very difficult to remove. A **safety** razor blade or a scalpel can be used to scrape away the ink, but take care not to cut yourself.

A variety of ink erasers are available; however, some are likely to damage the surface of the paper. **Plastic erasers**, especially those which contain a solvent which dissolves the ink as you use them, are probably the best type to use.

Large drawing offices use **electric erasers**, but they are rather expensive for school use.

Mistakes on white paper can be covered with white ink or poster paint. If you use typist's correcting fluid take care to use it in a well-ventilated area as the **fumes may be harmful**. It is also possible to glue a small piece of white paper over the mistakes as this may not be visible when the artwork is photocopied or printed.

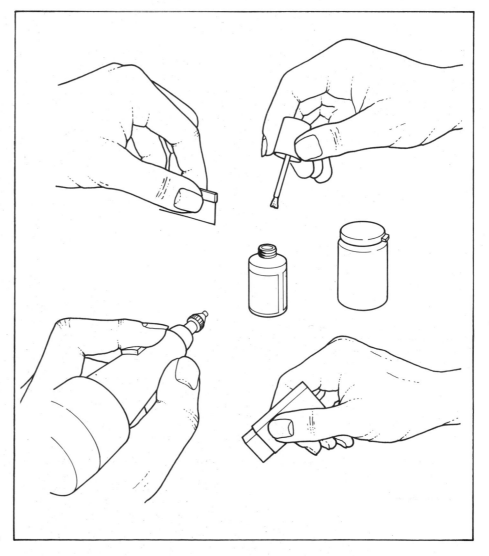

fig 7.7. Removing inks

WORKING WITH INK

Ink can be applied to many different types of paper including layout paper and good-quality tracing paper. Try to avoid using very soft, absorbent paper as it is likely to cause the ink lines to run or bleed and the paper fibres may also block or clog the nib of the pen.

When making finished drawings in ink, use a heavy-weight paper. Good-quality cartridge paper will be suitable for both line work and ink or colour washes. If you intend to apply a wash to your drawing, it is a good idea to stretch your paper first to prevent it from wrinkling. Page 46 shows how to do this. When drawing very highly detailed work in line only, then a hard, smooth surface will give best results. Bristol board is useful as it has a white drawing surface with one side smooth and the other slightly textured. Illustration board and fashion board can also be used.

fig 7.8. Paper and board

PREPARATION

You should always prepare your work in pencil first. Use a hard pencil such as a **4H**, very lightly, so that the lines can be rubbed out after the drawing has been inked in. Technical illustrators often set out and construct their drawings using a special blue, non-print pencil. When the drawing is printed or copied the blue lines do not show up. Work carefully and avoid over-using the eraser. The surface of the paper can easily be damaged by too much rubbing out, making it difficult to ink in the drawing successfully.

Working in ink consists of three main techniques: **line**, **dot** and **wash**. A wide variety of effects can be achieved in black and white illustrations by using various combinations of these techniques. Lines, dots and wash are used to suggest surface textures, shape, form and light.

fig 7.9. Drawing and construction

fig 7.10. Ink, dots and wash

LINE

Line drawings can be very simple, showing the outline or the basic shape of objects. By varying the thickness and spacing of the lines, more details and information can be shown. The illustration in fig 7.11 shows how simple drawings can be changed by adding extra linework. **Hatching** and **cross-hatching** can also be used to improve line drawings. This is the term used to describe lines drawn close together to create texture and tone. Cross-hatching is used to shade a drawing and increase the three-dimensional effect. It can also be used to add interest to a drawing or draw attention to a certain part of it. By varying or graduating the textures produced, the illusions of space, depth and form can be created.

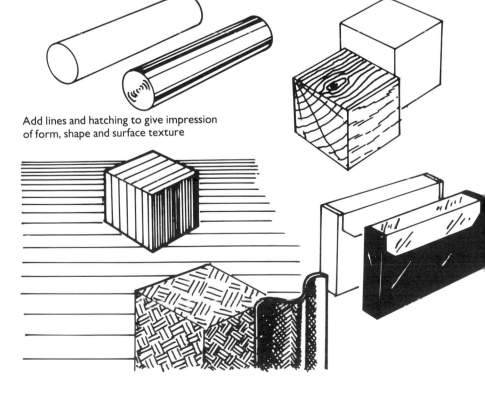

Add lines and hatching to give impression of form, shape and surface texture

fig 7.11. Rendering with line

QUALITY OF LINE

The lines should be black and dense to give good **contrast** against the paper. They must be sharp, clear and precise, not ragged, wobbly or spidery. If necessary, use a straight edge and **templates** or **flexi-curves** to help you draw curved lines. Drawing circles in ink can be difficult; however, it is possible to attach your pen to a pair of compasses with masking tape. Special compasses which will hold technical pens or felt-tips are also available and it is possible to purchase an adaptor which will allow you to fit a technical pen to a normal pair of compasses.

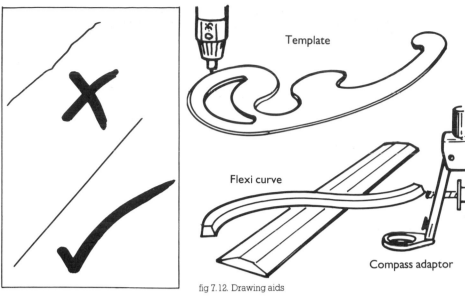

Template

Flexi curve

Compass adaptor

fig 7.12. Drawing aids

DOTS

Dots can also be used to create texture and give the impression of shape and form in the same way as hatching. Dots are produced by touching the tip of the pen on the paper. Do not press too hard or you may damage the nib of your technical pen. Darker areas of tone can be produced by using a thicker pen and putting the dots closer together. It is also possible to produce a graduated effect which can create an illusion of depth or distance. Technical illustrators sometimes use dots to texture an area of a drawing. They often use a rub-on dry transfer, known as '**Letratone**', rather than spending a long time making dots. The advantage of this system over a pen is that it is easy to produce a consistent tone over a large area. The disadvantage is that transfer sheets are rather expensive. Fig 7.13 shows the use of dots on a drawing.

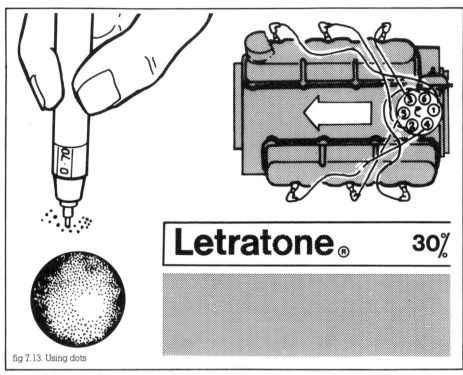

Letratone ® 30%

fig 7.13. Using dots

WASH

Areas of tone can be created by using ink washes. Drawing ink can be diluted to create different tones and then applied with a brush. Most types of inks can be diluted by adding **distilled water** or **natural rainwater**. Tap water may cause the ink to separate and give a spotted effect on the paper when it dries. The normal method of working with wash is to pencil in the drawing first and then work over it with waterproof black ink. When the ink has dried a series of washes can be applied using a brush. However, it is possible to construct the drawing in pencil, apply the washes and then draw in the details. Remember to stretch your paper **before** using washes to prevent it from wrinkling (see page 3).

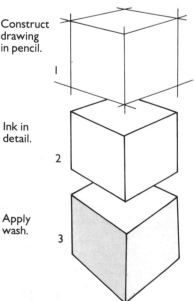

Construct drawing in pencil.

Ink in detail.

Apply wash.

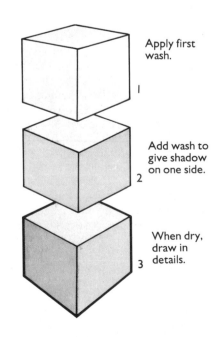

Apply first wash.

Add wash to give shadow on one side.

When dry, draw in details.

fig 7.14. Applying a wash

PERSPECTIVE

In technical illustration perspective is one of the most widely used systems or methods of drawing. Perspective drawings show an object as it really is, rather than distorting it as other drawing systems such as isometric and oblique tend to do. Perspective drawing has been covered in some detail earlier in this book, but there are other aspects of perspective which are of particular importance to the technical illustrator.

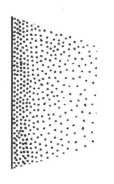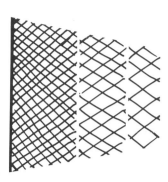

fig 7.15. Examples of aerial perspective

AERIAL PERSPECTIVE

When using tone it is possible to create the impression of distance or depth by using darker tones in the foreground of the drawing and allowing them to become progressively lighter as they recede into the background. This is known as atmospheric or aerial perspective. It can be simply, but effectively, achieved using rendering techniques such as dots or hatching.

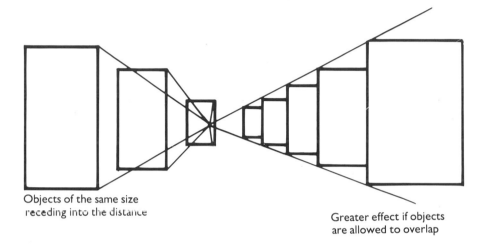

Objects of the same size receding into the distance

Greater effect if objects are allowed to overlap

fig 7.16. Overlapping

OVERLAPPING

Another good indication of depth can be achieved by using perspective to draw a series of objects of the same size receding into the distance, as shown in fig 7.16. The effect can be enhanced by overlapping the objects so they are partially hidden. This can be particularly effective if it is combined with other techniques such as aerial perspective.

DIVIDING AREAS

Perspective can be used to divide an area into small areas which appear to become smaller in proportion as they recede into the background. This is done by drawing a line to represent eye level, marking the vanishing point and then dividing the front edge of the area as required. Each of the points which mark the divisions is then connected to the vanishing point as a radial line. A diagonal line is then drawn across the area to be divided and a horizontal line is drawn at each intersection of the radial lines and the diagonal. The finished effect gives the impression of depth and distance. This type of drawing is particularly useful when architectural views are drawn. Fig 7.17 shows the stages involved in the division of an area.

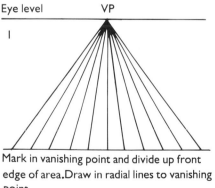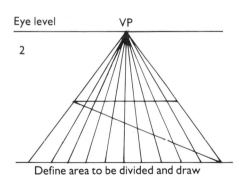

Mark in vanishing point and divide up front edge of area. Draw in radial lines to vanishing point

Define area to be divided and draw in diagonal line

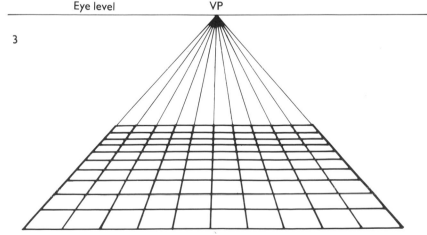

fig 7.17. Dividing an area

SHADOWS

fig 7.18. Shadows can help to describe the shape of an object

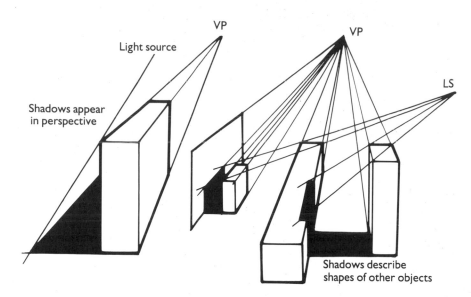

fig 7.19. Shadows with the light source in the same plane as the object

Shadows can give important visual clues to the **shape**, **form** and **nature** of objects. In some forms of technical illustration it is worth including shadows. Many architectural drawings show positions of shadows and they can be very effective in some pictorial views. If the addition of shadows is to be successful, they must be drawn as realistically as possible. Perspective can be used to obtain a realistic shadow effect. Fig 7.19 shows the effect of shadows on objects when the light source is in the same plane as the objects themselves.

It is possible to use a combination of perspective and shadows to give the impression that the light source is behind the objects, as shown in fig 7.20. First decide on the position of the light source (LS) and draw a perpendicular line down from it to the horizon line (HL). The point at which the two lines meet is the vanishing point of the shadows (VPS). Draw lines through the bottom corners of the objects and point VPS, then draw lines from point LS and the top corners of the objects until they intersect the lines drawn from the bottom corners. Join up the points of intersection to form the shadow areas. The shadows can then be rendered using any suitable method.

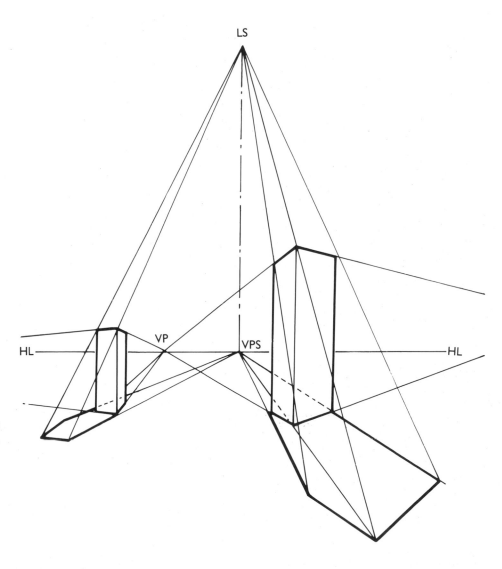

fig 7.20. Shadows cast from a light source behind the objects

EXPLODED DRAWINGS

In an exploded drawing, the parts of an object are drawn as though they are opened up and taken apart, giving the impression that they have been neatly **exploded**. Fig 7.21 shows the components of a car braking system which has been taken apart and 'exploded'. (Note the use of dots or Letratone in this drawing.)

This type of drawing is used for sales material and spare part catalogues. It allows parts to be quickly and easily recognised, even by people with little or no technical knowledge. In the parts departments of garages, exploded drawings are printed onto small sheets of clear plastic film, known as **microfilm**, and used to identify engine parts. Microfilm is used with a microfilm **'reader'** or viewer which projects the image onto a screen so that it can be seen easily. Thousands of items of information can be stored in this way and referred to when required.

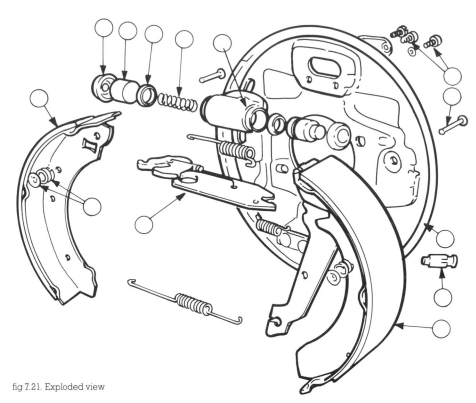

fig 7.21. Exploded view

Exploded drawings show how the parts of an object fit together and relate to each other, but they do not really show how the object works. Almost any drawing system can be used to make exploded drawings. For example, they may be drawn using **isometric**, various types of **perspective** or **axonometric** methods. They may be drawn vertically or horizontally. The way in which they are drawn depends very much upon the object and the information to be conveyed.

When making an exploded drawing, it is important that each part of the object can be seen easily. The illustrator will often arrange the parts so that they overlap each other slightly. This gives the drawing an impression of depth, but it also helps to show how the parts relate to each other and how they fit together.

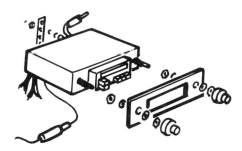

fig 7.22. Exploded view of a car radio

MAKING EXPLODED DRAWINGS

Exploded drawings may look rather complicated but, providing you understand how the object fits together, they are not all that difficult to draw. First decide on which drawing system to use (e.g. isometric, perspective) and then make a rough pencil sketch. It helps a great deal to have the object in front of you to work from, if this is possible. When you are happy with your pencil sketch, you can develop the drawing using ink, tone or colour. Why not try making an exploded drawing for yourself? Take a simple ballpoint pen, carefully take it apart and draw the components 'exploded' as in fig 7.23.

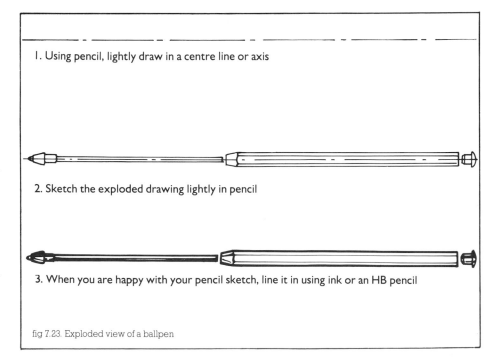

1. Using pencil, lightly draw in a centre line or axis

2. Sketch the exploded drawing lightly in pencil

3. When you are happy with your pencil sketch, line it in using ink or an HB pencil

fig 7.23. Exploded view of a ballpen

The drawing of the pen in fig 7.23 is a very simple horizontal exploded drawing. It is drawn 'straight on' and gives very little impression of form or depth. It is possible to create a three-dimensional effect by using a drawing system such as isometric or perspective. The drawing in fig 7.24 shows a calculator drawn in isometric which has been vertically exploded. This type of drawing may look quite complicated, but if you follow a few simple rules they are easy to produce. First of all study the object so that you fully understand how it is assembled and then make a rough pencil sketch of the layout. Begin by drawing the part which will appear to be nearest and then work back from there, overlapping each part as you draw them in. Overlapping gives the impression that one part is in front of another. If you explode a drawing too far it may not appear obvious to the viewer how the object fits together.

Fig 7.25 shows an exploded drawing of a cassette, drawn using two-point perspective. The basic shapes were drawn in roughly in pencil, then, when a satisfactory layout had been achieved, the details were drawn in. The advantage of perspective drawings over isometric and oblique drawings is that they appear to be more natural.

When you have constructed the drawing you can make it look more realistic by adding tone or rendering to show the material from which it is made. You will notice that in fig 7.24 a

heavier outline has been used around each part of the calculator. This is to make the separate parts stand out from each other.

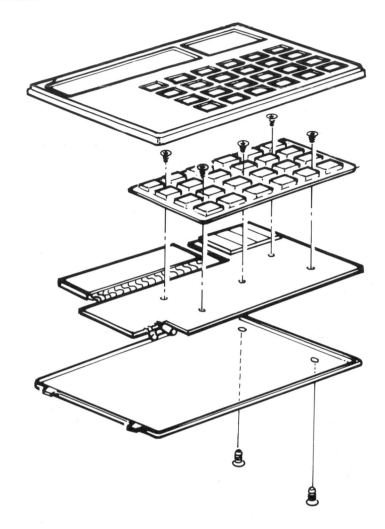

fig 7.24. Exploded view of a calculator

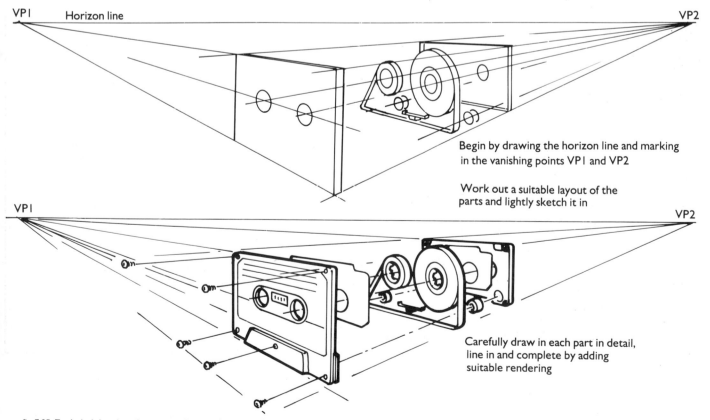

Begin by drawing the horizon line and marking in the vanishing points VP1 and VP2

Work out a suitable layout of the parts and lightly sketch it in

Carefully draw in each part in detail, line in and complete by adding suitable rendering

fig 7.25. Exploded drawing of a cassette drawn using two-point perspective

SECTIONS

Sectional drawings are used to show the inside of an object or the internal workings of a machine or other piece of equipment. They can be used to show internal construction details which may not be obvious from a normal drawing or photograph. Examples of sectional drawings are found in workshop manuals and other forms of technical information. Sales brochures and promotional posters also make use of this technique, especially when technical detail and innovation is a selling point. Sectional drawings can be roughly divided into two types of drawing: **the formal section** and the **cut-away section**.

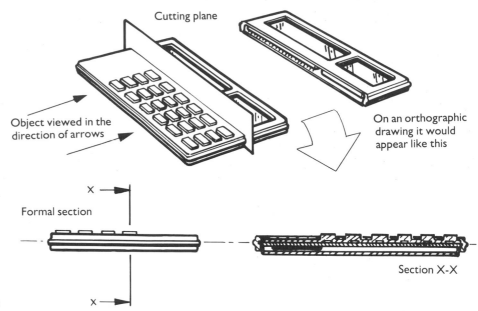

Cutting plane

Object viewed in the direction of arrows

On an orthographic drawing it would appear like this

Formal section

Section X-X

FORMAL SECTIONS

The formal section is used in orthographic drawings to show internal details of objects which cannot be shown using the normal plan and elevations. They are also used when the internal details are too complicated for them to be shown using hidden detail lines. The cutting plane is shown on the plan or elevation and the arrows show the direction of the view. The parts of the object which the cutting plane appears to cut through are shaded or hatched using 45-degree lines spaced about 4 mm apart. Formal sections are covered fully in chapter 9.

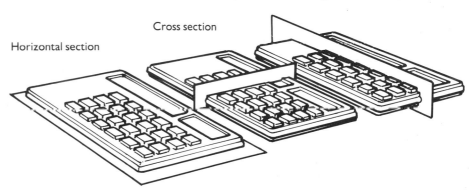

Longitudinal section

Cross section

Horizontal section

fig 7.26. Sections

It is not always necessary to draw a full sectional view of an object. For example, if the object is symmetrical it can be shown by using a **half section**. The other half is shown as an exterior view of the object. This also has the advantage that it saves space on the drawing. You will notice that some formal sectional views are not hatched. If hatching makes the drawing confusing and misleading, then it can be left off.

Formal sections tend to be used for conveying highly technical information, often to skilled people who can understand this type of drawing easily. They are also associated with drawings used to communicate how to make things.

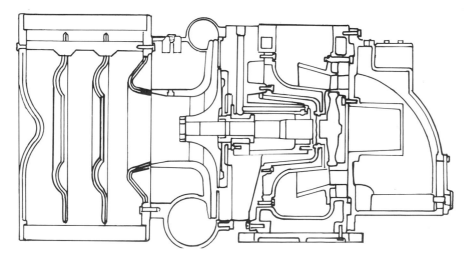

fig 7.27. Example of a formal section (small frame turbocharger)

CUT-AWAY SECTIONS

Cut-away sections are one of the most popular ways of showing the construction and internal workings or details of an object. Manufacturers use them to show how their products work and are made. Motor car manufacturers produce such drawings to help illustrate sales brochures. Manufacturers of large equipment, such as turbines and earthmovers, make use of the cut-away section on posters and sales leaflets which promote their products (fig 7.28). The cut-away section is probably one of the best-used graphic techniques available to the illustrator.

fig 7.28. Cut-away section

The cut-away section offers many interesting graphic possibilities to the illustrator. Like the exploded drawing, it can be drawn using a variety of drawing systems. Perspective and isometric are among the most commonly used. Cut-aways are usually part sections, as they give a much better impression of the shape and form of the object. Various parts of the object are removed to show important internal details. Exactly which outer part of the object is removed depends upon the internal details to be shown. This type of drawing offers the illustrator great scope to experiment with a variety of different techniques and mediums. Many cut-away drawings are coloured using airbrush techniques, while others combine the use of drawing with photography. It is also possible to produce sections which combine photographs with line drawing and airbrush work.

fig 7.29. Cut-away section

To make a cut-away section

Begin making a cut-away section by choosing a suitable drawing system and sketching in the object. Decide where to cut the object in order to show the internal details. Try to make the cut straight so that it will show the outer shape clearly. When complete, line in the drawing and add colour or rendering.

Lightly sketch in the object

↓

Decide which part to cut away

↓

Straight cuts will show the outside shape

↓

Line in the drawing and add colour or rendering

fig 7.30. Making a cut-away section

Cut-away sections are often found in motor car maintenance manuals. Many of these drawings are produced by a combination of graphic techniques. For example the illustration shown in fig 7.31 also includes the use of the **ghosted view**. Some areas are not actually cut away, but shown as though they are transparent. Some parts are drawn as outlines only, allowing the parts behind them to be seen. Cut-aways like this are produced in black and white and colour. Many car manufacturers produce very good airbrush-coloured cut-away posters and wall charts to illustrate their models.

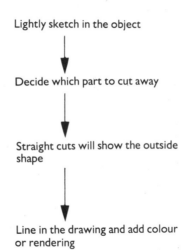

fig 7.31. Cut-away and ghosted view together

121

PRESENTING INFORMATION

The technical illustrator may be required to present technical and statistical information in a graphic form. Data presented numerically may be difficult for the layman to understand, but may be more easily understood if it is presented in a diagrammatic form. The illustrator may have to produce graphs or diagrams to show facts, trends, performance, relationships or comparisons. This area of technical illustration allows scope for inventiveness and encourages the use of a variety of graphic techniques and forms of presentation. With a little imagination, data and statistical information can be made visually exciting and more readable.

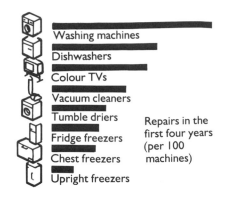

fig 7.32. Bar chart

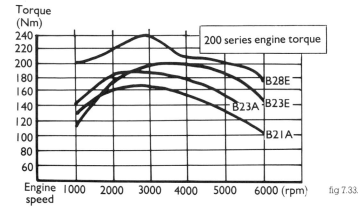

fig 7.33.

GRAPHS

Graphs are the traditional method of showing information graphically and probably the one you are most familiar with. They are used to show the relationship between two factors such as time/distance or speed/power. The graph can take the form of a series of straight lines or a curve, depending on how it is being used. The graph in fig 7.33 shows the torque produced by the engines in the Volvo 200 series of motor cars. It shows the engine power at certain engine speeds and also compares it with the other engines available in the same range of cars. The graph in fig 7.34 presents its information in a more visually attractive way. It shows how the lead content of petrol has been decreased in recent years, and also poses the question, when will it be removed completely?

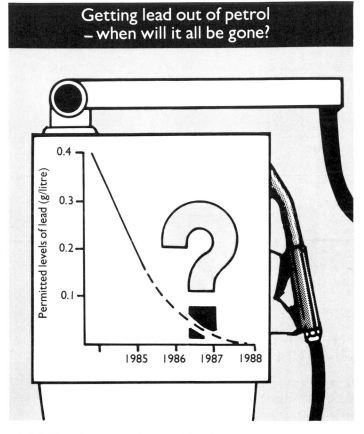

fig 7.34. Information presented in a more interesting way

BAR CHARTS

Bar charts show information more graphically than the traditional graph. They can be drawn horizontally or vertically, but the vertical chart is usually referred to as a **column chart**. The information is shown by a series of bars or columns each of the same width, with a space equal to the width left between each bar or column. Single bars or columns are sometimes used as a proportionate chart. The bar represents the whole, and the parts of it show proportions or percentages of the whole. Fig 7.35 is a bar chart which shows and compares the nutritional content of a food product.

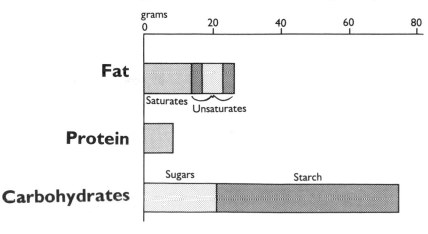

fig 7.35. Bar chart

HISTOGRAMS

Histograms are similar to bar charts. They use two axes, and the bars or columns are drawn close together so that they form a stepped curve, giving an appearance similiar to a graph. The histogram in fig 7.36 shows the daily average temperature in Madrid and is an example of the kind of information which might be required to be shown graphically in a travel brochure.

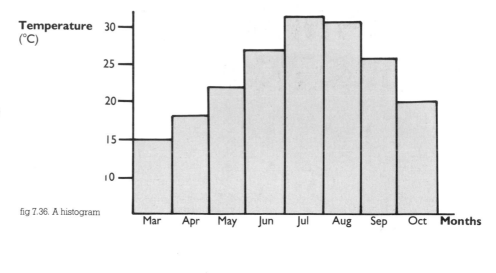

fig 7.36. A histogram

Availability of durable goods

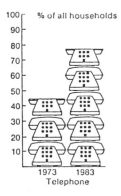

fig 7.37. A pictogram

PICTOGRAMS

Pictograms use symbols or simple pictures to represent information. They are very useful when presenting information to people who are not used to dealing with figures. Fig 7.37 shows an example of a pictogram.

PIE CHARTS

A circle is used to represent the whole and it is then divided into sectors, rather like cutting a pie. The sectors are proportional to the quantities or component parts involved. Fig 7.38 shows a pie chart drawn three-dimensionally rather than as a flat circle.

fig 7.38. A pie chart

Containers found on beaches

3D CHARTS

Three-dimensional charts are popular for illustrating comparisons and are usually visually interesting. They can take the form of simple columns or bars drawn using one of the three-dimensional drawing techniques (fig 7.39), or they can use shapes and forms which represent, or are associated with, the objects being shown. They allow the illustator to make use of a variety of graphic techniques and materials in order to create an interesting effect.

fig 7.39. Three dimensional chart

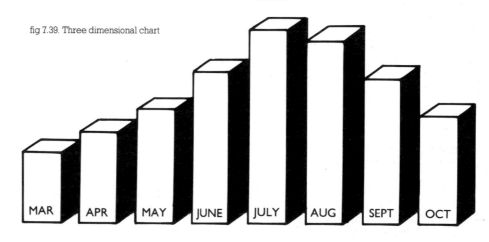

MATRICES

A matrix can be used to make a quick and simple comparison. It can also be used as a checklist. Matrices are sometimes used on distance diagrams, to show how far apart certain places are. Fig 7.40 shows a matrix used in a car accessories sales brochure.

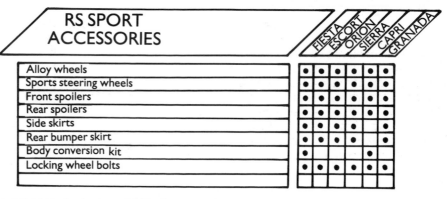

fig 7.40. Matrix showing the availability of car accessories

COMMUNICATING INSTRUCTIONS

Once a product has been designed and manufactured it is the technical illustrator's job to design and produce the instructions which relate to operating, using and maintaining the product. These may be instructions to the user regarding the layout of the controls or instructions showing how to carry out periodic routine servicing. There are several ways of showing this kind of information graphically, including flow charts and diagrams, sequential drawings and operational drawings.

Fig 7.41 is an example of an instructional drawing. It shows the layout of the interior of a motor car and is the type of drawing you are likely to find in the owner's instruction book.

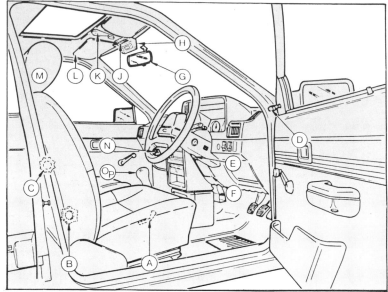

fig 7.41. The use of instructional drawings

FLOW CHARTS

PREPARATION — Represents the beginning, modification or end of process

PROCESS — Used to show part of general process.

DECISION — Indicates that decision has to be made and leads to other paths being followed

INPUT/OUTPUT — Shows something added to or taken away from process

TERMINAL/INTERRUPT — Delay, halt or interruption in process

fig 7.42. Data processing symbols

Flow charts show graphically the stages or operations involved in a process. The **British Standards Institute** has a recommended procedure for doing this which is outlined in the booklets BS4058 and PP7307. Each stage in the process is shown by using a standard symbol to represent the action taken. The sequence of actions is linked with a flow line and arrows showing the direction of flow. The main data processing symbols used represent the process, preparation, terminal/interrupt, input/output and decision. Fig 7.42 shows the symbols and explains their use.

Flow charts can be drawn vertically or horizontally. Vertical charts always start at the top and horizontal charts at the left-hand side. When making flow charts, take care to keep the layout clear and simple so that it can be followed easily and, to avoid confusion, make sure that the flow lines do not cross. Fig 7.43 is an example of a flow chart which shows how to carry out a simple task. Flow charts can also be used to find faults when a piece of equipment is not working properly. Workshop manuals often include a fault-finding diagram to help the user rectify simple faults.

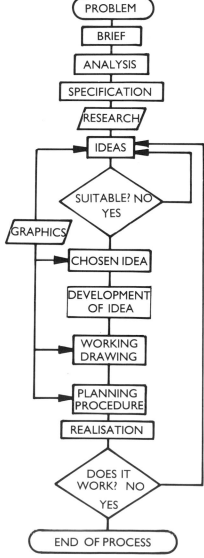

fig 7.43. The design process as a flow chart

SEQUENTIAL DIAGRAMS

A picture or diagram can often communicate instructions much more clearly than written or verbal instruction, which can sometimes be difficult to understand. Sequential diagrams are used for this purpose and show an **operation** or **sequence of operations**. They may show how to use a product or piece of equipment, how to assemble or make something. The instructions to self-assembly furniture or a construction kit are usually conveyed using sequential diagrams. Fig 7.44 shows part of the instruction sheet for a plastic model kit. It shows how to assemble the car, step by step, with the minimum use of words. You will also notice that it is an exploded drawing which uses ribbon arrows to show where each part fits. Sequential diagrams can be drawn using any suitable drawing system. The choice of system will depend on the type of object, the instructions to be conveyed and the level of detail required. When making a sequential diagram you should always aim to let the picture tell the story. Labels and captions will be required, but try to keep written instructions to a minimum. You must also try to achieve a balance between providing too much information and not enough. Usually the simpler the diagram, the more effective it is. Some people refer to sequential diagrams as flow diagrams, but this is not strictly correct. They are really diagrams which show a sequence of actions or operations. They may also be called operational diagrams.

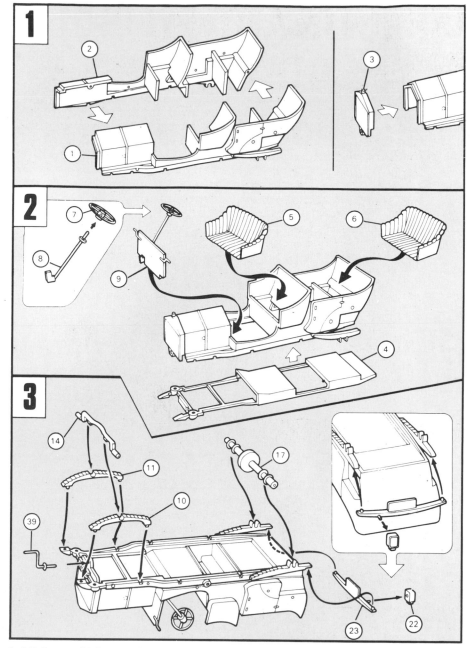

fig 7.44. A sequential diagram system from a modelling instructions sheet

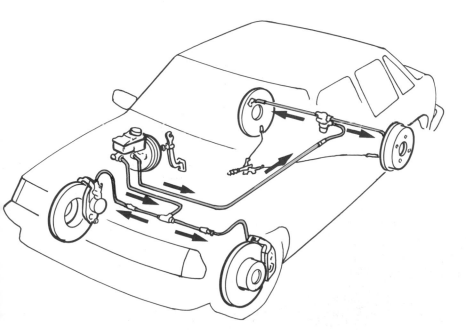

fig 7.45. A flow diagram

FLOW DIAGRAMS

The term flow diagram is used here to describe an illustration which shows a **movement or operation from start to finish**. The whole movement is shown as a complete sequence on one drawing. Fig 7.45 is a flow diagram showing the hydraulic braking system on a motor car. It shows the movement of the brake fluid along the brake pipes to the wheel cylinders when the pedal is depressed. Flow diagrams can show the power flow of an engine, the flow of oil in a lubricating system or anything else which has movement or flow.

CIRCUITS AND SYMBOLS

Technical illustrators are often required to draw circuit diagrams. These may be for electronic, electrical, pneumatic or hydraulic circuits. Most motor car or motorcycle workshop manuals contain a wiring diagram. Some electrical products such as TVs and videos often have a circuit diagram supplied with them and these are often found at the back of the instruction booklet. They are very useful when carrying out repairs or fitting accessories to motor vehicles. They are used in industry when dealing with control system on various products. Electronic circuit diagrams are essential when designing and building your own projects. The diagram in fig 7.46 is taken from a workshop manual and shows part of a car wiring diagram. They are usually printed in black and white with the colours of the wires shown by a letter code.

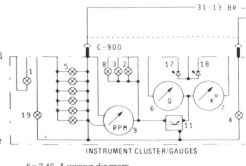

fig 7.46. A wiring diagram

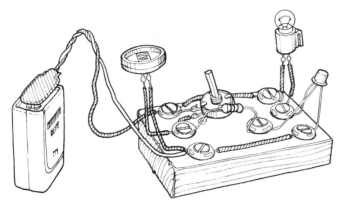

fig 7.47. A simple electric circuit

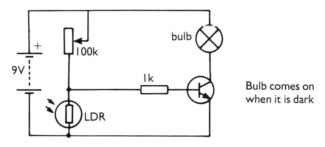

fig 7.48. Circuit diagram of a simple electric circuit

It would be very time-consuming for the illustrator to draw every component and connection separately in a three-dimensional drawing. It would also make the drawing difficult to understand and could lead to misinterpretation. Instead, a form of graphic shorthand is used.

Shorthand is a form of notation. It uses simple symbols to represent words and enables secretaries, for example, to write very quickly. In graphic shorthand symbols are used to represent components, with the connections between them shown by lines. This type of drawing is known as a schematic diagram. It is a very simple method of showing graphically how a system works. Fig 7.47 shows a simple circuit constructed on a modelling board. The circuit itself is very simple, but the way it is drawn could lead to confusion. Fig 7.48 shows the circuit drawn as a schematic diagram. Once the symbols are understood it is simpler and easier to understand.

Wherever possible, schematic diagrams should be drawn using the correct British Standard symbol. These can be found in the **BSI booklet PP7307**. In some cases you may need to design your own symbols to use on a drawing. You will then need to identify each symbol clearly using a legend or key somewhere on the drawing.

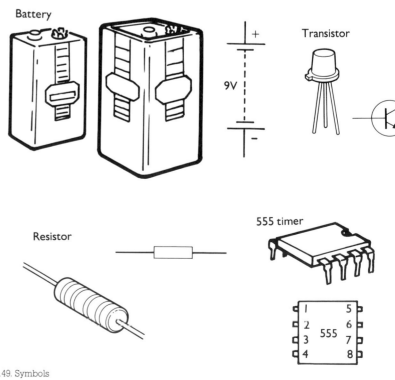

fig 7.49. Symbols

Symbols are also used to show circuits and components in **micro-electronics**, **pneumatics** and **hydraulics**. Fig 7.50 shows a pneumatic circuit and the same circuit is drawn in the form of a schematic diagram in fig 7.51.

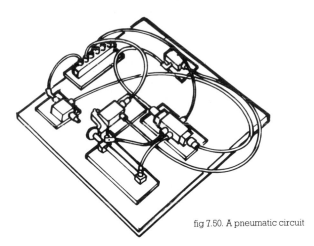

fig 7.50. A pneumatic circuit

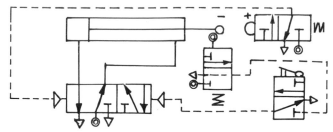

fig 7.51. Circuit diagram of pneumatic circuit

Some of the more common symbols are shown in fig 7.51. There is no need to try and learn them off by heart, as you will soon become familiar with them as you draw them. Plastic stencils of the symbols are available and are used in the same way as lettering stencils. Dry transfer symbols are also available, but they tend to be rather expensive if you have a lot of drawings to produce.

Other information can be shown in the form of schematic diagrams. Maps, for example, use symbols to represent buildings and places. Route maps for buses and trains are usually simplified to make them easy to understand. The London Underground map is a very good example of this (fig 7.53).

Table 1. Selected electrical and electronic graphical symbols

Description	Symbol	Description	Symbol
Direct current	—	Fuse	
Alternating current	~		
Positive polarity	+	Resistor, general symbol	
Negative polarity	−	Variable resistor	
Variability		Resistor with sliding contact	
Pre-set adjustment		Potentiometer with moving contact	
Primary or secondary cell		Heating element	
Battery of primary or secondary cells		Capacitor, general symbol	
Alternative symbol		Polarized capacitor	
Earth or ground		Voltage-dependent polarized	

fig 7.52.

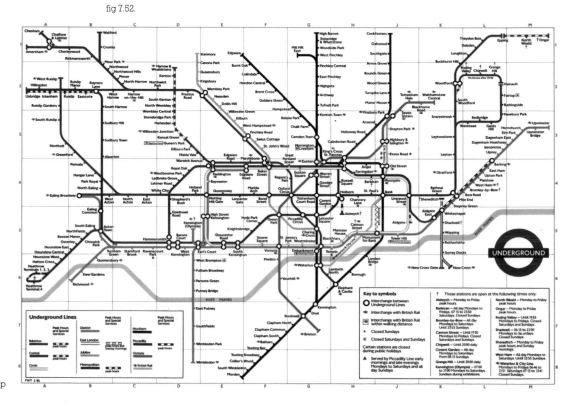

fig 7.53. London Underground map

127

COLOUR

Colour has a limited use in technical illustration, as much of the work of the illustrator is reproduced from line or tone drawings in black and white. Design graphics and other areas of Design and Communication rely much more on the use of colour. Despite this, there are occasions when excellent use is made of colour. For example, colour is used on cut-away sections and in the presentation of information. It is also used in the layout of technical booklets and brochures. Fig 7.54 shows an example of the use of colour.

Methods of applying colour are described fully on pages 44–47, but the technical illustrator is likely to use two methods which have not been previously described. These are the use of coloured plastic film and paint or ink sprayed onto the work.

fig 7.54. A colour cut-away section

FILM

fig 7.55. Applying coloured film

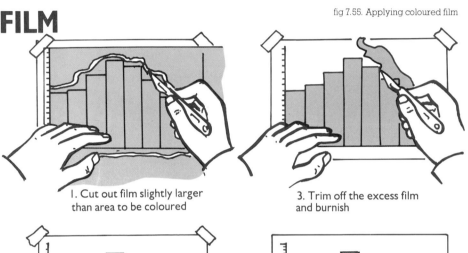

1. Cut out film slightly larger than area to be coloured

2. Place film in position and smooth out with fingers

3. Trim off the excess film and burnish

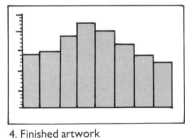

4. Finished artwork

Acetate sheet is used for applying colour to diagrams, charts and maps. It is a transparent, coloured film which is available in a wide range of colours with either matt or glossy finishes. Film would normally only be used for quality presentation and display work as it is rather expensive to use in large quantities. The drawing or diagram is made in the normal way and the coloured film is then applied. It is placed over the drawing and cut out, slightly larger than required, using a sharp scalpel. The backing is then removed and the film placed in position. It is smoothed onto the drawing carefully with the fingers and any air bubbles removed. The excess film is trimmed away with the scalpel and the coloured area burnished to make sure that it will not peel off. If a burnishing tool is not available, the handle of a spoon or any smooth, flat object can be used.

A dry transfer film is also available in a wide range of translucent and opaque colours. It is applied in a similar way to film except that it does not have to be cut out with a scalpel. The outline of the area to be coloured is scored with a pointed, but not too sharp, object and the area is then burnished up to the outline. The sheet of film is then peeled away, leaving the coloured area on the work. The backing sheet is placed over the work and it is burnished in the same way as you would dry transfer lettering. Technical illustrators use this method to give uniform areas of colour to charts and diagrams when presenting information in graphic form. The main disadvantage in terms of school use is cost. However, it may be well worth considering for the final realisation of a piece of project work.

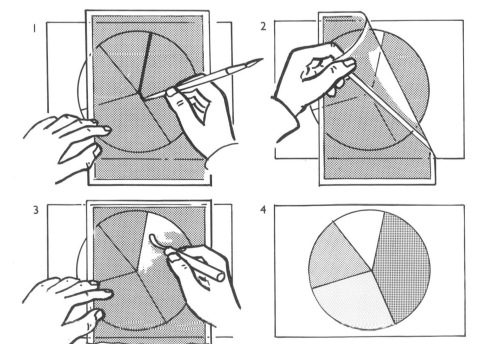

fig 7.56. Dry transfer film

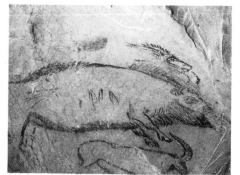
fig 7.57. A cave painting

SPRAY TECHNIQUES

A variety of coloured effects can be achieved by spraying paint or ink onto a drawing in a number of ways, ranging from spattering with an old toothbrush to spraying with an expensive airbrush. Spray techniques are used widely by the technical illustrator for creating realistic and detailed effects. They are used for cut-away sections and ghosted views as well as final presentation drawings which show what an object will look like.

It is believed that powdered paint was blown through a hollow pipe and onto the walls of caves as long as 35,000 years ago. Similiar techniques are still used today to create texture, and add interest and detail to an illustration. These techniques are fairly simple and with a little practice you should be able to use some of them in your work.

fig 7.58. Using an old toothbrush to spatter paint on to paper

SPATTER

Ink or paint is loaded onto an old toothbrush and spattered onto the paper. This is done by drawing a pallete knife or similar flat tool back over the bristles, allowing them to 'flick' back and spatter droplets of ink or paint onto the paper. Some interesting effects can be achieved, but it is difficult to put a uniform covering onto the paper.

DIFFUSER

A diffuser, available from art material shops, for spraying fixative onto drawings, can be used to spray ink or paint. The material is mixed to the correct consistency and then sprayed by blowing through the diffuser as shown in fig 7.59. A similar method is to use a perfume sprayer or atomiser.

fig 7.59. Using a diffuser

fig 7.60. Aerosols

AEROSOLS

Aerosols of paint, such as car touch-up and enamel sprays, can be used on graphic work. A wide range of colours are available, including metallic effects as well as matt and gloss finishes. They can be expensive if large areas have to be sprayed, and care is required when storing and disposing of the cans. Do **not** leave them near heat or in direct sunlight and never puncture them, even if empty. Refillable aerosols are available. They consist of a can of propellent, such as compressed air, connected via a valve to a jar which can be refilled with paint. Providing they have been diluted to a suitable consistency, almost any type of paint or ink can be sprayed.

AIRBRUSHES

Airbrushes tend to be expensive, but a simple, cheaper alternative is available. This consists of a felt-tipped pen sprayed by a blast of air. The air is stored in a can and is controlled by a valve. As the valve is depressed, the air blows through the tip of the pen and sprays the ink onto the paper. The conventional airbrush is a small precision spray gun powered by air from a compressor. Originally, the airbrush was used to colour and retouch photographs, but it is now used widely to produce illustrations for instruction manuals, magazines and technical posters.

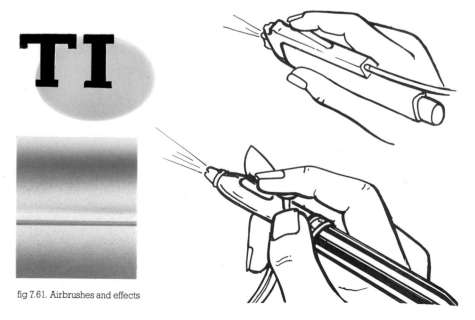
fig 7.61. Airbrushes and effects

MASKING

Before applying colour with any of the spray techniques, the work must be masked to avoid over-spraying the surrounding areas of the drawing. There are several quite simple ways in which this can be done, but it does require a little planning.

CARD STENCILS

One of the most inexpensive methods of masking is to make stencils from thin card. The required shapes are cut from the card using a sharp modelling knife or scalpel. Care must be taken to ensure that the finished stencil lays flat on the paper, otherwise there is a chance that the paint may stray underneath it as it is sprayed. Stencils can be held down with weights or they can be lightly stuck down with Blu-tack or a rubber-based adhesive.

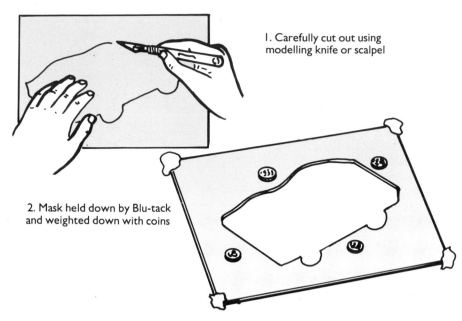

1. Carefully cut out using modelling knife or scalpel

2. Mask held down by Blu-tack and weighted down with coins

fig 7.62. Making card stencils or masks

fig 7.63. Newspaper and masking tape

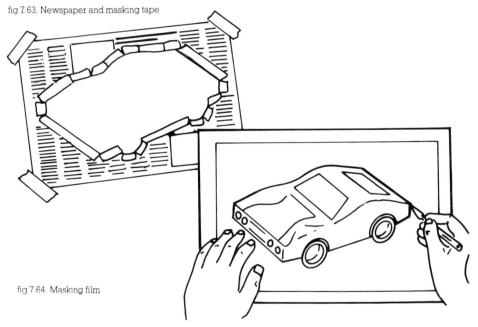

fig 7.64. Masking film

PAPER STENCILS

Newspaper and masking tape is another easy and inexpensive way of making masks or stencils. You will need to make sure that the print on the newspaper does not rub off onto your drawing and also that the masking tape does not tear or damage the surface of the paper when it is lifted off.

MASKING FILM

A masking film known as **Frisket film** is available from art material suppliers. This is a transparent film which has a slightly sticky back so that it does not damage the paper as it is lifted. A sheet of film is usually applied over the artwork and areas are removed as required by cutting with a scalpel.

MASKING FLUID

When masking small, detailed areas, a liquid masking film can be used. This is a rubber-based solution which is painted onto the paper and left to dry. Once dry it will act as a resist and can easily be removed by gently rubbing with the fingers without damaging the surface of the paper.

When applying colour with any of the spray techniques, begin by spraying the darker colours first, and work through to the lightest. Details and highlights can be applied last. When the masks have been removed the edges can be sharpened up and the highlights touched in with a very fine brush.

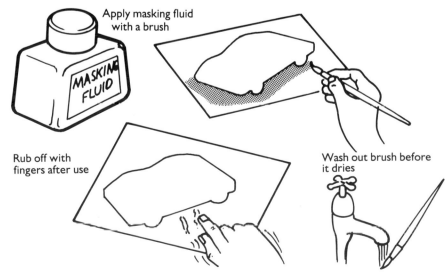

Apply masking fluid with a brush

MASKING FLUID

Rub off with fingers after use

Wash out brush before it dries

fig 7.65. Using masking fluid

USING THE AIRBRUSH

Airbrushes need a supply of **compressed air** either from a stored source such as an aerosol canister or from a small compressor. Car tyres can be used as a source of air, but the pipe to the airbrush must be fitted with a filter or a moisture trap to make sure that the work is not spoilt by condensation. The air pressure required varies according to the material being sprayed. Inks and watercolours will spray well at between 15 and 20 lb, while enamel paints may require up to 35 or 40 lb. The compressor or canister is usually fitted with a simple pressure control or regulator.

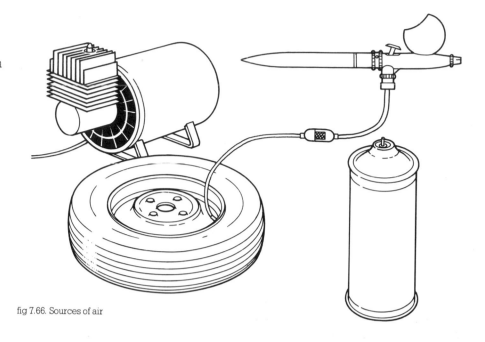

fig 7.66. Sources of air

PREPARATION

The paint or ink needs to be diluted to a suitable consistency for spraying. It should be mixed to about the same consistency as milk. If you are mixing your own colours it is wise to strain them through a piece of muslin, which will remove any lumps and prevent the airbrush from blocking during use. Special airbrush paint is available, pre-mixed to the correct consistency and free from lumps. The paint is loaded into the airbrush reservoir using a pipette or eyedropper.

fig 7.67. Filling the airbrush

AIR BRUSH INK

SPRAYING

Practise spraying on a piece of scrap paper. Hold the airbrush about 100 mm away from the paper and move it horizontally across the sheet. Be sure to release the control valve before you stop moving, otherwise blots and spots will appear on your work. Fig 7.68 will give you an idea of what the work should look like and help you to identify your mistakes. This is only intended as a basic introduction to airbrushing. Practise for yourself and try out some of the masking techniques shown in this chapter.

CLEANING THE AIRBRUSH

After you have finished using the airbrush it **must** be thoroughly cleaned. Put clean water in the reservoir and spray until there is no trace of paint or ink. Dismantle the airbrush, remove the needle and carefully wipe it. The body of the brush can then be cleaned out. Once it is clean it can be re-assembled, taking **great care not to damage or bend the needle**.

fig 7.68. Identifying mistakes

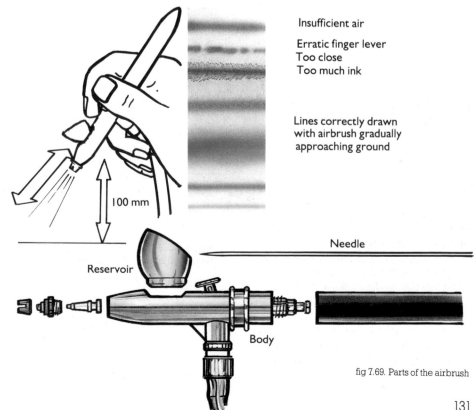

Insufficient air

Erratic finger lever
Too close
Too much ink

Lines correctly drawn
with airbrush gradually
approaching ground

100 mm

Needle

Reservoir

Body

fig 7.69. Parts of the airbrush

131

EXERCISES

1. The statistics in fig 7.70 represent the performance of various models in a range of motor cars. Using this information and some of the techniques of technical illustration solve the following design problems:

a) Design a bar chart to compare the fuel consumption of the models across the range.

b) Design a three-dimensional chart to compare the top speed of the models in the range.

c) Design a simple line graph which will show the acceleration of the XR4i.

2. Take a simple object such as a torch or a bicycle pump and make an exploded drawing of it.

3. Design a lubrication chart for a new bicycle. It should be no larger than 100×150 mm, so that it can be attached to the bicycle when sold.

4. Make a sequential drawing to show how to replace the batteries in your pocket calculator. This is the type of drawing which might be included in an instructional leaflet.

5. Collect examples of technical illustration from magazines, car brochures, instructions and sales and promotional material. Cut them out and keep them in a scrap book for future use. If you cannot cut them out, sketch them and record the details. Scrap books and sketch books can be very useful as a resource when you need to find how something works or how to present an idea.

6. Make a flow chart to show how to mend a puncture in a cycle or motorcycle tyre. Be careful not to confuse this with a flow diagram.

7. Choose a simple object such as a pencil box or a cassette tape box and make a cut-away section of it to show the contents inside.

8. Make an exploded drawing of a 13 amp plug. Use colour to show the correct wiring of the plug.

9. Make a sequential drawing to show how to fit a 13 amp plug. Include a method of checking the fuse in the diagram.

	1.6 SALOON	2.0 SALOON	2.0 ESTATE	2.3 SALOON	XR4i
	(5-speed)	(5-speed)	(5-speed)	(Automatic)	(5-speed)
Maximum speed (mph)	101‡	114‡	111‡	109	128
Overall fuel consumption (mpg)	33.0	28.3	27.5	20.9	21.4
Fuel consumption (mpg) at:					
30 mph	55.4	●	●	36.7	●
50 mph	46.9	●	●	31.8	●
70 mph	35.8	●	●	26.7	●
Range on full fuel tank (miles)	429	368	358	272	282
Acceleration (seconds):					
0–30 mph	3.8	3.0	3.2	4.2	2.7
0–40 mph	6.5	4.8	5.2	6.3	4.1
0–50 mph	9.3	6.8	7.4	8.7	5.8
0–60 mph	13.0	9.3	10.1	11.9	7.7
0–70 mph	18.3	13.4	14.4	16.4	10.4
Standing start ¼ mile	19.1	17.1	17.7	18.7	15.9
40–60 mph in top gear	16.2	15.2	16.9	6.9†	8.7

© *Autocar,* IPC Transport Press Limited.

● Data not available   † In 2nd gear   ‡ In 4th gear

fig 7.70. Car performance statistics

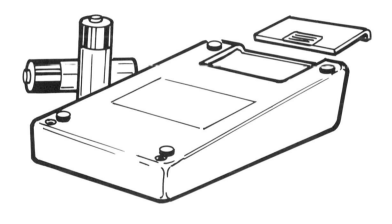

fig 7.71. A pocket calculator

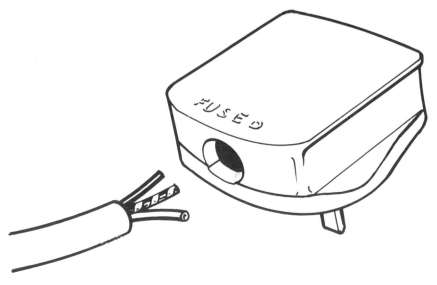

fig 7.72. 13 amp plug

COMPUTER GRAPHICS

An airline pilot overshoots the runway while attempting to land and crashes into a housing estate. The pilot is perhaps rather embarrassed, but since the scene is completely generated by computer, no one has been hurt in this simulation landing.

At an international athletics meeting a huge 'screen' can display the results of a race. A large number of lights on a board and controlled by a computer are used to form the letters in the message.

Images and information generated and stored in computers are now commonly seen. The computer is a powerful tool; vision is a powerful means of communication. Computers and vision combine to follow to form a revolutionary means of communication – computer graphics.

The impact of a video game with its flashing and moving display is an example of the power of computer graphics.

The nature and quality of the images is dependent on the power of the machines used to produce them. Personal computers will produce graphics that are rather 'lumpy' and coarse. The machines that can produce the stunning displays and store a great deal of information are far more costly, some still costing millions of pounds. The cost is being reduced and the power is increasing. Machines that were used only five years ago in industry are now being produced at prices that allow them to be used in the school and home.

Computer graphics can be defined as **modelling** (describing an object in terms of lines, solids and colours), **storage** (of the model in the memory of the computer), **manipulation** (changing the model by altering its shape or size or merging two models together) and **viewing** (the computer model from a particular view point and depicting what is seen).

fig 8.1. Stunning visual effects from a Nimbus computer running a PLUTO graphics system

fig 8.2. Athletics stadium showing the large screen

fig 8.3. An old style drawing office

fig 8.4. A new style drawing office

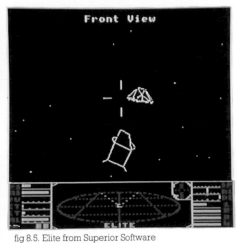

fig 8.5. Elite from Superior Software

133

COMPUTER INPUTS

KEYBOARD

The keyboard is the general purpose interface between the operator and the computer. The keys are connected to logic circuitry that changes the finger press to a special code. This code is given the name ASCII (American Standard Code for Information Interchange). There are 256 different codes representing numbers letters (upper and lower case), punctuation marks and various other codes. This code is fed into the computer where it can be operated upon by the computer language and the program.

MOUSE

The ball underneath the mouse box is rolled on a table top. These devices are used to move the cursor around the screen. Drawing programs use them. It is possible to write on the screen as through you were writing or sketching a picture on a piece of paper. The device also has three buttons that are used to input information. At present the mouse is the most favoured input for graphical uses.

MAGNETIC DISC

The data required to run the program or the information upon which the program operates, must be stored in a permanent form unless it is to be lost every time the computer is switched off. (This only applies to data held in the RAM). To rewrite a list of data every time we wish to use it in the computer is rather pointless, just as it would be to rewrite a telephone directory when looking for a telephone number. The data is stored by being sent to one of a number of devices. The disc, either a 'floppy' 5.25" or a 'cassette' 3.5", is the most common method you will use to store the data while not in the computer. The information is sent at high speed from the disc directly into the computer for use, it can then be sent back just as quickly when you have finished. The disc drive is, therefore, not only an input device, but also an output device.

fig 8.6. Computer using a disc and mouse as inputs

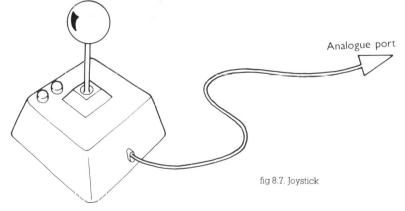

Analogue port

fig 8.7. Joystick

JOYSTICK

A device that looks a little like an aeroplane joystick is used to input information to the computer. It sends positional information, used in games and drawing programs.

TRACKER BALL

A tracker ball is used to input information in the sameway as a mouse, but has the ball on the top. Fingers are used to rotate the ball. Positional control can be closely monitored and adjusted with this device.

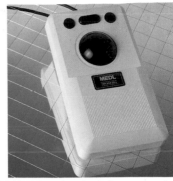

fig 8.8. The Marconi tracker ball; a mouse on its back

fig 8.9. Graphics showing a tablet and puck in use

GRAPHICS TABLET

A graphics tablet is a pencil like probe, or a puck with a crossed hair targetting device which is used on a special drawing area to send positional control signals to the computer. The advantage of this input can be seen when a drawing is to be traced into the computer. It is easier to trace a map of the British Isles than to draw it freehand.

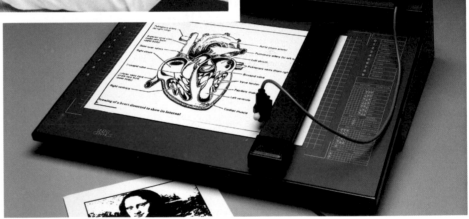

fig 8.10. Image from Plotmate

IMAGE SCANNER

Using a light sensitive scanning head fixed to a plotter, it is possible to register light and dark. It is possible, therefore, to scan a picture and to enter this into memory for further manipulation.

VIDEO DIGITISER

The image from a video recorder or camera can be digitised and saved in the computer memory as a series or codes. Pictures can be drawn on the screen from this data and can then be manipulated by various graphics programs.

fig 8.11. Video image

fig 8.12. Video image

COMPUTER OUTPUTS

VISUAL DISPLAY UNIT

The computer can send information to many different devices. The most common device is called a visual display unit or VDU. Often a television is used to provide this output. The information sent to the screen is in the form of a code turning on a certain colour at a certain place.

The VDU can be used to show lines and shapes and can show drawings as well as words. The VDU can be made to animate pictures, and is extensively used in computer 'games'.

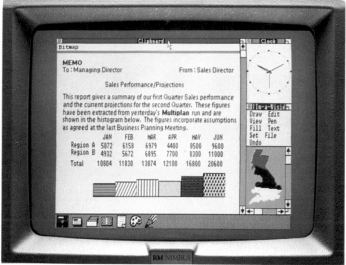

fig 8.13. Use of graphics as information is displayed on a word processing screen

fig 8.14.

DISC AND TAPE

Disc and tape can be used to receive information from the computer. It can then be stored until required. These give a permanent method of storing data.

fig 8.15. 3D imaging

PRINTER

The data displayed on the screen can be made into 'hard copy' by sending the information to a printer.

Daisy wheel printer

These are only used for printing words from a word processor. The quality of lettering is very good, but they are rather slow in operation.

Laser printer

These printers are capable of very high resolution, making very fine detail possible. The pixel size is very small, so lines seem smooth and not made from blocks as with a dot matrix printer. These printers are still very expensive, but the price is slowly falling. They will print at high speed: 10 A4 pages per minute are possible with some machines. The quality of the lettering and drawing is as good as professional printing machines such as those used to print this book.

fig 8.16. Screen in use creating a drawing

Dot matrix printer

These printers have a printing head simular to the pixels (see page 138) on the screen. The dots printed can be made to represent lettering, a newspaper style photograph or a line drawing. The print is in the form of small blocks of print making diagonal lines difficult to represent. These printers are much cheaper than daisy wheel printers and work at much higher speeds.

fig 8.17. Black and white print out from dot matrix

fig 8.18. Complete A4 page dumped on an Integrex printer

Ink jet printer

As the name suggests, these printers squirt a jet of ink at the paper. They can use coloured inks to produce colour pictures. They are rather costly and the operation can be slow.

PLOTTERS

Plotters are used to produce drawings and charts of very high quality. Different coloured and types of pens can be used and can plot on paper, card, acertate sheet or drafting film.

fig 8.20. Roller bed plotter

fig 8.19. Plotmate plotter

VIDEO

Any picture that can be displayed on the screen can be stored on a video tape as a single frame, or as a series of moving pictures as they are generated by the computer. It is possible for a computer generated sequence to be stored one frame at a time like a cartoon and then played back as a 'movie'.

SCREEN DISPLAY

The drawing is always displayed on the VDU screen while it is being processed or being drawn. The quality of line and colour is dependent on both the quality of the VDU and the ability of the micro to store the information required for detailed drawings.

The BBC computer can display graphics in different 'modes'. Mode 0 has the most definition and can display the finest lines. However, the memory capabilities of this micro is such that only two colours can be displayed. Mode 2 has 16 different colours available, but the definition is poor, and the drawings become rather 'lumpy'. Fig 8.21 shows the different modes and their resolution available on the BBC micro.

Professional graphics stations in industry require a very high resolution with many colours available to the user. This requires great amounts of data storage space and the ability to do many calculations in a very short space of time.

The IBM compatible personal computers and the Acorn Archemedes are now able to produce graphics that reach professional standards, at a much lower cost.

Graphic capabilities, Acorn BBC micro

Mode	Graphics	Colours	Text
0	640 × 256	2	80 × 32
1	320 × 256	4	40 × 32
2	160 × 256	16	20 × 32
3	Text only	2	80 × 25
4	320 × 256	2	40 × 32
5	160 × 256	4	40 × 32
6	Text only	2	40 × 25
7	Teletext	Display	40 × 25

fig 8.21.

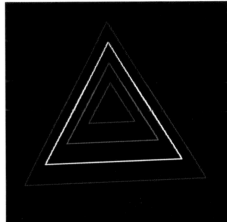

PIXELS

The screen is divided into blocks called pixels. The BBC micro can divide the screen into 640 × 256 squares. That means that 163,840 different squares can be one of two colours. The memory required to do this is quite large, 20k. If we wish the pixels to be more than two colours, the storage space required is much larger. Some graphics stations have a resolution of 1000 × 1000 and a possibility of 500 different colours available at each pixel. The size of the computer store required for these high quality graphics is in the order of 4 Megabytes of RAM. Fig 8.22 shows the different sizes of the pixels at two different modes.

fig 8.22. Relative pixel sizes

LETTERS

The styles of the letters used on a micro are called fonts. To say there are 10 different fonts available means that 10 different styles of lettering are available to the user. The standard letters are based on a block of 8 × 8 pixels. High resolution modes give small letters, allowing up to 80 characters across the screen. Low resolution modes can only give up to 20 characters, but in many different colours. The graphics designer must choose the mode that he or she requires upon the requirements of the graphics.

It is possible to design different fonts for special requirements. Some programs allow the user to do this, while some have fixed fonts.

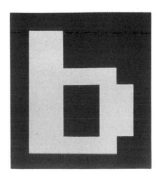

fig 8.23. Standard letter font

RASTER GRAPHICS

This type of graphics refers to the method of storage of information and its manipulation. Raster graphics is pixel graphics, the data stored is telling the computer what colour each pixel must be to produce the required effect. This is used for 'artistic' type drawing packages where a visual effect is most important. Examples of this style are to be seen under the heading computer art on pages 142–143.

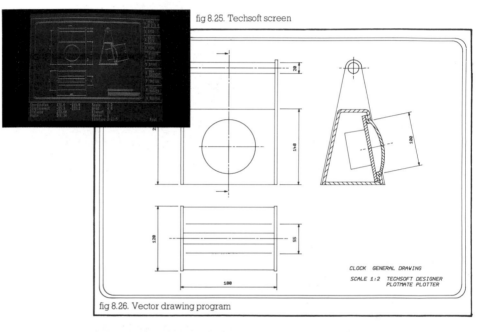

fig 8.24. Raster drawing

VECTOR GRAPHICS

The information for drawings that are used in industry as 'working drawings', are produced as vector drawings. A vector is a line that has size and direction. The drawing is plotted as a series of points joined with straight lines. These depict a 3D object, but as the screen is only 2D, some projectional method of drawing is used, much the same as would be used to draw a product on paper. Both orthographic and isometric projections are used, often on screen at the same time. The storage of the drawing in this manner allows the drawing to be manipulated, rotated, stretched, reflected and measured. Examples are to be found in the computer aided design section.

fig 8.25. Techsoft screen

fig 8.26. Vector drawing program

3D GRAPHICS

Often the requirement is for a non technical drawing of a component, possibly to use as an advertising drawing or to give a more pleasing visual effect. Vector and raster graphics can be used in combination to produce visually solid drawings from vector information. Compare the drawings of a fan in vector lines (fig 8.27) or as a 3D solid (fig 8.28). Which is easier to understand? Which can have most technical information on display?

The production of visually solid objects that can be rotated and otherwise manipulated requires great computing power, many millions of calculations must be performed at high speed.

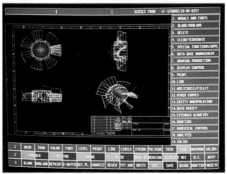

fig 8.27. Fan wire

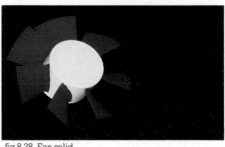

fig 8.28. Fan solid

HARD COPY

All drawings can be displayed on the VDU, but this is of a temporary nature. A more permanent copy, a 'hard copy', is usually required.

A raster drawing in many colours with both drawings and text, would use a colour printer for the best effect. Some printers are now able to produce A3 drawings at fast speeds.

A vector drawing could use a printer, but best results are found by using plotters with different pens. Drawings up to A0 size are produced in this manner.

GAMES

Computers have been used as 'games' machines since they began to appear. The early machines were only capable of very simple graphics: it was only possible to move pixel blocks around the screen. Early games that had very simple moving graphics include table tennis and brick out of the wall.

The advance in the technical possibilities and the programming techniques has produced a whole new world of interactive games.

The impact of the space invader programs of the 70s was tremendous, the age of the video arcade game was upon us.

The need for greater graphics qualities has led to the development of very sophisticated games programs for computers. These games are communicating devices between the player and the computer. The awareness of this communication is very necessary for any programmer. The development of computer games has had a great effect on all graphics on the computer.

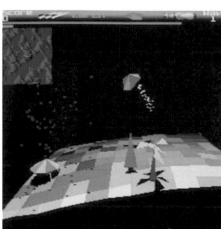
fig 8.29. REVS

fig 8.30. Strykers run

fig 8.31. Computer game

TELETEXT

Televisions are now used as communication devices, both through the programmes and also Ceefax and Oracle, two teletext information services.

The 'information' is built up into pages that can be called up by a number. The difference between teletext pages and a book or leaflet is that updating is possible. An example of this is shown in the reporting of cricket matches and their scores. A newspaper can only print and report on the latest score at printing time, while a teletext score card can be updated as often as required as the match develops.

Electronic communication is becoming very common. If you go to a travel agent to book a holiday the agent will probably use a television screen and computer to link up with travel firms by telephone line. The agent will use the computer to dial the number of the firm or service agency and obtain the latest information. The computer can also be used to send information to the travel firm, in the form of your booking for the holiday of your choice, that has just been checked for availability.

This system can be used not only to book flights and rail tickets, but can also link you to your bank or credit card company. You can get information on your account or even have your money sent directly to the travel agent without using any paper money or a cheque.

This communication is dependent on there being a telephone link between the computers, both text and pictures can be sent anywhere in the world.

fig 8.32. British Rail Oracle

DESK TOP PUBLISHING

Desk top publishing (DTP) is the name given to the method used to produce written and drawn information using a computer. Newspapers are an example where DTP could be of use. The text is typed into a computer memory using a wordprocessing program. This text can then be manipulated in size, shape or type of print style that is to be used. This means that we can change the text very easily to suit our design for the whole page.

Drawings are created with drawing programs. They can also be manipulated in shape, size or even magnification. Pictures from a video camera through a digitiser can also be used.

This allows the designing of the page to be accomplished with ease and great speed. It is possible to try many different layouts using the same information.

These DTP programs could help us to communicate ideas and information. The shape of the text blocks mixed with the drawings will have a bearing on the impact of the information that you are trying to communicate.

Using colour jet printers, A4 sized sheets can be produced in full colour with drawings and text (see fig 8.18, page 137). The use of laser printers allows us to produce a quality of output that is almost as good as this book. Project work of the highest standard can now be produced using computer techniques.

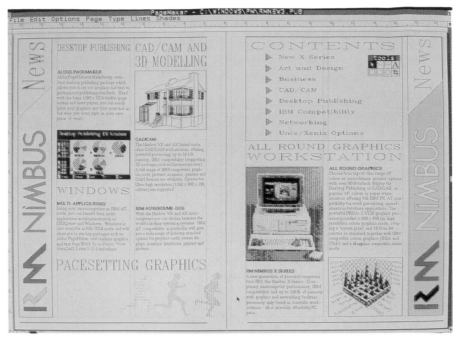

fig 8.33. Desk top publishing

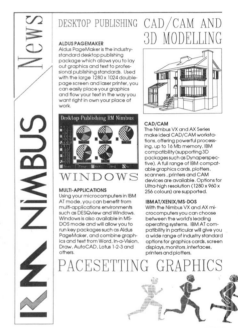

fig 8.34. Print out of pages

fig 8.35. AMX pagemaker

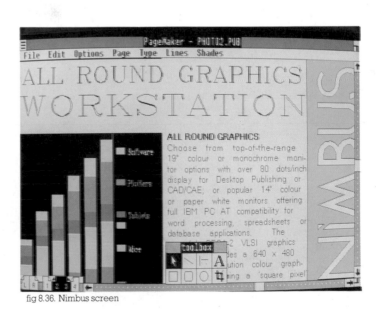

fig 8.36. Nimbus screen

COMPUTER ART

Artists and designers have always used any materials and techniques that are available to them. Early men used natural pigments and a wall as his canvas. Today many different materials and methods of expression are available to artists, whether it is a spray can and a wall or a computer and its screen. The computer should be regarded as an extension of the artists imagination, giving him a different medium with which to work.

Computer art is based on pixel or raster graphics, using the screen as the canvas. The ability to draw or paint computer pictures depends on three main components, first the power of the computer to cope with the manipulations required, second the program to enable the generation of the art on the screen and third the imagination of the user.

Within programs, the drawing of lines and shapes is relatively simple. A program to draw a rectangle on screen is easily written, however, being able to change the shape of the rectangle while still visible on the screen needs a much more powerful program.

Mathematically-generated drawings can be used. Programs are all about manipulation of numbers. Fractal curves are mathematically-generated. Fig 8.38 shows a fractal tree grown mathematically, starting with a line that splits into a specified fraction of the length of the start line. The division then moves on another stage splitting each branch again into subdivisions. Adding a random element to the spacing and the lengths of the branches produces a tree that looks more natural (fig 8.39).

It is also possible to produce curves from mathematical equations. Simple curves and graphs are usually drawn using two axes. To draw curves using more than two axes is difficult. It is possible to model a vase or goblet mathematically from an equation (fig 8.40). Combining both techniques will allow pictures to be created (see fig 8.41).

fig 8.37. 3D bottles

fig 8.38. Fractal tree, regular

fig 8.39. Fractal tree, random

fig 8.40. Mathematical curve

fig 8.41. Vase and tree combined

The ability to create is essential in all drawings, the ability to create and modify easily is a test of a good program. Art packages usually have a drawing screen area with a series of choices around the sides or top edge. Pull down menus give the user choices. If lines are to be drawn, the user can pull down the 'lines' menu and select from perhaps five or six different types of lines and different thicknesses.

The user of the package will have methods of creating simple shapes at their fingertips. Squares, rectangles, triangles, circles and ellipses are generally available. The shapes can be line drawings or solid colours, to the artists choice. The better programs allow the position and size of these shapes to be altered.

Fig 8.42. Typical computer art screen showing colour and drawing

Fig 8.43. Computer drawn house

Fig 8.44. Plants showing only the finished artwork

Lines

Simple lines can be used to join shapes to produce drawings. The user selects a pencil and can either draw freehand or as straight lines. Freehand drawing gives control to the artist, but is not an easy technique to master, no easier than drawing with a pencil. Drawing straight lines usually involves rubber banding. Here the artist draws a line from one point to another in a straight line, the computer shows on the screen a straight line between that start and finish point following the pencil as directed. This allows for adjustment by eye until the line is in the correct place, then it is fixed in position. Freehand drawing is fixed directly on the screen as the pencil is moved, however wobbly the line is.

Colour fill

It should be possible to flood fill an area with colour. If a shape is outlined, the fill routine will colour this area. The colour could be a solid colour or a texture representing bricks, pebbles or even a tartan. If the shape is not fully outlined, it is possible that the colour will leak out and cover unwanted areas.

Spray paint

There should be various facilities available within an art program that allow the user to produce not only solid colours, but also more natural shades. This can be achieved using the computer as an airbrush, with various widths of spray available. The spray can be a solid colour on the screen or could be a 'splatter' spray, allowing subtle shading to be achieved.

Erase

The programs will allow the user to rub out lines or part lines that are not wanted. Areas can often be defined and erased. Individual pixels can be removed if the program allows magnification of an area of the screen. Some rubbers allow for selective colour removal.

Zoom

The user will often need to see the picture in close detail. Zoom facilities allow this to be achieved. A square or rectanglar area is selected and enlarged, allowing the user to see each one of the many pixels that make up the picture. It is then possible to have very close control over the artwork.

Ikons

Ikons are small pre-defined groups of character blocks. It is possible to design an ikon in the shape of a hand, pencil or spray brush which are seen on program screen as symbols to help in understanding the program facilities. It is also possible to design ikons in the shape of electronic symbols or simple components. Drawing diagrams from lines and selected symbol ikons becomes a very easy way of producing circuit drawings. These ikons are stored in a library of shapes that is then available to the artist.

Fig 8.45. Racing car

Colour

We see objects in colour. If all our art is in black and white much of the quality can be lost. The ability of the program to depict colour depends on the facilities and memory of the computer. Most home computers can show up to eight different colours on the screen at a time. Some show flashing colours, though this is of limited use if a hard copy is required, flashing ink is not yet available!

A professional graphics station will be able to show possibly a thousand shades. The memory required for this colour definition is very large and the cost is still high. Computers in schools can be expected to draw using 256 different colours. This requires a computer with at least half a megabyte of memory available.

Text

Art programs will allow the user to write on the picture area. Different sizes and shapes of fonts are available. Fig 8.18 on page 137 shows that lettering and drawing can be mixed. Here we see differently coloured text and a very detailed drawing.

Project work

It is now possible to produce models of artwork of a very high standard. It should be remembered that however good the program, the designer needs to be highly skilled to produce the best results. Some examples of raster graphics can be seen on these pages.

Fig 8.16.

Fig 8.47. AMX Super Art

144

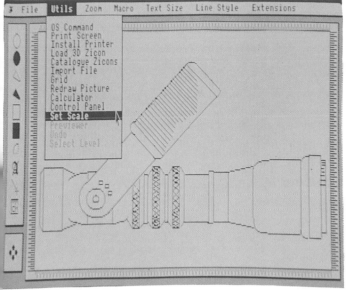

Fig 8.48. AMX designer

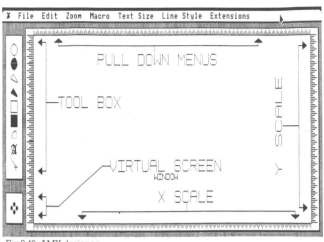

Fig 8.49. AMX designer

Fig 8.50. Mirror soft

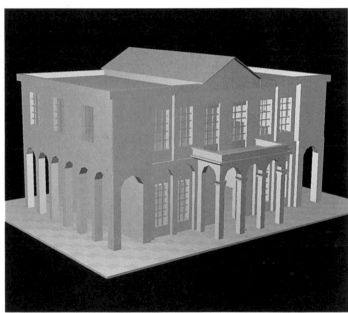

Fig 8.51. Pluto

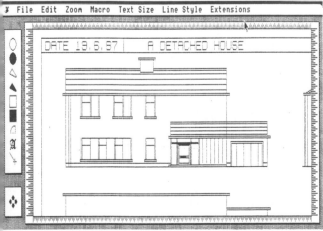

Fig 8.52.

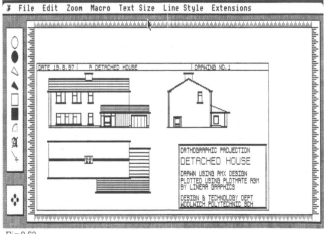

Fig 8.53.

HARD COPY

This is the name given to the paper version of the screen drawings. Most printers in schools are of the dot matrix type. The printout is in black, on white paper. Coloured paper and coloured printer ribbon (usually only red is available) can be used to produce special effects. This type of printer represents colour by different shades or tones of grey.

Colour jet printers will give a direct hard copy in colour as their name suggests. Graphics programs should have 'dump' routines to suit different printer types.

Graphic design work to be printed in large numbers is produced in a different manner. A photograph of the screen gives a slightly distorted image, due to the shape of the screen. This is not an entirely suitable method of producing work of the highest quality. The coloured artwork, whether computer printout, photograph or painting, has to be printed as only four colours. For each colour, black, red, blue and yellow, a printing 'plate' is made. Green is produced in the usual way by mixing blue and yellow, some black can be added for dark green and so on for all the colours we use.

The graphic design work is scanned and a master is produced for each of the colours. When printing, the paper is printed four times, once for each plate, as you would expect. This makes the printing costs of coloured books much higher than those for black and white printing.

Computer generated graphic work is already split into the colours, as each pixel can be only one colour at a time. If the program is designed to print only one colour at a time we can use a simple dot matrix printer from which the printer can make the plates.
Fig 8.54 shows a screen shot of a piece of graphic design; the colours are easily seen. The computer used can only show four colours at a time. Here white, red, black and yellow were used. Figs 8.55, 8.56 and 8.57 show the prints of the separate colours. Shading and patterns have been used to produce more than four colours. The fourth colour on the screen, white, is the paper colour and does not require a plate to be made. Fig 8.58 is the colour version printed from the three plates.

Fig 8.54. Screen shot

Fig 8.55. Colour 1 black

Fig 8.56. Colour 2 red

Fig 8.57. Colour 3 yellow

Fig 8.58. Full colour print produced from Microbrush AB Design

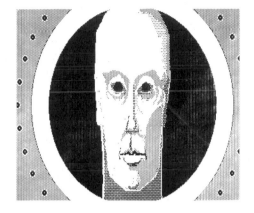

Fig 8.59. Face, colour 1, black   Fig 8.60. Face, colour 2, red   Fig 8.61. Face, colour 3, yellow

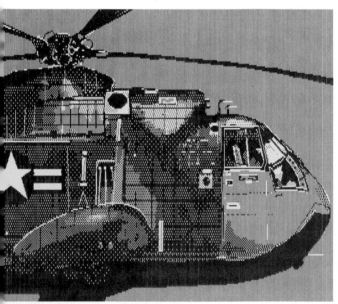

Fig 8.62. Helicopter printed black on blue paper

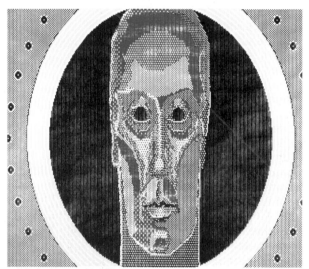

Fig 8.63. Face, colour printed

Fig 8.64. Helicopter printed black on white

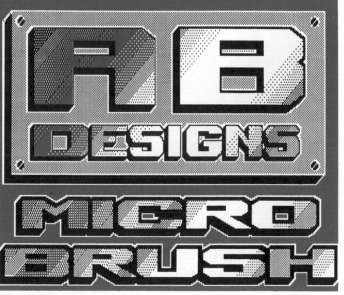

Fig 8.65. Colour print, name plate

COMPUTER AIDED DESIGN

Computer aided design (CAD) covers many different aspects of product design and in many instances is linked with computer aided manufacture (CAM). The computer can be used in many different areas, from the technical research data (information) and market research data, to the data required to control a large milling or printing machine. This data can be inter-related and drawn upon easily by other departments, The market research data will be related to, perhaps, surveys done on various consumer goods. Large numbers of people are questioned on their attitudes to consumer products, and information is also gathered on the people themselves. This information is entered into the computer as a data file and can then be questioned. For example, the researcher could need to know the percentage of people who are female, have children, drive a car and work part time. This information could influence whether a certain product is to be marketed or not.

The design department will need data in the form of drawings and component or cutting lists. The drawings are entered into the computer as a series of measurements. The object being drawn is 3D, but can only be drawn on a 2D screen or paper. A system of drawing must be used to portray this 3D object.

Two drawing systems that are used are orthographic and isometric projection. Often both systems are displayed on screen at the same time. The designer will have a library of standard components or parts of components. For example, it would be a waste of time to draw line by line every single nut and bolt holding a sewing machine together. It is much easier to ask the computer to collect a nut and bolt of a certain size from its library and draw it at a certain place. This is one of the advantages of computer designing, being able to place a complete component from

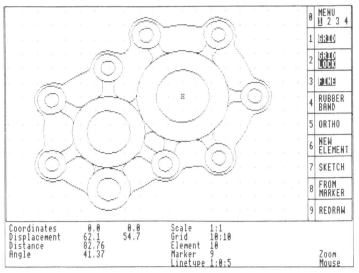

0	MENU 1 2 3 4			
1	GRID			
2	GRID LOCK			
3	FINE			
4	RUBBER BAND			
5	ORTHO			
6	NEW ELEMENT			
7	SKETCH			
8	FROM MARKER			
9	REDRAW			

Coordinates	0.0	0.0	Scale	1:1
Displacement	62.1	54.7	Grid	10:10
Distance	82.76		Element	10
Angle	41.37		Marker	9
			Linetype	1:0:5

Zoom
Mouse

SCREEN LAYOUT

0	MENU 1 2 3 4
1	MOVE
2	MIRROR IMAGE
3	ROTATE
4	ALTER SIZE
5	CIRCLE
6	TANGENT NORMAL
7	ARC
8	SPECIFY LINE
9	HATCH

0	MENU 1 2 3 4
1	ZOOM
2	ZOOM OFF
3	SCALE
4	GRID SCALE
5	PAN
6	LINE TYPE
7	DELETE
8	CHANGE MARKER
9	MODIFY

0	MENU 1 2 3 4
1	TEXT
2	DIM LINE
3	PLOTTER
4	CALL FILE
5	SAVE
6	ADD FILE
7	RESET
8	SALVAGE WORK
9	RESTART

Fig 8.66. Computer aided design   **ALTERNATIVE MENUS**

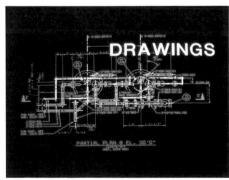

Fig 8.67. Drawing

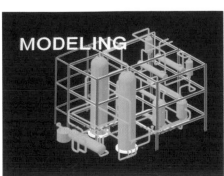

Fig 8.68. Modelling

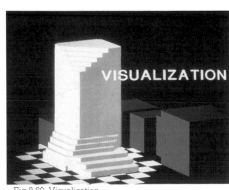

Fig 8.69. Visualisation

memory at a single stroke, never again needing to draw it line by line.

The drawing is not a pixel image of an object as in computer art programs, but a visual representation of vector information. This enables the computer to hold a 3D model in its memory in the form of mathematical data. The program is able to manipulate this data to draw the visualisation of the object on the screen or paper.

It is possible to rotate the whole object and draw it on screen again, viewed from a different angle. If the computer is very powerful, as industrial design computers are, this rotation can be seen to be continuous. The drawing is redrawn so fast that the object seems to be turning slowly on the screen. It is often difficult to visualise the back of an object, but by turning on the screen it is possible to see all sides of the object at will. The graphics used in the game Elite are of this nature. Rotating a wire frame diagram takes far less memory space than rotating solid 3D shapes that are required in a design environment.

The programs that draw in this manner such as Autocad, Techsoft Designer, Compas from British Thornton and Superdraft are very complicated pieces of software. They are not as powerful as programs used in industry, but are getting much closer. The new 32 bit machines of the next generation of computers will be capable of this sort of design work. There are many facilities available to the user on these programs. The drawing is entered into data store, usually by a mouse or the keyboard, in the form of positional information, ie. so far up, down, back or forward from the last point. On the screen it registers as a visual line. The drawing is not restricted to the size of the screen. The screen is to be regarded as a window on to a much larger drawing beyond. The drawing can be scaled down and

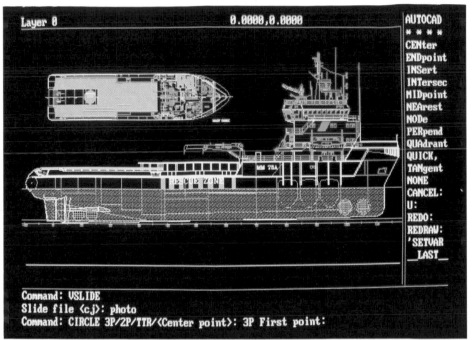

Fig 8.70. Autocad

Fig 8.71. Crane on computer

shown in its entirety or scaled up and only a small part shown in detail.

An example of the use of CAD can be seen in its use by a manufacturing company who make large generating machines to order. Each one is fitted to the customers requirements. The customer can specify the positioning of any controls on the control panel, which will vary depending on the customer's specific requirements. The control panel is displayed on the screen for design alteration. The customer can point to switches and indicators and move them across the screen into the required positions. The customer can manipulate the drawing program, he or she is not drawing lines, but moving groups of lines depicting a certain component. When the customer is satisfied, the layout is fixed. Unknown to him he has altered much more than the obvious drawing on the screen. Linked with each component drawing is other information: how big a hole and what shape is required to be cut in the panel, how far from the corner this will be, how much the component will cost, is it in stock, does it need ordering and how long is delivery on this item, and much more. This ability to layer drawings, showing only the information required at one time, helps to select the important information required by machines cutting holes or costing departments pricing the generator.

DRAWING TECHNIQUES AND TERMINOLOGY

Lines have a starting point and a finishing point. They also have a direction and can be drawn in different line types, such as solid, broken or centre line.

Ortho: lines drawn with this facility are automatically rendered as true vertical or true horizontal lines. This can be very useful when drawing rectangular shapes in orthographic views.

Curves: any lines that is not straight, is a curve. This can include circles, ellipses and arcs.

Circle: it is possible to draw a circle to suit many possible variations, such as:

1. Centre, radius.
2. Centre, point.
3. Radius, touch two lines.
4. Radius, touch line, arc/circle.
5. Radius, touch arc/circle.
6. Radius, touch two points.
7. Three points.
8. Radius, point touch line.
9. Radius, point, touch arc/circle.

These combinations should be catered for.

Arc: an arc is part of a circle and again can be specified in different ways:

1. Fillet.
2. Centre, point, angle.
3. Radius, touch two lines.
4. Radius, touch line, arc/circle.
5. Radius, touch two arc/circle.
6. Radius, touch two points.
7. Three points.
8. Radius, point touch line.
9. Radius, point, touch arc/circle.

Fillet: a fillet is a special curve, a curve joining two lines usually on the corner of an object to soften a sharp corner. The straight lines are drawn first and a curve is then inserted touching the lines. There will be two short lines to be removed sticking out at the sharp corner. These can be removed selectively, the better programs expect this to be done and prompt you with flashing lines.

Tangent normal: these lines need to be drawn with accuracy if circles and lines are to join exactly when drawing a product. The program should help by providing a means to do this.

Follow the sequence involved in drawing a simple component. Try to find where the different operations that are described will be needed during the process of creating this drawing.

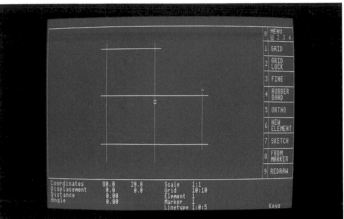
Fig 8.72. Layout lines

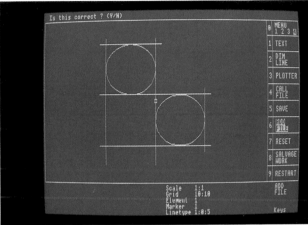
Fig 8.73. Circles added

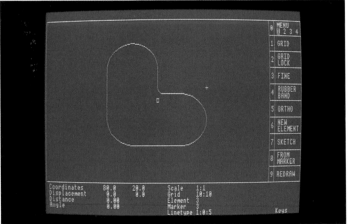
Fig 8.74. Outer shape

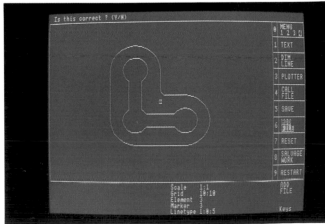
Fig 8.75. Cut-out drawn

Hunt: finding an exact position of two crossing lines or a point can be very difficult. This often leads to un-joined or crossing lines when viewed at high magnification. The hunt facility allows you to move close to a point and then ask the computer to hunt for the nearest point on the drawing. The program will select the exact point and then ask you if this is the point you required as a check.

Grid: the program can draw a series of dots across the screen at a set distance apart. The scale of these grids can be changed. They are not present on the final drawing, they are there simply to guide you when drawing.

Gridlock: the cursor is only allowed to move in steps, the size being specified by the grid. This is often an advantage. To be able to move to exact mm rather than to a fraction of a mm can help with accuracy. Drawing printed circuits requires the designer to move in steps of 0.1 inches. The grid could be set to this size then the cursor locked to move only in steps of the required size. This is of great assistance when positioning the components.

Hatch: hatching a drawing is required to show the cut face when a sectional view is given. A series of parallel lines are drawn at 45°. If the outer line of an area is given with any islands specified, the program will then automatically hatch the area at the selected line spacing. This can be a slow part of the program. Many calculations and checks have to be performed by the computer to find all related outlines and islands.

Zoom: zooming allows the designer to enlarge areas of the drawing to see detail more clearly.

Pan: panning allows the designer to look around the drawing. The screen shows only a window onto the drawing. This window view can be moved around to show details that were previously out of sight. Imagine looking through a telescope at the view out of the window. Only a small part of this view is visible. To see more, the telescope must be moved side to side or up and down. This is called panning.

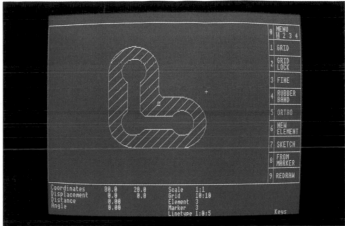

Fig 8.76. Hatch

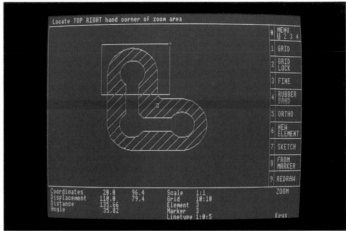

Fig 8.77. Depicting zoom area

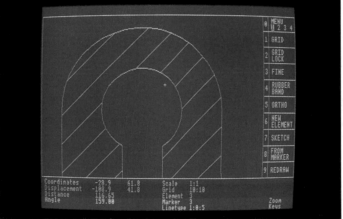

Fig 8.78. Zoomed area

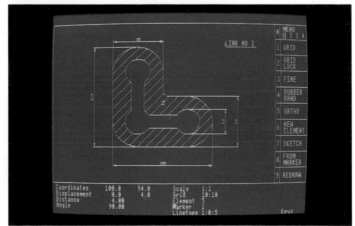

Fig 8.79. Final drawing

Element: a component such as a nut and bolt or electronic component, or a larger component such as a kitchen cupboard can be drawn as an element. This element can then be stored in a library of shapes which can be retrieved later and used again. This ability to collect elements from a library allows us to place whole groups of lines at a time. One reason for using a computer system is this ability to assemble a drawing from pre-drawn elements, so saving time and money. A designer of kitchen layouts does not want to draw cabinets and drawer units line by line, it would take too long. He simply selects the element for each unit from the library and places them in the correct places on the kitchen plan. It is possible to lift these elements and move them around the layout to suit a customer's ideas. Large kitchen furniture retailers often offer this service to their customers.

Repeat: an element can be drawn more than once using a repeat routine. Imagine drawing a speaker grill with lots of slots for the sound to emerge from. If we can draw one slot as an element and then repeat draw at a specified spacing, say six times, this will be much easier than drawing the same slot with rounded ends seven times.

Rotate: a rotated element can be drawn, twisted through an angle, then redrawn. The ability to repeat and rotate could be used to draw a bicycle wheel. One spoke and a little of this tyre and tread is drawn, this is then rotated and repeated to draw all the other spokes and the rest of the tyre until they join to make a whole wheel.

Reflect: a reflected element is redrawn on the other side of a reflection axis. The new part of the drawing is a mirror image of the original element. Reflecting a drawing is often used when drawing a shaft or other round object viewed from the side. A silhouette of one side need only be drawn, the other side is then reflected about the central axis.

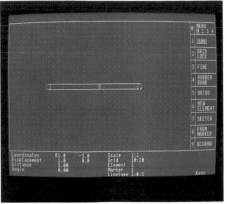
Fig 8.80. One slot

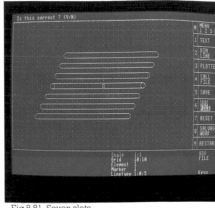
Fig 8.81. Seven slots

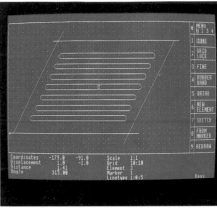
Fig 8.82. Shape outline

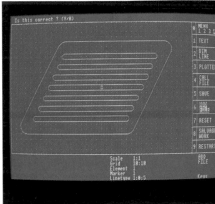
Fig 8.83. Fillet corners

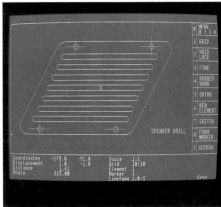
Fig 8.84. Finished drawing

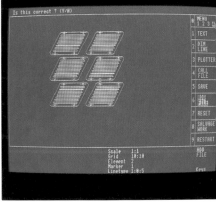
Fig 8.85. Repeat

Fig 8.86. Rotate

Scale: it is possible to draw an element at a different scale. This makes it possible to draw one standard nut, for example, and then scale it to different sizes to suit the application. This makes it unnecessary to keep library drawings of different sized nuts.

The whole drawing can be scaled, as is normal practice. It is difficult to always draw full size. Map makers would have problems finding a piece of paper large enough!

Using a complex drafting program need not be a complex operation. The better programs are user friendly. They use pull down menus and on screen information. This allows the drawing to proceed without spending time searching through manuals to find how to do a certain operation. In the end the product produced is only as good as the designer, not the tools he or she uses.

3D VISUALISATION

It is often important to produce a drawing that is more of an artistic drawing than a technical drawing. Isometric projection goes some way towards this end. With a wire frame drawing in isometric it is possible to give a better impression of an object to a non technical person. This can be enhanced by the removal of hidden lines at the back of the object which can confuse the viewer. Removal of these lines can be either automatic in the better programs, or requiring the designer's rubber in the simpler programs. Solid objects are easier to recognise than wire frame drawings. Programmers have gone to much trouble to produce modelling programs that can draw solid shapes. The drawing is built from solid shapes either placed on or removed from the screen. To draw a simple tube, the designer builds up a solid cylinder then removes a second cylinder from the middle. Producing a complex shaped object can take a great deal of time. Once produced, the mathematical model of the shape will allow the designer to rotate the object at will to allow viewing from all sides. This gives a very good visual impression of the 3D object being portrayed.

Fig 8.87. A civil engineering project, a dam, drawn to suggest a 3D object

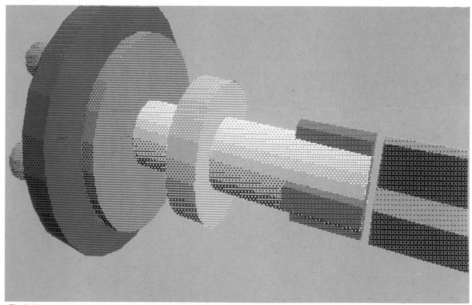

Fig 8.88. Solid 3D visualisation of a component

Fig 8.89. Helicopter

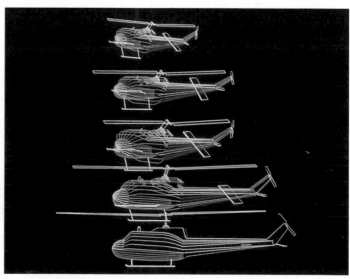

Fig 8.90. Helicopters

TECHNICAL ILLUSTRATION

It is possible to produce drawings on a computer using a drafting program.

The production of words on a computer requires a word processor. This allows words to be entered and the layout altered to suit our requirements.

It the two systems are combined it is possible to produce pages of high quality print that include diagrams and words. Most technical publications require this mixture of text and diagrams. Follow the sequence of photographs showing the development of one such page.

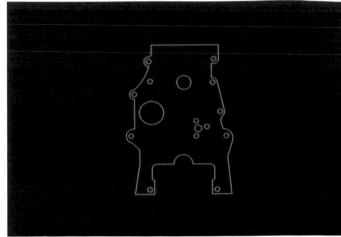

Fig 8.91. Block 2D

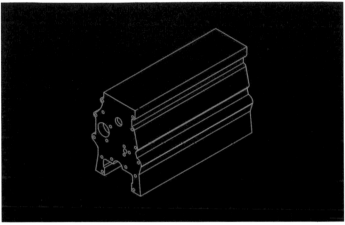

Fig 8.92. Block 3D

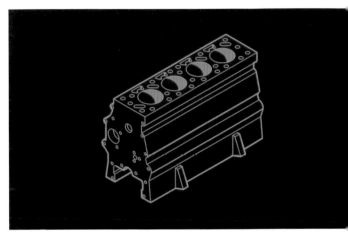

Fig 8.93. Holes and bosses

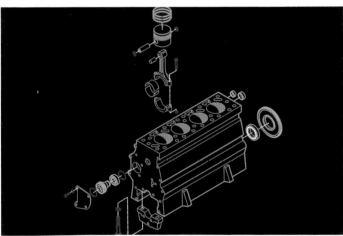

Fig 8.94. Piston and block

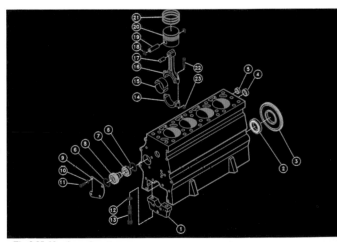

Fig 8.95. Numbered parts

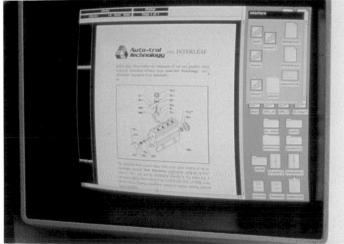

Fig 8.96. Building text and graphics

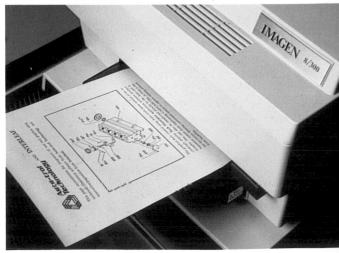

Fig 8.97. Laser printer

FILMS

Science fiction films have been searching for realism and spectacular screen effects since the days of Flash Gordon in the 1930s. Computer graphics have been helping to solve the problems that have arisen in the film industry due to declining audiences and the introduction of television and video. The trend has been towards bigger and better effects. The results were such film series as Star Wars, Star Trek and Superman.

The first feature film to use computer graphics was Westworld produced in 1977. It starred Yul Brynner, whose eyesight took the form of a mosaic of 'quantized' patterns. This is now a familiar video effect, often seen on television.

For the film 2001, a 55 foot model was manipulated and filmed to simulate the flying of the spaceship. It is now possible to do away with the physical model and allow the computer to hold a representation (mathematical model) of the object. This object can then be modelled directly on the screen.

The film Tron, produced in 1982, used computers during a sequence of a computer game. The light cycle was wholly computer generated. The generation or 'razzing up' of the cycle shows the stages of computer generation, from a wire frame through solid and on to the shading of the form.

The use of computer generated sequences is now an integral part of the film industry.

Think about films that you have seen, were there any computer generated sequences?

TELEVISION

Thanks to television, we all know about computer graphics. Commercials, children's programmes, science documentaries and news programmes have all drawn upon the resource and skills of computer graphics.

Channel 4's logo was an early example of moving computer graphics.

Have you seen any of the adverts and programmes shown on this page? New adverts and simulations are appearing every day. Is the effect that they create helping to communicate the ideas?

Fig 8.98. Light cycle drawing from Tron

Fig 8.99. Light cycle from Tron

Fig 8.100. Channel 4 logo

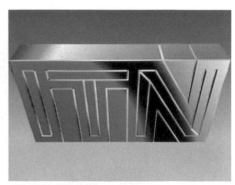
Fig 8.101. TV graphics

Fig 8.102. TV graphics

Fig 8.103. Norwich Union advert

Fig 8.104. Sports sequence

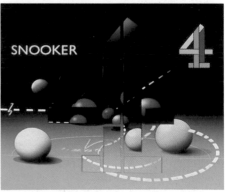
Fig 8.105. Sports sequence

GRAPHIC DESIGN

With a graphics program it is possible to produce a drawing, such as a logo, that can be then modified for many uses. The logo for a local swimming club was designed as a project to help improve the image of the club. The logo was constructed from circles, arcs and straight lines. If only one had been required it would have been quicker to draw the logo on paper. When a slightly smaller or larger version is required the computer is able, with a simple instruction, to re-draw to the correct scale. This would be much more difficult with paper and pencil. The position of the lines,

logo and other information can be designed on screen and altered eaasily to the club's requirements. Positions can be changed and the plotter is then set to draw, producing another exact drawing.

The plotter is able to draw directly onto acrylic sheet with spirit based pens, enabling a large logo to be made for the notice board. Smaller logos and printing was used to produce gala programs, news and result sheets. The plotter will draw on screen printing material so that prints on hats, swimming costumes and T-shirts are all possible. This is all achieved by modifying the original logo drawing.

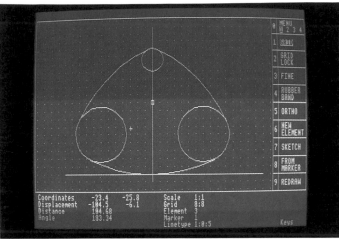

Fig 8.106. Building logo

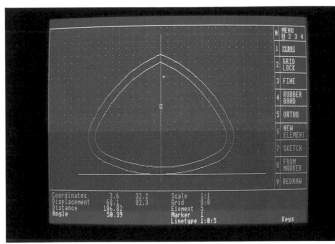

Fig 8.107. Building logo

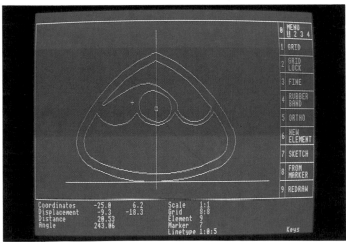

Fig 8.108. Logo

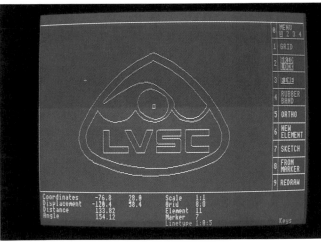

Fig 8.109. Logo and letters

Fig 8.110. Separate logo components

Fig 8.111. Complete logo

Fig 8.112. Logo on clothing

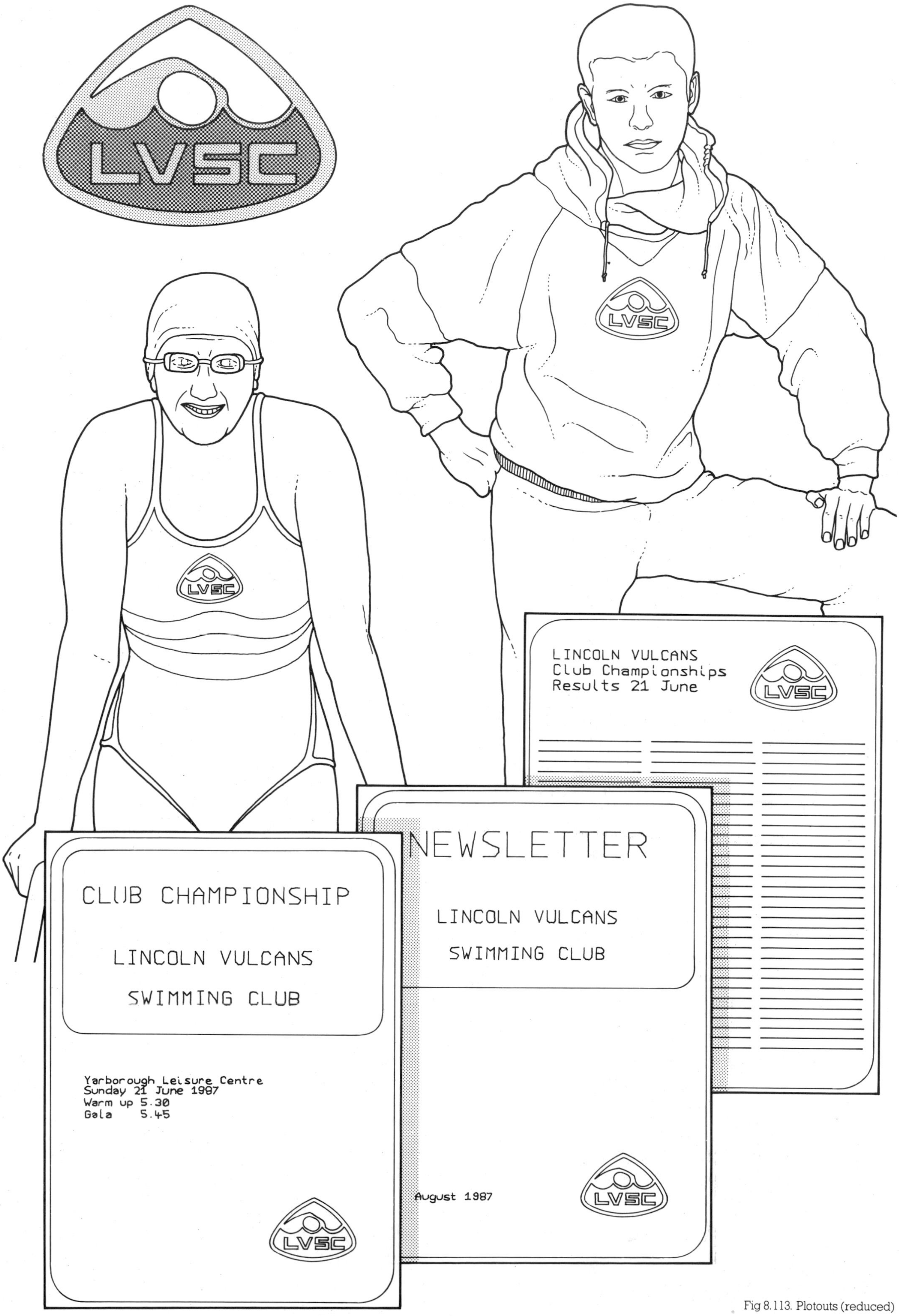

LINCOLN VULCANS
Club Championships
Results 21 June

CLUB CHAMPIONSHIP

LINCOLN VULCANS

SWIMMING CLUB

Yarborough Leisure Centre
Sunday 21 June 1987
Warm up 5.30
Gala   5.45

NEWSLETTER

LINCOLN VULCANS

SWIMMING CLUB

August 1987

Fig 8.113. Plotouts (reduced)

PRINTED CIRCUIT BOARDS

Printed circuit boards are used in all electronic devices. The increase in sophistication of these devices increases the complexity of the electronic circuitry. Computer graphics can be used to great effect to help a designer produce these boards.

A circuit board is a composite material. It is comprised of a layer of copper to form the conductors for the electrical paths, and a series of layers of glass reinforced plastic (GRP), often wrongly called 'fibre glass'. Electrical components such as resistors, transistors and integrated circuits are fastened to this board. Holes are drilled, the leads and pins go through the board and are soldered to the tracks of copper on the other side. The unwanted copper has been previously etched away. The lines joining the pins and solder pads must be routed to join without ever crossing or touching other lines. The lines can be drawn on a screen and altered until the correct layout has been achieved.

Two such programs are shown below. Both produce a 'master' circuit on paper or drafting film. The master is used with a photographic method to transfer the lines to the board. Many boards can then be made from this master copy of the circuit. One program uses a printer output, which requires a transparency to be made using a photocopier. The other draws using a plotter directly onto the copper for one off boards, or onto drafting film for mass production.

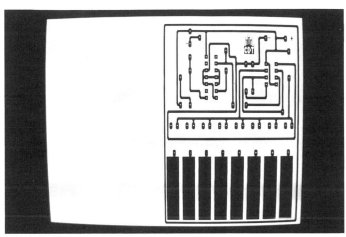

Fig 8.114. Diagram

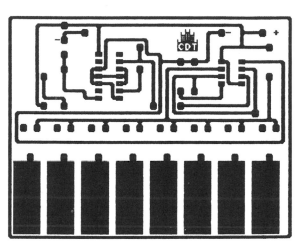

Fig 8.115. Printout

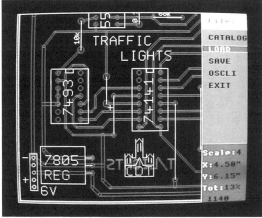

Fig 8.116. Screen Lintrack

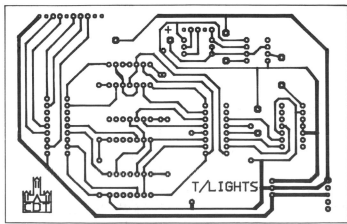

Fig 8.117. Plotout

Fig 8.118. PCB

ENGINEERING DRAWING

Engineering drawing provides a vital link between the **designer** and the **manufacturer**. The importance of this is shown in the illustrations on this page where the working drawing fulfils an important role between the designer's ideas and the end product.

When an article has been designed, detailed drawings are sent to the manufacturer so that production can begin. To make sure that these drawings are fully understood, and not misinterpreted, they are produced to **British Standards**. These give the basic rules for engineering drawing and are outlined in a booklet available from the British Standards Institution, 2 Park Street, London W1A 2BS. All drawings in this chapter are produced to these standards.

fig 9.1. The drawing office

fig 9.2. The working drawing

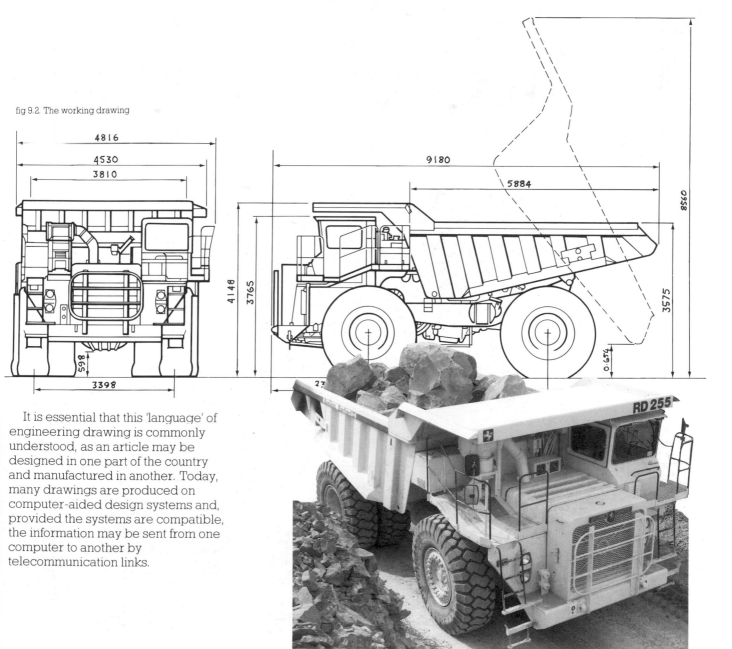

It is essential that this 'language' of engineering drawing is commonly understood, as an article may be designed in one part of the country and manufactured in another. Today, many drawings are produced on computer-aided design systems and, provided the systems are compatible, the information may be sent from one computer to another by telecommunication links.

fig 9.3. The end product

TYPES OF LINE

———————————————	**THICK CONTINUOUS** Visible outlines and edges
———————————————	**THIN CONTINUOUS** Dimension lines, projection lines, hatching lines and outlines of adjacent parts
— — — — — — — —	**THIN, SHORT DASHES** Hidden outlines and edges
—————— · ——————	**THIN, LONG CHAIN** Centre lines
——— · ——— · ———	**THICK, LONG CHAIN** Cutting planes
∿∿∿∿∿	**THICK, WAVY LINE** Short break lines and irregular boundary lines

fig 9.4. Types of line

PAPER SIZES

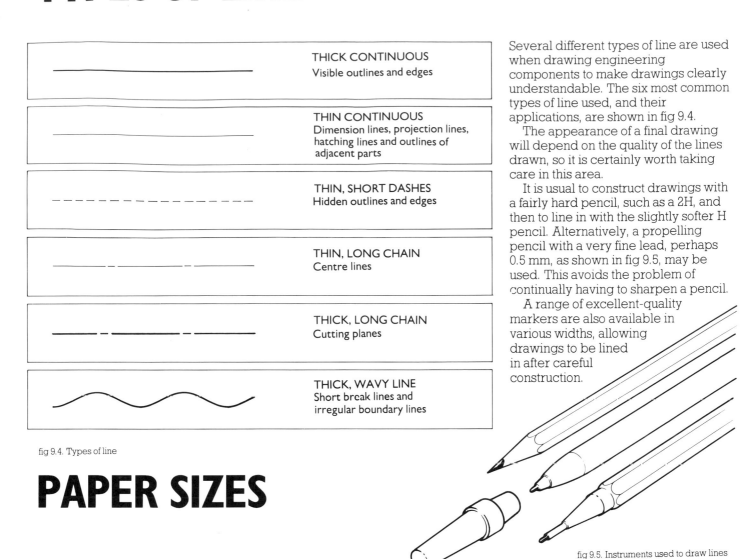

Several different types of line are used when drawing engineering components to make drawings clearly understandable. The six most common types of line used, and their applications, are shown in fig 9.4.

The appearance of a final drawing will depend on the quality of the lines drawn, so it is certainly worth taking care in this area.

It is usual to construct drawings with a fairly hard pencil, such as a 2H, and then to line in with the slightly softer H pencil. Alternatively, a propelling pencil with a very fine lead, perhaps 0.5 mm, as shown in fig 9.5, may be used. This avoids the problem of continually having to sharpen a pencil.

A range of excellent-quality markers are also available in various widths, allowing drawings to be lined in after careful construction.

fig 9.5. Instruments used to draw lines

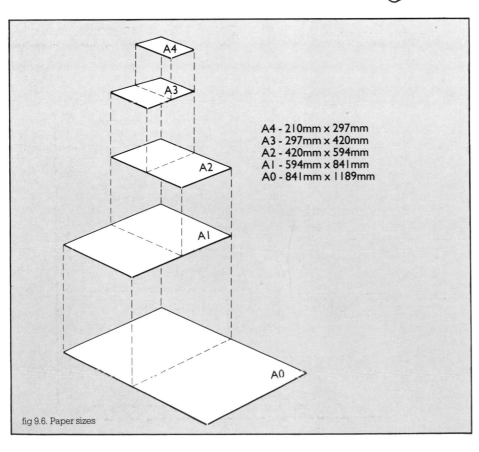

A4 - 210mm x 297mm
A3 - 297mm x 420mm
A2 - 420mm x 594mm
A1 - 594mm x 841mm
A0 - 841mm x 1189mm

fig 9.6. Paper sizes

The sizes of paper that are commonly available are shown in fig 9.6. In industry, the larger-size papers such as A0 and A1 are used for original drawings. These may be reduced to smaller sizes by reproduction methods when further copies are required.

Schools rarely have the equipment available to cope with the largest sizes of paper. Therefore, we tend to use either A3, A2 or occasionally A1 for engineering drawing. It is essential that the paper is large enough to show all the necessary detail. This usually makes A4 unsuitable for our purposes.

It is important to use good-quality paper or problems may arise when 'lining in' a drawing with marker pens and when erasing lines. Poorer quality papers will often have a surface that proves unsuitable for this.

SELECTING A LAYOUT

It is important to set work out on a sheet of paper in an **organised and presentable** manner. This will make the finished drawing more pleasing to the eye than one which has been positioned on the paper with little thought.

It is usual to begin by drawing a border around the paper, perhaps 10 to 20 mm in width. All drawing should be contained within that border.

There are certain items of information that any engineering drawing must include if it is to satisfy the requirements of the British Standards. These are outlined in fig 9.7, but in more detail they are:

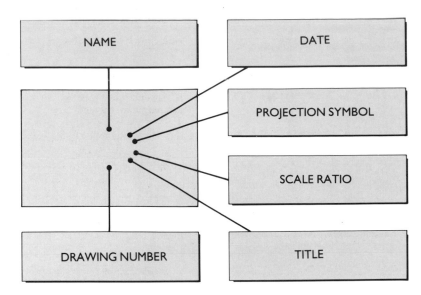

fig 9.7. Information an engineering drawing must include

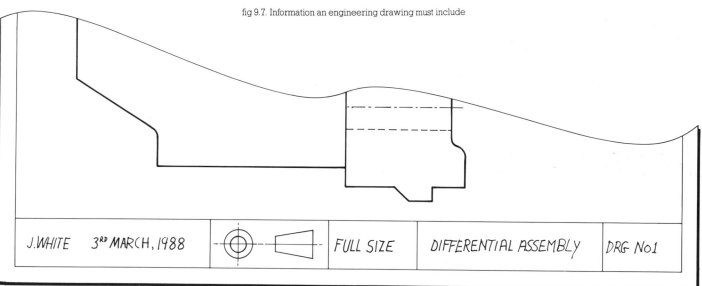

fig 9.8. Ways of arranging information

1. The name of the person that has made the drawing.
2. The date on which the drawing was made.
3. The first or third angle projection symbol.
4. The scale or ratio to which the drawing was made.
5. The title of the drawing.
6. The number of the drawing.

This information should be positioned at the bottom of the drawing stretching from the left to right-hand side. Fig 9.8 shows a suitable way of arranging this.

When the drawing shows several components, it may include a parts list, such as the one shown in fig 9.9, on the right-hand side of the paper. This identifies each part with a name and number which can then be labelled on the orthographic views.

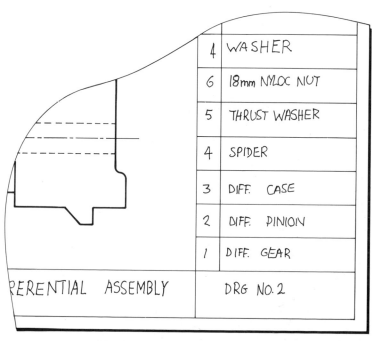

fig 9.9. Parts list

DRAWING TO SCALE

Wherever possible, it is desirable to draw an object to its **actual size**. This would mean that a 10 mm hole would be drawn 10 mm in diameter on the paper. However, this is not always possible, because some objects, such as the RD250 Dump Truck, are too large to fit on the paper. Similarly, some electrical components will be too small to be drawn actual size if the minute detail is to be understandable. In either case we must draw to a scale.

Choosing the scale can be a problem, because we need to avoid the kind of difficulties shown in fig 9.10. In the first case the object was reduced by too great a factor, making it appear insignificant in the centre of the paper, and in the second case by not enough to allow all the required elevations to be positioned on the paper.

Some of the scales you may find useful are shown in fig 9.11. In each case the first number represents the size used on the drawing, compared with the second number, a size from the object. This means that a drawing made to a scale of 2:1 is an **enlargement**, while 1:2 is a **reduction**. The consequences of using a 1:2 scale are shown in fig 9.12.

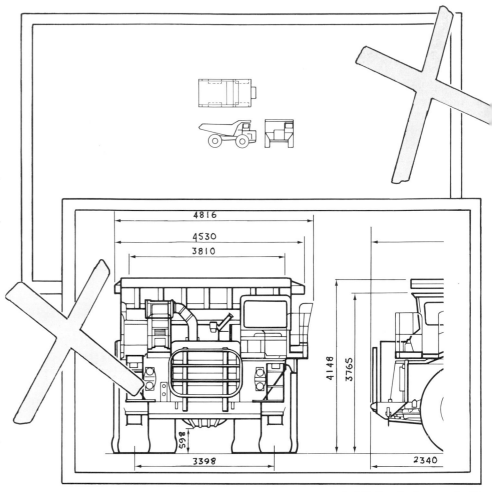

fig 9.10. Choosing the correct scale

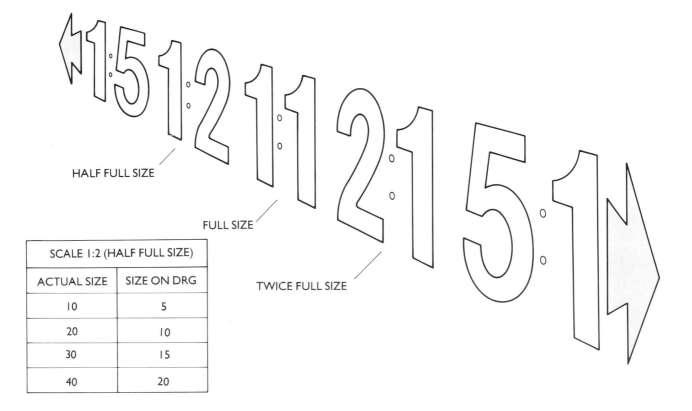

HALF FULL SIZE

FULL SIZE

TWICE FULL SIZE

SCALE 1:2 (HALF FULL SIZE)	
ACTUAL SIZE	SIZE ON DRG
10	5
20	10
30	15
40	20

fig 9.12. Working to a scale

fig 9.11. Scales commonly used in engineering drawing

DRAWING TO STANDARDS

LETTERING AND NUMERALS

Good-quality lettering is essential in engineering drawing if notes, measurements, part numbers and labels are to be clearly understood. Stylized lettering should be avoided, as it can be difficult to interpret and is usually unnecessary. The type of lettering shown in fig 9.13 is ideal for use on engineering drawings.

There are three ways of applying lettering. The first is by rubbing **dry transfers** onto the paper with a pencil. This method produces very professional-looking results, but the sheets can be expensive and difficult to apply well. The second is **freehand**, usually drawn between construction lines. This can become quite acceptable with a little practice. The third method is by the use of **stencils** which can again produce very good results, but can be rather time-consuming when large amounts of text are required.

fig 9.13. Lettering methods

ABBREVIATIONS

There is rarely sufficient space on an engineering drawing to write out all the required information in full and if there were it would tend to detract from the drawing. To shorten the amount of text that has to be applied, a series of abbreviations has been developed by the British Standards Institute. The most common of these are shown in fig 9.14; it can be seen that a considerable amount of lettering can be saved by using the abbreviations. For example, the word millimetre is shortened to mm and countersunk to CSK.

Diameter (before the dimension)	∅
Diameter (in a note)	DIA
Radius (before the dimension)	R
Chamfered	CHAM
Millimetre	mm
Centimetre	cm
Metre	m
Countersunk	CSK
Countersunk head	CSK HD
Centre line	L
Number	No.
Square (before the dimension)	□
Square (in a note)	SQ
Outside diameter	O/D
Inside diameter	I/D
Threads per inch	TPI
Hexagon	HEX
Hexagonal head	HEX HD
Across flats	A/F
Round head	RD HD
Right hand	RH
Left hand	LH
Pitch circle diameter	PCD
Counterbore	C'BORE
Figure	FIG
Drawing	DRG
Material	MATL
Centres	CRS

fig 9.14. Abbreviations

DIMENSIONING

All drawings need to be dimensioned so that it can be seen what size the object is in real life regardless of the size it has been drawn. The British Standards Institute has laid down certain rules concerning the application of these dimensions to a drawing. The three main points that should be remembered are shown in fig 9.15 and are as follows:

1. All measurements must be read from the **bottom** or **right**-hand side of the paper.

2. **Limit lines** should be drawn out from the object and numbers written above a **dimensioning line** stretching between these.

3. **Smaller measurements** should be placed **closer** to the drawing.

However, there are particular ways of dimensioning common features such as **diameters**, **radii** and **holes** and these are explained in figs 9.16 to 9.19.

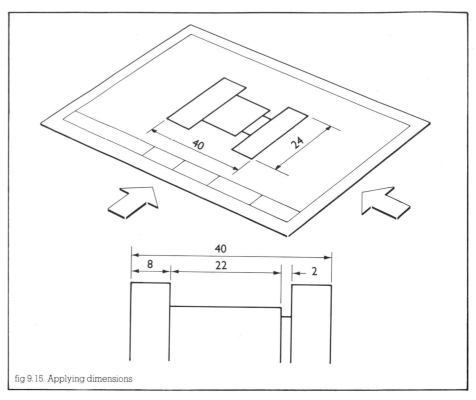

fig 9.15. Applying dimensions

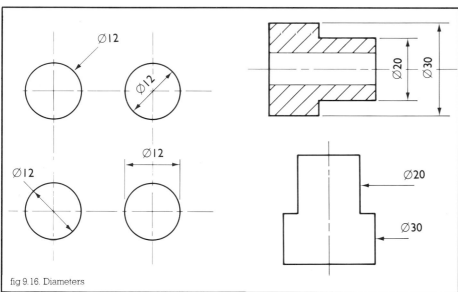

fig 9.16. Diameters

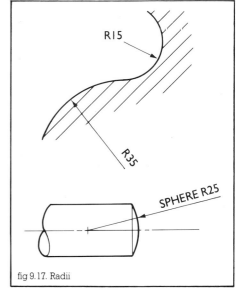

fig 9.17. Radii

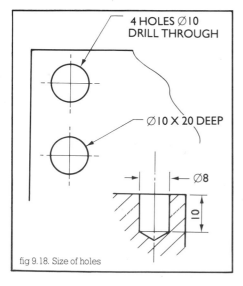

fig 9.18. Size of holes

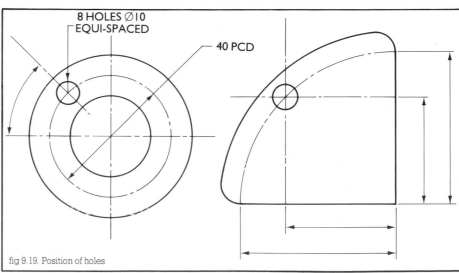

fig 9.19. Position of holes

164

INTERNAL AND EXTERNAL THREADS

It is not possible to show all the details of each threaded part in an engineering drawing. Therefore, the British Standards Institute has recommended ways of representing **internal and external threads**.

The most common of these is shown in figs 9.20 and 9.21, where it can be seen that the hole or piece of bar is drawn first as it would be if it had no thread. The thread is then shown by adding a thin line on the outside of the hole in the case of an internal thread, and on the inside of the bar for an external thread. This is fairly logical when one considers that an internal thread is cut with a **tap** and an external thread with a **dye**.

There are many different types of thread, but the **metric** type are becoming increasingly common. They are labelled in the following manner – M36 × 4. The M indicates that this is a metric thread, the 36 that it is 36 mm in diameter and the 4 that the pitch is 4 mm.

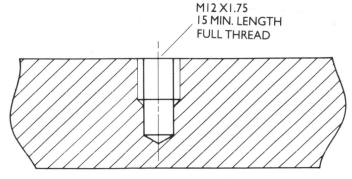

M12 X 1.75
15 MIN. LENGTH
FULL THREAD

fig 9.20. Dimensioning a threaded hole

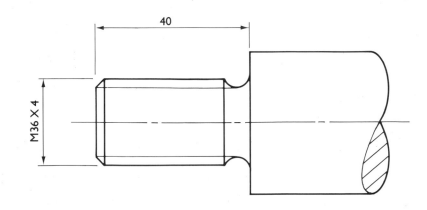

fig 9.21. Dimensioning a screw thread

HEXAGONAL-HEADED NUT AND BOLT

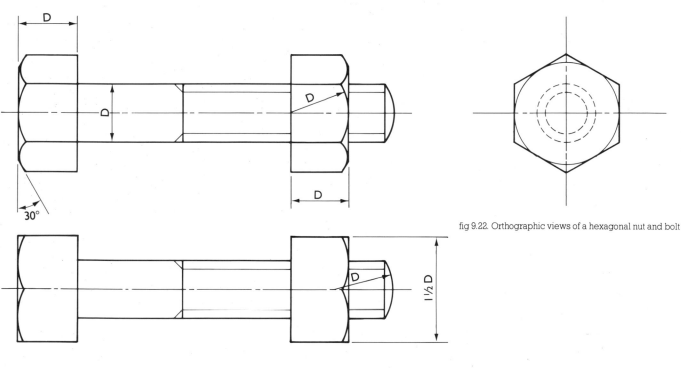

fig 9.22. Orthographic views of a hexagonal nut and bolt

A standard **hexagonal-headed nut and bolt** can be completely drawn out once the value of 'D' (the diameter of the shank) is known. Fig 9.22 illustrates how all the parts relate to the value of 'D', with the exception being the length of the bolt which is usually stated separately.

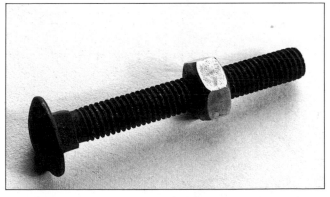

SET SCREWS AND WING NUTS

Set screws are defined as having a thread which runs the entire length of the shank. They are available with several different types of head, three of which are shown in fig 9.23. They are often screwed into internally threaded blind holes to hold items in position.

An alternative method of fastening a component is to tighten a stud into an internally threaded blind hole and then use a hexagonal nut on the protruding end.

Grub screws are used to tighten pulleys onto shafts.

Thumb screws and **wing nuts** are similiar to a set screw and hexagonal nut, but they are designed to be turned by hand. This is most useful where the component has to be removed frequently, but is not satisfactory where a more permanent fixing is required.

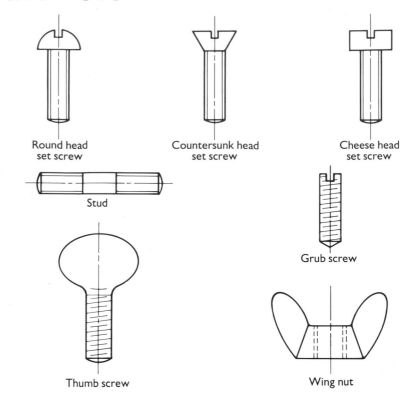

Round head set screw

Countersunk head set screw

Cheese head set screw

Stud

Grub screw

Thumb screw

Wing nut

fig 9.23. Set screws

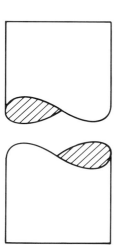

fig 9.24. Round-solid shaft

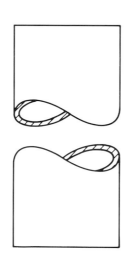

fig 9.25. Round-tube shaft

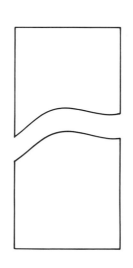

fig 9.26. Square or rectangular shaft

BREAKS

It is not always possible to draw the entire lengths of shafts in drawings. Where they need to be broken at the two ends or in the middle, the conventions shown in figs 9.24 to 9.26 are used. It is essential that the correct convention is used or it may not be clear whether the shaft is solid or a tube, or round or square in section.

KNURLING

Knurling is used to add grip to a component so that it can be turned by hand without there being a danger of slipping. The operation of knurling is carried out on a **lathe** and is, therefore, usually applied to bars that are round in section. The conventions for showing two different types of knurling are illustrated in figs 9.27 and 9.28.

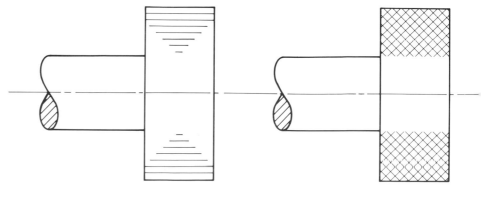

fig 9.27. Straight knurling

fig 9.28. Diamond knurling

ORTHOGRAPHIC PROJECTION

Two angles of projection are used to display orthographic views. These are shown in fig 9.29, where the block has been suspended between angles 1 and 3 and the views projected onto the surrounding walls. Each method of projection requires three views to be drawn (**front**, **end** and **plan**), and arranged in the ways shown in fig 9.29, according to the angle of projection used.

Today **third angle** is mainly used in America and **first angle** in Great Britain, though it it likely that third angle will become universally accepted in the future. Examination syllabuses require a working knowledge of each.

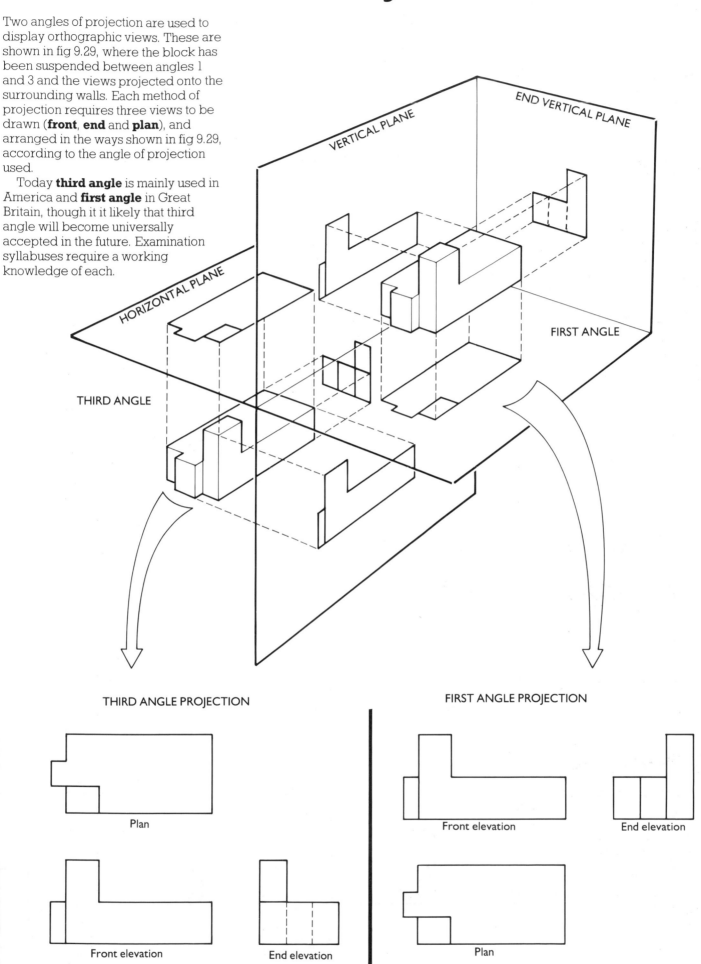

THIRD ANGLE PROJECTION

Plan

Front elevation

End elevation

FIRST ANGLE PROJECTION

Front elevation

End elevation

Plan

fig 9.29. First and third angle projection

FIRST ANGLE PROJECTION

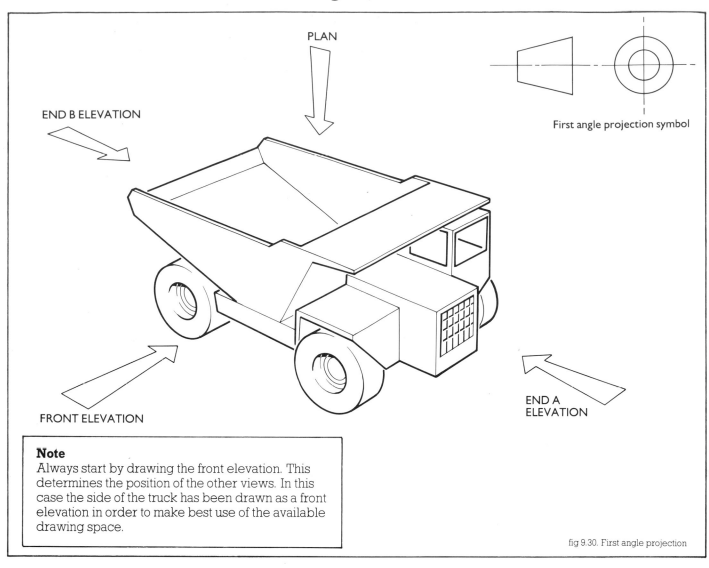

PLAN

END B ELEVATION

First angle projection symbol

END A ELEVATION

FRONT ELEVATION

Note
Always start by drawing the front elevation. This determines the position of the other views. In this case the side of the truck has been drawn as a front elevation in order to make best use of the available drawing space.

fig 9.30. First angle projection

In **first angle projection**, the front, end and plan views are drawn as shown in fig 9.31. This means that each view has to pass over an existing drawing to the position where it is drawn. The plan view is therefore drawn below the front view, and the end views on the side furthest away from their position

on the front view. The **symbol** used to show that a drawing is drawn in first angle projection (fig 9.30) is usually included in the title block.

It is common practice to show at least three views of an article, because each shows only two dimensions and together they combine to give the

trained eye a three-dimensional picture of the object. When all the views are drawn, one is usually projected from another, though in fig 9.32 only the side of the RD250 Dump Truck is shown so that the detail can be fully appreciated.

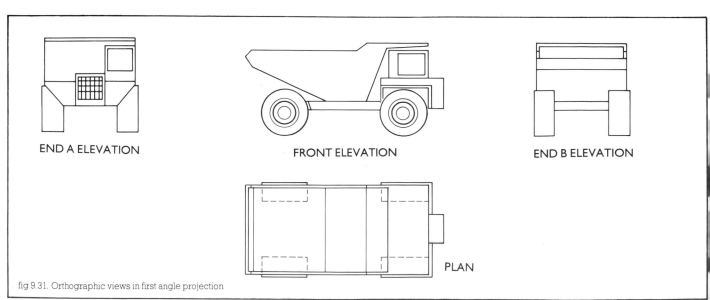

END A ELEVATION

FRONT ELEVATION

END B ELEVATION

PLAN

fig 9.31. Orthographic views in first angle projection

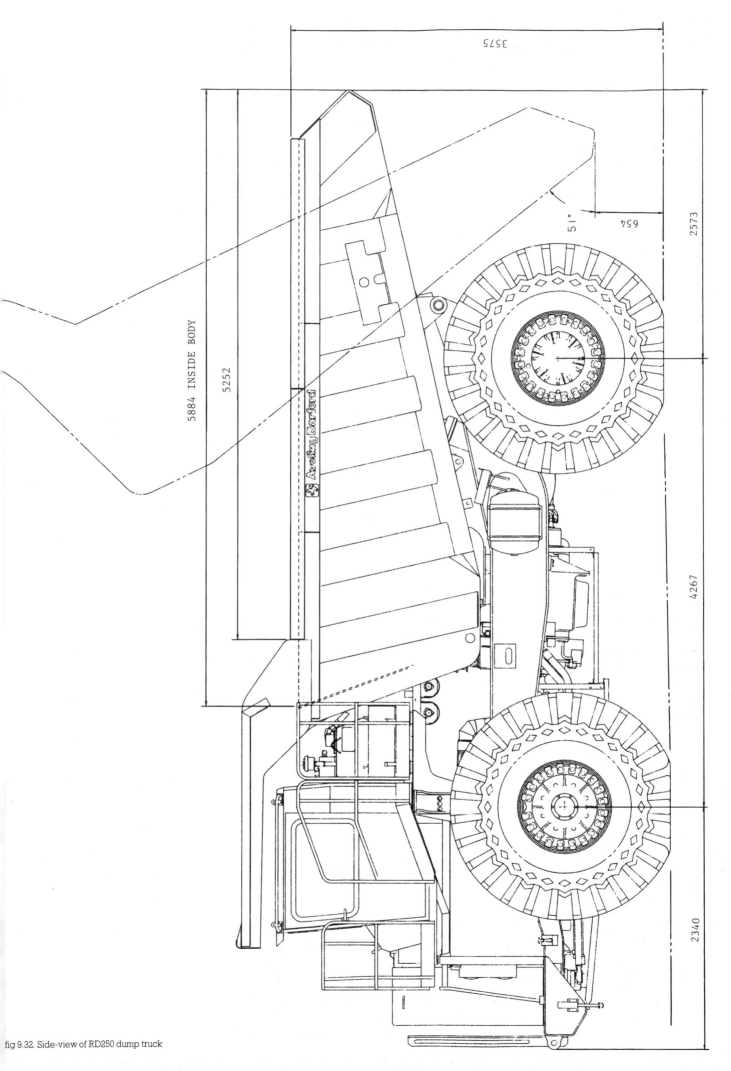

fig 9.32. Side-view of RD250 dump truck

3575

51°

654

2573

5884 INSIDE BODY

5252

Aveling Barford

4267

2340

THIRD ANGLE PROJECTION

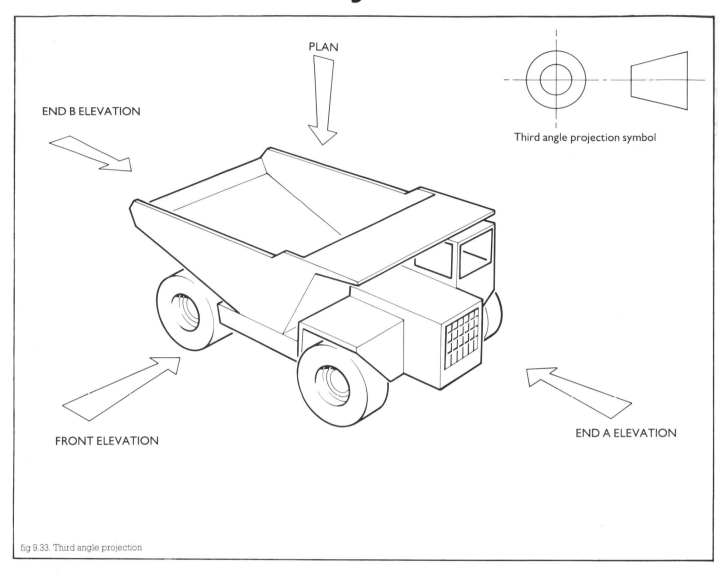

END B ELEVATION

PLAN

Third angle projection symbol

FRONT ELEVATION

END A ELEVATION

fig 9.33. Third angle projection

When working in **third angle projection** the front, end and plan views are drawn as shown in fig 9.34. This means that the views simply open out from the front views. The plan view is therefore drawn above the front view, and the end views on the side nearest their position on the front view.

The **symbol** used to show that a drawing is drawn in third angle position (fig 9.35) is usually included in the title block.

As with first angle projection it is common practice to show at least three views of an article because each shows only two dimensions and

together they combine to give the trained eye a three-dimensional picture of the object. When all the views are drawn one is usually projected from another, but in fig 9.35 only the end view of the RD250 Dump Truck is shown so that the detail can be fully appreciated.

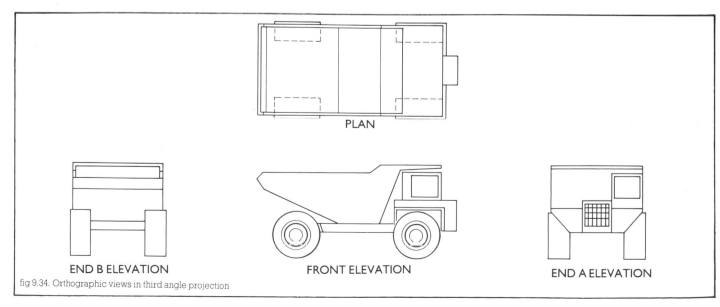

PLAN

END B ELEVATION

FRONT ELEVATION

END A ELEVATION

fig 9.34. Orthographic views in third angle projection

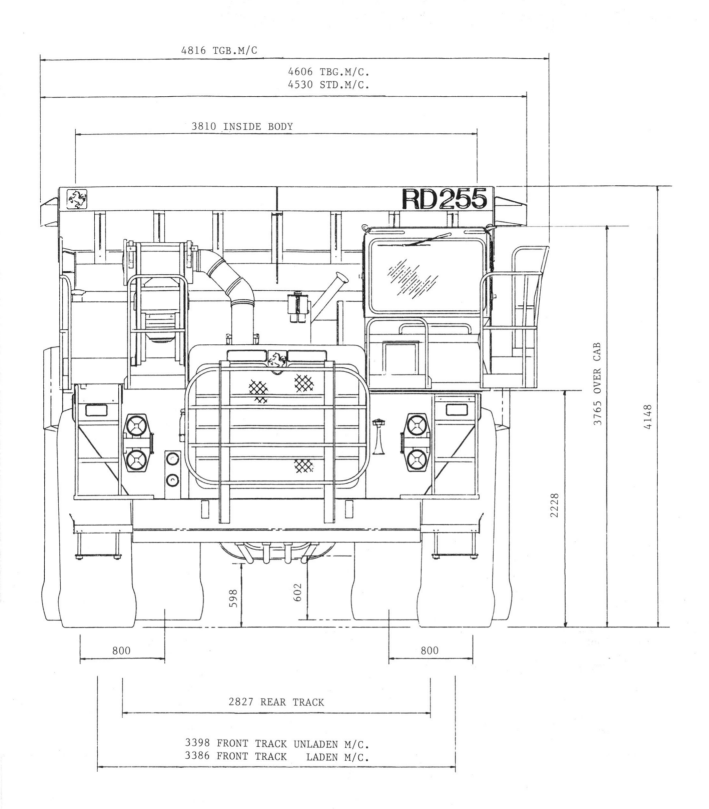

4816 TGB.M/C

4606 TBG.M/C.
4530 STD.M/C.

3810 INSIDE BODY

RD255

3765 OVER CAB

4148

2228

598

602

800

800

2827 REAR TRACK

3398 FRONT TRACK UNLADEN M/C.
3386 FRONT TRACK   LADEN M/C.

fig 9.35. End-view of RD250 dump truck

AUXILIARY VIEWS

We have looked at two methods of drawing front, end and plan views of an object – first and third angle projection. In most cases this will be quite sufficient to allow you to build up a complete picture of the object in your mind. However, there will be occasions when an **extra view**, called an **auxiliary view**, is required to show parts that cannot be seen fully in the front, end or plan views or to find out the **true shape** of a surface.

Fig 9.36 shows an example of an auxiliary view. Here the RD250 Dump Truck has been drawn from an angle of 45° above the rear. The resulting view does in fact show three dimensions: length, width and height. However, the height and length are not true representations because they are considerably foreshortened due to the position of the viewpoint.

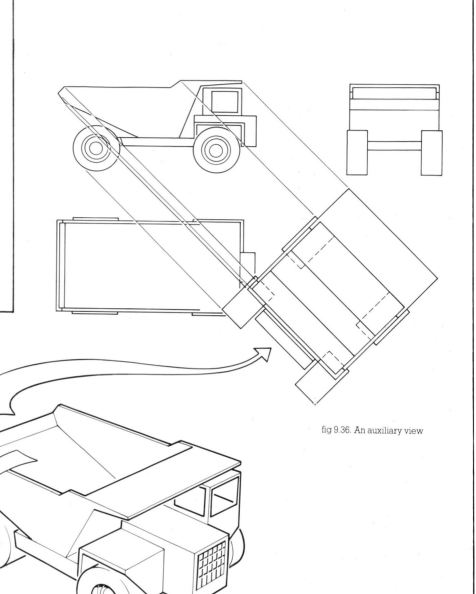

fig 9.36. An auxiliary view

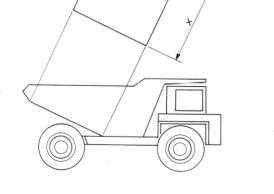

True shape of surface

fig 9.38. Finding the true shape of a surface

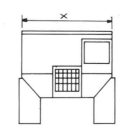

fig 9.37. RD250 dump truck

An auxiliary view can be drawn from any point around the object. It is constructed by drawing lines **parallel** to the viewpoint and then plotting in the new view by taking distances from either the end or plan views.

It is not always necessary to draw an auxiliary view of the entire object because one may only wish to find out the true shape of a particular surface. For example, in fig 9.38 lines have been projected at right angles to the base of the rear of the Dump Truck. The distance 'X', which is the width of the base, is taken from the end view. It is impossible to see the true shape of the base in either the front, end or plan views because it is an inclined surface.

SECTIONAL VIEWS

So far, we have only been concerned with drawing the outside of the object. The only way which we have used to show the inside of the article is dotted lines which represent **hidden detail**.

However, a much more satisfactory way of examining the inside of an object is to imagine that it is cut into two, one half being removed and the remainder drawn. These views are called sectional views and are usually drawn in conjunction with the front, end and plan views. Therefore, one may have external front and end views with a sectional plan view.

Figs 9.39 to 9.41 illustrate how vertical cuts produce sectional front and end views, and horizontal cuts produce sectional plan views. The line on which the object is cut is called a **cutting plane** and is shown by a thin, long-chain line. This is thickened at

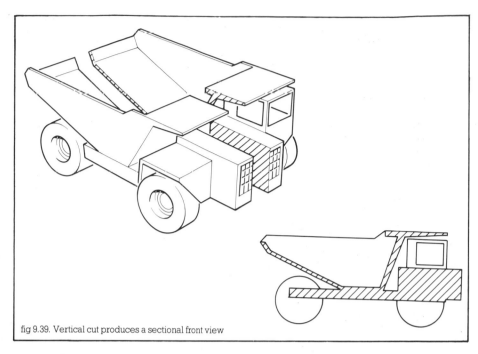

fig 9.39. Vertical cut produces a sectional front view

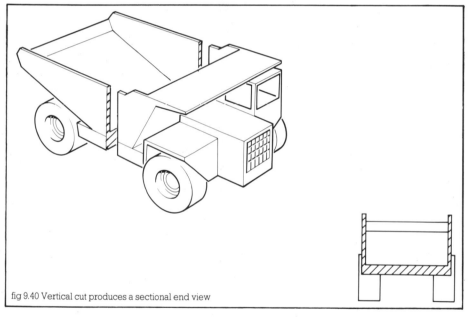

fig 9.40 Vertical cut produces a sectional end view

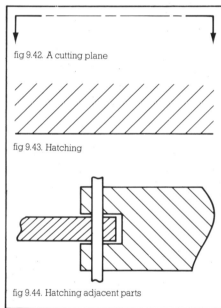

fig 9.42. A cutting plane

fig 9.43. Hatching

fig 9.44. Hatching adjacent parts

either end and with arrows added to show the direction of the view (fig 9.42). The part of the object behind the arrows is imagined to have been removed for drawing purposes.

Surfaces that have been cut are **hatched** with **45°** lines as shown in fig 9.43. If the cutting plane passes through an open space, this is not hatched, but details are drawn of what is behind that space. There are some components, such as nuts and bolts, that are cut, but not hatched.

Where an object is made up of several parts, adjacent pieces are hatched in opposite directions whenever possible, as illustrated in fig 9.44.

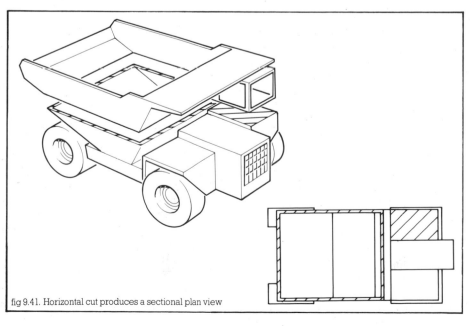

fig 9.41. Horizontal cut produces a sectional plan view

HALF SECTIONS

It is not always necessary to show an article sectioned along its entire length. If it is **symmetrical** about a centre line one half can be sectioned and the other left as an external view. This is shown in fig 9.45, where a more informative view has been created by drawing a half section.

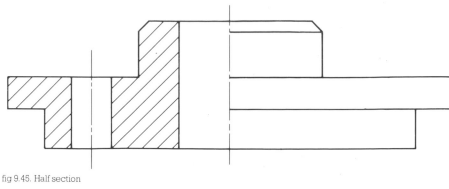

fig 9.45. Half section

PART SECTIONS

In some cases part of an external view can be shown as a section. This is particularly useful where a pin, such as the one shown in fig 9.46, only requires the end part to be sectioned in order to show the hole that has been drilled in it.

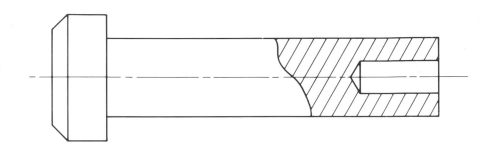

fig 9.46. Part section

REVOLVED SECTIONS

Revolved sections can be drawn at intervals along an external view. These are **rotated** through **90°,** showing what would be seen at that point if the article were cut. It is possible to remove these from the drawing and place them to one side, providing the point at which the section was taken is clearly labelled.

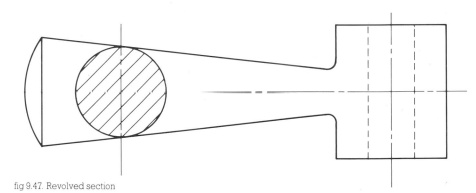

fig 9.47. Revolved section

EXCEPTIONS

On page 00, it was stated that all surfaces that are cut by a cutting plane are, with a few exceptions, hatched with 45° lines. Figs 9.48 to 9.50 show three exceptions to this. They are **ribs**, **shafts** that are **cut along their length**, and **fastening devices** such as **nuts**, **bolts**, **set screws** and **rivets**.

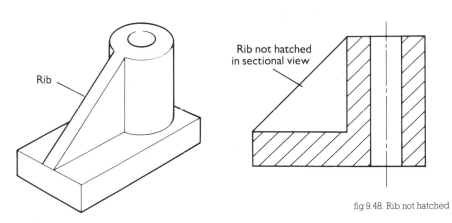

Rib

Rib not hatched in sectional view

fig 9.48. Rib not hatched

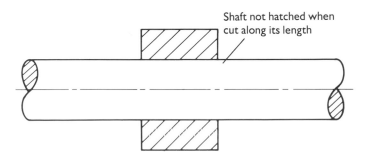

Shaft not hatched when cut along its length

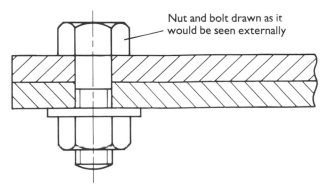

Nut and bolt drawn as it would be seen externally

fig 9.50. Nut and bolt not hatched

Figure 9.52 shows a sectional view produced by industry. Here the RD250 Dump Truck has been sectioned along the cutting plane shown in fig 9.51. The truck is made up of many hundreds of parts, therefore only the main body is sectioned and the engine, gear box and differential are shown as external views. To attempt to section through and hatch all these parts would have produced an extremely detailed drawing which would have needed to be drawn on a much larger scale than this if it was to be of any value. As it is, the view that is given is very useful because it has taken away the body of the truck and shown where the parts are positioned underneath.

fig 9.51. Cutting plane for sectioning RD250 dump truck

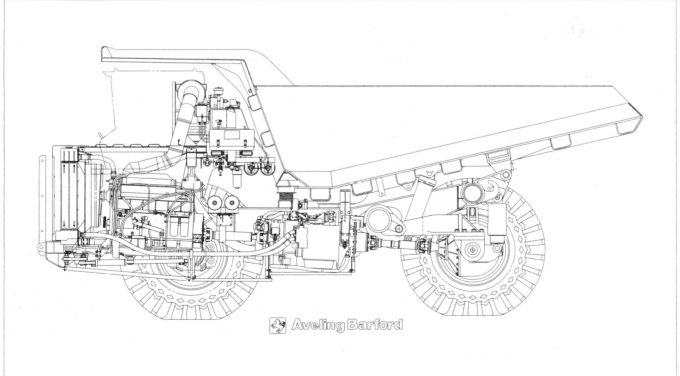

fig 9.52. Section through an RD250 dump truck

ASSEMBLY DRAWING

Very few, if any, pieces of engineering exist as **single components** in their own right. Even the very simplest assemblies are made up of several components, and a complicated product such as the RD250 Dump Truck has many thousands of parts. These all need to be **assembled** in the correct manner to produce the final article.

In the case of one relatively simple assembly in the RD250 Dump Truck, the differential, there are over 60 separate pieces. These can be seen in the **exploded drawing** in fig 9.53, which very clearly shows the **relative positions** of each part. Each component will have been drawn out as an engineering drawing exercise, as shown in fig 9.55, before manufacture. It is essential that the drawings are accurate, as the components may be manufactured in several different places then brought together for assembly. If there are any inaccuracies in the drawing or manufacturing techniques, problems will be encountered at this point.

A sectional view through the assembled centre part of the differential is shown in fig 9.54. You may be required to construct this kind

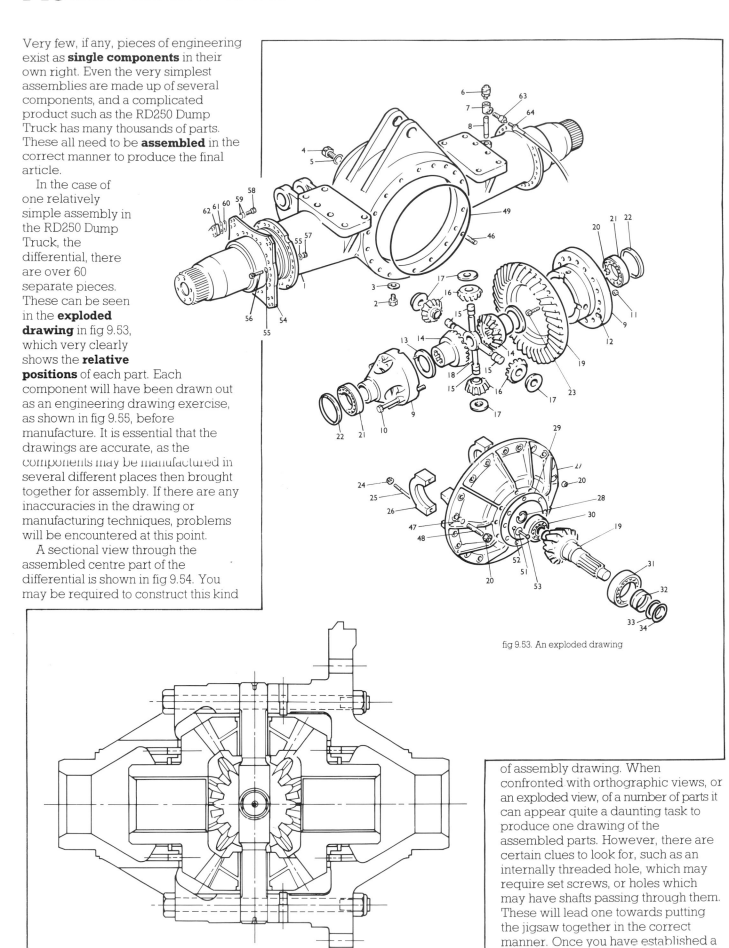

fig 9.53. An exploded drawing

fig 9.54. A sectional view of part of the assembled differential

of assembly drawing. When confronted with orthographic views, or an exploded view, of a number of parts it can appear quite a daunting task to produce one drawing of the assembled parts. However, there are certain clues to look for, such as an internally threaded hole, which may require set screws, or holes which may have shafts passing through them. These will lead one towards putting the jigsaw together in the correct manner. Once you have established a picture in your mind, or made a sketch of how the pieces fit together, the drawing of the assembled parts can be started.

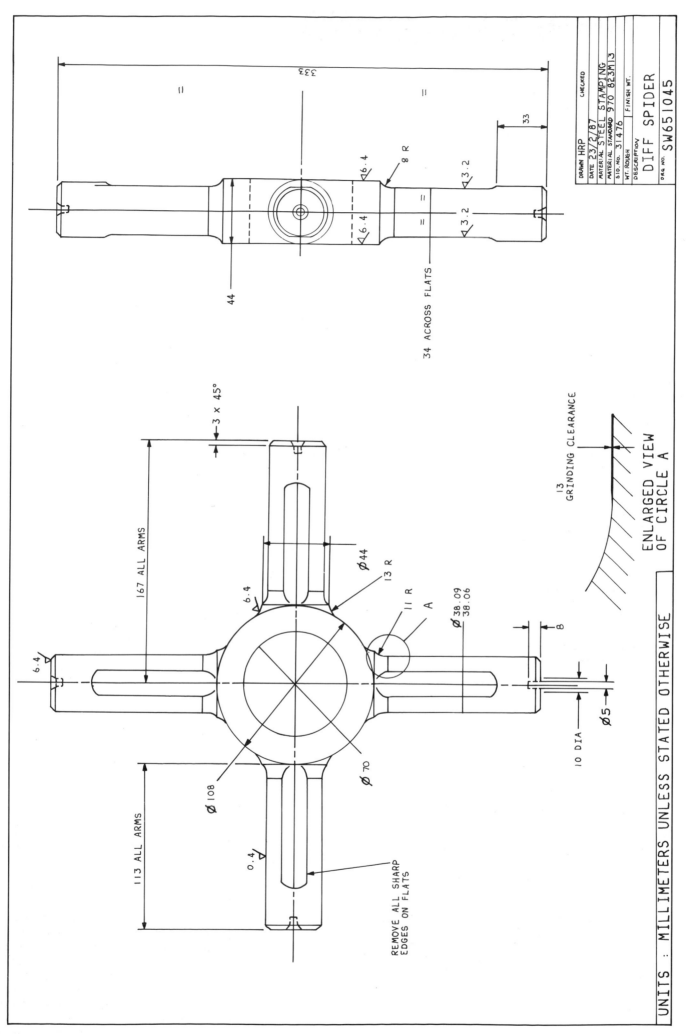

fig 9.55. Orthographic views of one component

DEVELOPMENTS

A development is the true shape of a flat piece of material that is required to make a three-dimensional object. In industry many components, such as hoppers, ducting and casings are made by folding sheet metal and joining the edges. The rear of a model of the RD250 Dump Truck shown in fig 9.56 is to be made from cardboard, but it could easily be made from other sheet materials such as acrylic or tin-plate. The shape of the piece of material that is required to make this is shown in fig 9.57. Folds are indicated here by dotted lines or thin construction lines with the outline being thicker. The glueing tabs necessary to hold it together are not shown on the development, but are added in the way shown in fig 9.58.

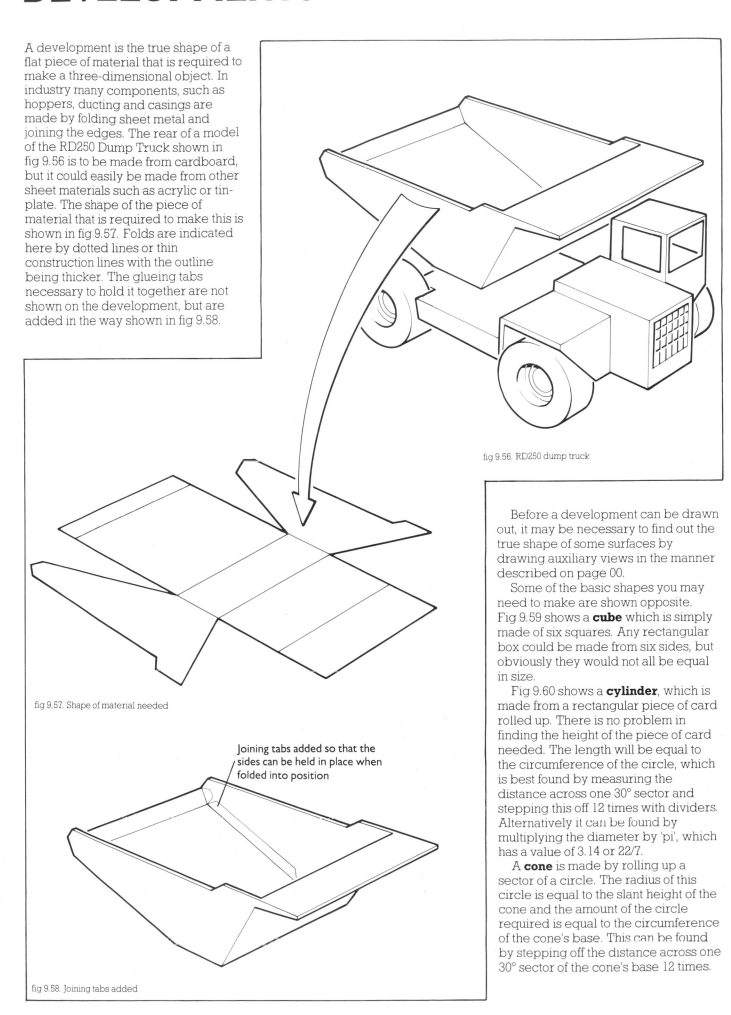

fig 9.56. RD250 dump truck

fig 9.57. Shape of material needed

Joining tabs added so that the sides can be held in place when folded into position

fig 9.58. Joining tabs added

Before a development can be drawn out, it may be necessary to find out the true shape of some surfaces by drawing auxiliary views in the manner described on page 00.

Some of the basic shapes you may need to make are shown opposite. Fig 9.59 shows a **cube** which is simply made of six squares. Any rectangular box could be made from six sides, but obviously they would not all be equal in size.

Fig 9.60 shows a **cylinder**, which is made from a rectangular piece of card rolled up. There is no problem in finding the height of the piece of card needed. The length will be equal to the circumference of the circle, which is best found by measuring the distance across one 30° sector and stepping this off 12 times with dividers. Alternatively it can be found by multiplying the diameter by 'pi', which has a value of 3.14 or 22/7.

A **cone** is made by rolling up a sector of a circle. The radius of this circle is equal to the slant height of the cone and the amount of the circle required is equal to the circumference of the cone's base. This can be found by stepping off the distance across one 30° sector of the cone's base 12 times.

FURTHER DEVELOPMENTS

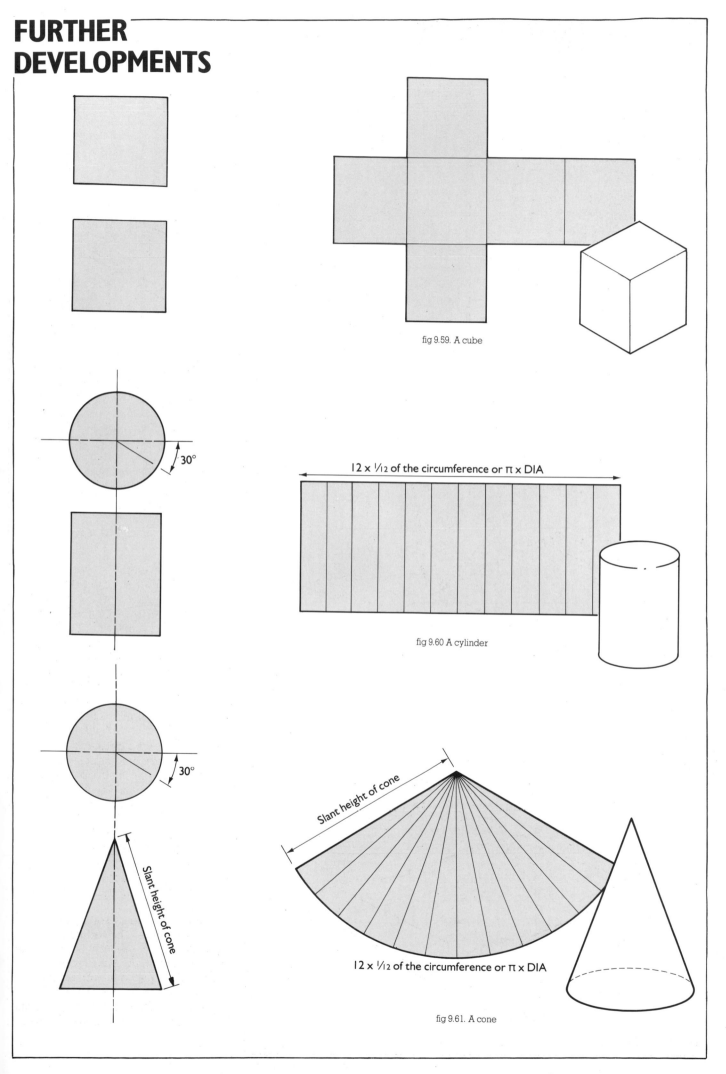

fig 9.59. A cube

30°

12 x ¹/₁₂ of the circumference or π x DIA

fig 9.60 A cylinder

30°

Slant height of cone

Slant height of cone

12 x ¹/₁₂ of the circumference or π x DIA

fig 9.61. A cone

DRAWING FROM OBJECTS

It is common practice to make drawings of an object and then manufacture it. However, there may be times when this process needs to be reversed, for example, when a particular part needs replacing and there are no drawings available to send to a manufacturer. Therefore, the object has to be measured, as in fig 9.62, and new drawings made. In Design and Communication courses it is a most valuable exercise to take an existing article, such as the pencil sharpener shown in fig 9.62, and to produce a series of engineering drawings of it (figs 9.63 and 9.64). This can form the basis of a study which can later be turned into a design exercise by showing possible modifications.

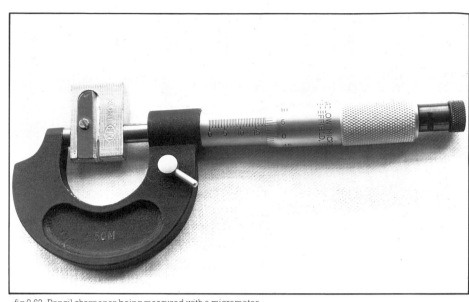

fig 9.62. Pencil sharpener being measured with a micrometer

fig 9.63. Orthographic views drawn in first angle projection

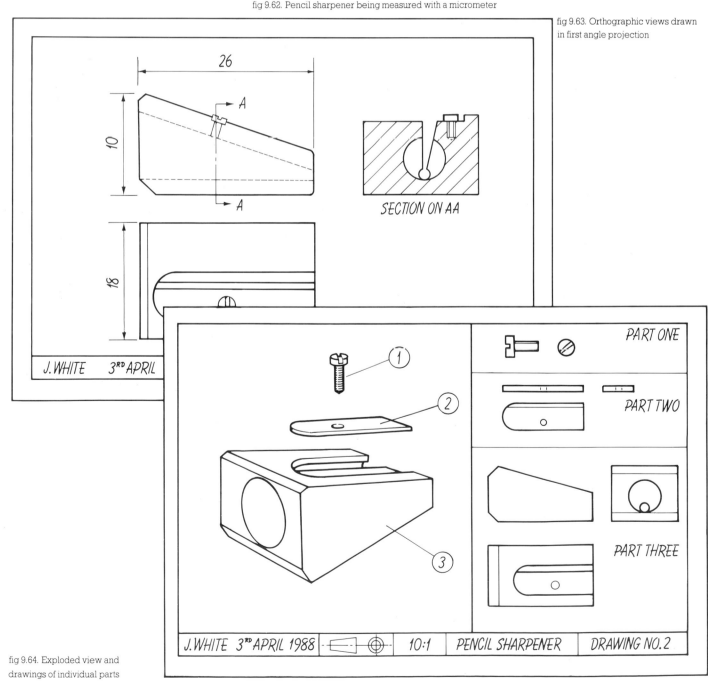

fig 9.64. Exploded view and drawings of individual parts

STORAGE AND REPRODUCTION TECHNOLOGY

In the past, it was common practice for a draughtsman to make individual drawings of an object and then when further copies were required the process was repeated. This was very costly in terms of hours. Today we are much more advanced in our methods of storage and reproduction of drawings.

Many design departments store drawings on 35 mm film in a card index system as shown in fig 9.65. Two copies of each drawing are kept on **film**, one for working purposes and the other under security in case the original is damaged. When a drawing is required the film is loaded into a machine and can be printed off to the appropriate size. This saves space by not having to store lots of large drawings and also saves draughtsmen's time by not having to redraw a component when a further copy is required.

The latest computer technology is widely used both to make drawings and then to store the information so that it can be redrawn at any time. A large amount of information can be stored on a disk that can then be used on similar machines in different parts of the world. It is also possible for the information to be transmitted from one computer to another via telecommunication links. You may be able to store some of your own drawings on a computer system. The

fig 9.65. Drawings stored on film

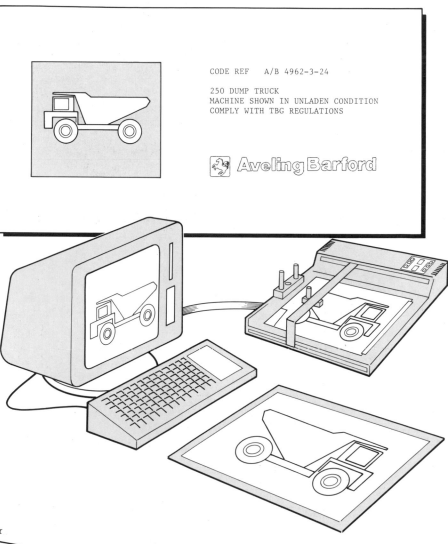

CODE REF   A/B 4962-3-24

250 DUMP TRUCK
MACHINE SHOWN IN UNLADEN CONDITION
COMPLY WITH TBG REGULATIONS

Aveling Barford

fig 9.67. Enlarging and reducing drawings with a photocopier

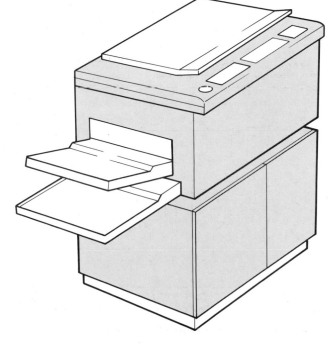

fig 9.66. Storage and reproduction of drawings through a computer system

programming will be time-consuming, but time will be saved when a repeat drawing is required.

Perhaps the easiest way of reproducing drawings in schools is by using a **photocopier**, many of which have an enlargement and reduction facility. They are particularly useful where many repeat drawings have to be made of the same article. In such cases the original drawing can be kept so that it can be photocopied when required.

EXERCISES

1. Write out in full what the abbreviations given below are short for.

a) DIA   d) CSK   g) PCD
b) mm   e) A/F   h) R
c) MATL   f) C'BORE   i) I/D

2. Fig 9.68 shows part of an engineering drawing which contains several different types of line. State what each is called and its use in this drawing.

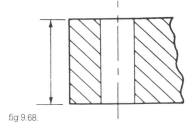

fig 9.68.

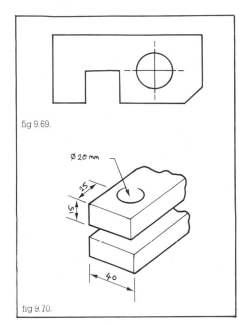

fig 9.69.

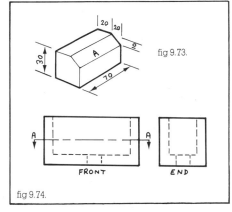

Ø 20 mm

25

5

40

fig 9.70.

3. Fig 9.69 shows the front view of a shape manufactured from mild steel. It has been drawn full size, but has not been dimensioned. Make a copy of it and fully dimension it using the conventions outlined in the British Standards.

4. In fig 9.70 two pieces of mild steel bar which are drilled with a 20 mm diameter hole have been drawn. These are to be fastened together with a hexagonal nut and bolt. Draw a full-size sectional view cut through the centre of the hole with the nut and bolt in position.

5. Sketch front, end and plan views in first angle projection of the block drawn in fig 9.71. Include the appropriate projection symbol in your answer.

6. Sketch front, end and plan views in third angle projection of the block drawn in fig 9.72. Include the appropriate projection symbol in your answer.

7. It is necessary to find the true shape of the surface 'A' shown in fig 9.73. This is to be achieved by drawing an auxiliary view of that surface. Draw out the front, end and plan views full size and include an auxilliary view showing the true shape of 'A'.

8. Sketch a sectional plan view of the block drawn in fig 9.74 which has been cut along the plane AA.

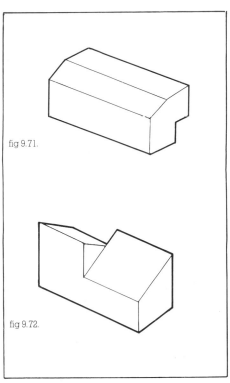

fig 9.71.

fig 9.72.

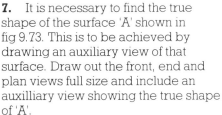

20 20

30

10

A

70

fig 9.73.

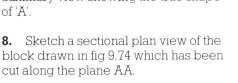

A   A

FRONT   END

fig 9.74.

9. The shapes shown in figs 9.75, 9.76 and 9.77 are to be made from a thin sheet material. Draw out the flat shape of the material (development) that would be required to make each. Show the folds by dotted lines, but do not include any tabs that may be necessary to join them together.

10. Take a simple object such as a plastic container, pen or simple workshop tool and produce two study sheets as shown on page 00. The first should contain orthographic views of the object and a parts list. The second should show details of the individual parts and an exploded view.

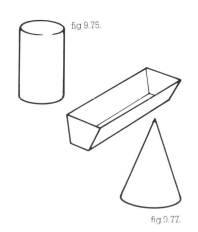

fig 9.75.

fig 9.77.

ENVIRONMENTAL DRAWING

Environmental drawing is an area concerned with making drawings of the surroundings in which we live. This can be a very broad area of study, because people's environments vary enormously. We will only attempt to highlight some common areas. Others, that are perhaps relevant to the particular area in which you live, may be interesting topics for you to explore.

The four main areas to be considered are **maps**, **street furniture**, **services** and **architectural drawings**. They are highlighted in fig 10.1, which shows a compilation of the types of things to be looked at in each of the areas of study. These are simply representative samples from each. They will be explored in greater depth later.

The first area is maps. Under this heading we will look at Ordnance Survey maps, street maps, three-dimensional maps and graphical representation of information in a map form. This is a very lively area and one that humans have been concerned with since the earliest times.

The second area is that of street furniture. A walk along any street will reveal many examples such as road signs, road markings, lighting and street names. However, we must also consider how this form of communication varies from region to region and from one country to another.

The third area to be considered is that of services supplied to buildings. It is worth noting that most buildings will usually have five services connected: these are gas, electricity, water, telecommunications lines and waste disposal. Each service has detailed drawings made of it to ensure a safe and efficient service.

The final area concentrates on architectural drawings and plans. Clearly any building has to be drawn out in great detail before construction can begin. This must not only include orthographic elevations, but also detailed drawings of such elements as electrical wiring, heating systems, interior design and work schedules.

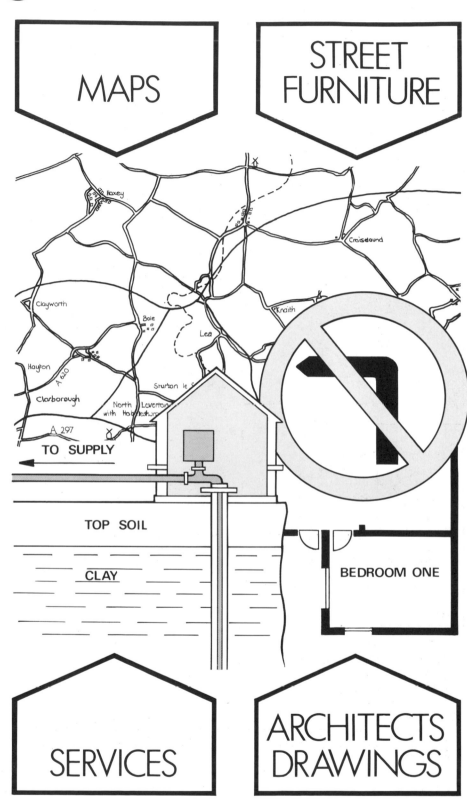

MAPS

STREET FURNITURE

TO SUPPLY

TOP SOIL

CLAY

BEDROOM ONE

SERVICES

ARCHITECTS DRAWINGS

fig 10.1.

MAPS

From the very earliest times, people have drawn **maps** of their environment. Initially this was necessary so that they could find their way from one place to another and be aware of the features they might find beneficial or dangerous. Today it is often a question of convenience rather than survival, with people using maps to see how to travel from one place to another as quickly as possible. However, people such as climbers, sailors and walkers rely heavily upon accurate maps to keep them safe.

Early attempts were often rather crude and relied largely upon the drawing of notable landmarks such as a hill, a tree, a forest or a river. These were very useful for primitive peoples, but were inaccurate, even though they were a remarkably good attempt considering the times in which they were drawn and the methods available. Claudius Ptolemy's attempt at mapping the British Isles, shown in fig 10.2, bears this point out by his production of a map in which it is difficult, if not impossible, to recognise the Britain we know today.

Nowadays we are much more highly organised and skilful in our attempts to draw maps. This is largely due to the **Ordnance Survey**. This organisation dates from 1791 when Britain found itself under threat of invasion from France. The British Army required accurate mapping of the south coast of England for military purposes at a scale of 1 inch to 1 mile. The necessary survey was carried out by the Board of Ordnance, a Crown organisation responsible for army engineering, artillery and other armaments at the time.

As the threat of invasion receded, civilian applications for mapping were identified. The **industrial revolution** was under way, with the associated

fig 10.2. The British Isles according to Claudius Ptolemy

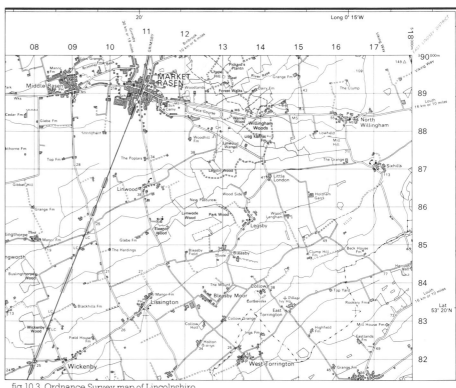

fig 10.3. Ordnance Survey map of Lincolnshire

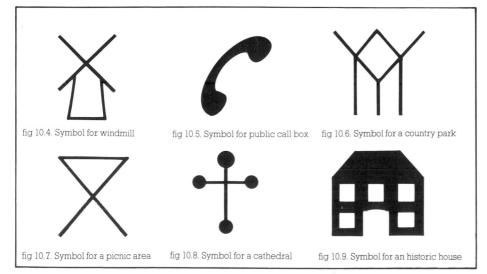

fig 10.4. Symbol for windmill

fig 10.5. Symbol for public call box

fig 10.6. Symbol for a country park

fig 10.7. Symbol for a picnic area

fig 10.8. Symbol for a cathedral

fig 10.9. Symbol for an historic house

rapid expansion of towns, roads and rail networks. Politicians, administrators, civil engineers and others were quick to recognise the value of accurate maps. By the mid-nineteenth century, the Ordnance Survey had assumed its modern role of providing a national survey for scientific, military, government and public uses. Today Ordnance Survey is a civilian government department with headquarters in Southampton and a network of small local survey offices throughout the country.

In any map, of whatever scale, it is not possible to draw every exact detail as it would look in an aerial

fig 10.10. Michaelgate, Lincoln

photograph. So that these maps can present the information in a clear manner, a standard set of **symbols** and **colours** is used to represent the objects. An example of this is shown in fig 10.4, the symbol for a windmill. Clearly it would have been difficult to draw the actual windmill with its exact number of sails onto the map. Further examples of symbols from maps are shown in figs 10.5 to 10.9.

Fig 10.5 shows a public call box, fig 10.6 a country park, fig 10.7 a picnic area, fig 10.8 a cathedral and fig 10.9 an historic house. There are many other features shown in the map in fig 10.3, including villages, road numbers and classifications, woods, rivers, railway lines and stations.

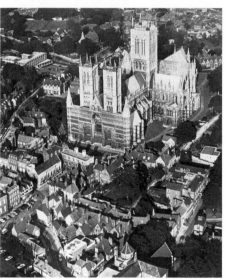

fig 10.11. Aerial view of Lincoln

STREET MAPS

Street maps are enlargements of certain areas of maps. They are often of urban areas, where it is difficult to show the great detail required to display such features as main roads, buildings and parks. They are necessary so that a particular location can be found within the maze of streets that make up our towns and cities.

Fig 10.10 illustrates how it is often not possible to see very far from our normal ground level position. This means that the particular place you may wish to find could be very close, but it cannot be seen as your view is obscured by buildings. By moving to an elevated position one can get a view similar to the one shown in fig 10.11. This is an **aerial photograph** that can quite easily be changed into a street map as drawn in fig 10.12.

It is sensible to iron out some of the bends in the roads and to use colour carefully to aid clarity. Of course the street names must also be added. Details that are unnecessary to the street map, such as the names of shops and hotels, are left out so that the finished map can fulfil its main function, which is to show street names and their layout.

You will find maps of this type positioned in most cities to help visitors find their way around. They often have items of particular interest such as the museum, castle and cathedral marked.

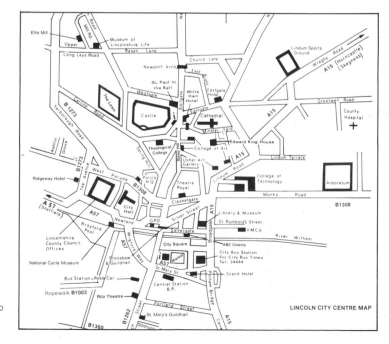

fig 10.12. Street map of Lincoln

GRAPHICAL REPRESENTATION OF ROUTES

It is often essential to present information not only in a clear and precise manner, as with Ordnance Survey maps, but also to use **graphics** to make the map visually more interesting and hopefully easier to understand. A selection of examples of this type of work is shown on these pages. Each has been selected for the different way in which it tackles the problem of displaying a route or information related to travel.

Fig 10.13 is an illustration taken from a British holiday brochure. It shows a map of England divided into different regions each identified by a letter. The price of the holiday can be found by choosing the correct horizontal line that states the area from which travel begins and the vertical column allows the selection of a hotel. The price of the break can be found where the two intersect.

MID SEASON 29 October–16 December & 3 March–28 April.

Price for 2 nights in £s		A	B	C	D	E	F	G		
HEATHROW PARK, IBIS HEATHROW		57	63	65	71	73	76			
ROYAL SCOT		55	61	63	69	71	74			
IBIS EUSTON		63	69	71	77	79	82	89	102	106
BLOOMSBURY PARK		63	69	71	77	79	82	89	102	10
HOSPITALITY INN PICCADILLY		67	73	75	81	83	86	93	106	110
KENSINGTON PALACE THE TOWER	Twin	75	81	83	89	91	94	101	114	118
	Superior	85	91	93	99	101	104	111	124	128
ROYAL TRAFALGAR ROYAL HORSEGUARDS	Twin	75	81	83	89	91	94	101	114	118
	Superior	85	91	93	99	101	104	111	124	128
ROYAL WESTMINSTER		85	91	93	99	101	104	111	124	128
THE CADOGAN, THE LOWNDES, THE SELFRIDGE		89	95	97	103	105	108		128	
CANNIZARO HOUSE		109	115	117	123	125	128			
1st Class Supplement		3	6	7	10	11	13			

fig 10.13. Illustration from a holiday brochure

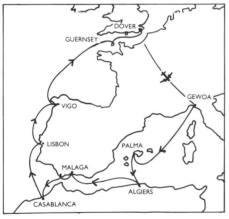

fig 10.14. Cruise route

Fig 10.14 is taken from another holiday brochure and shows the route for a cruise. It has been selected because it concentrates on the cruise route and ports of call to the exclusion of everything else. There are no countries or seas named, yet it is remarkably clear that the cruise begins by flying to Genoa and then cruising through the Mediterranean, before returning to Dover.

Fig 10.15 shows a route map to a famous landmark, Belvoir Castle. Here only the major roads have been shown with their identification numbers. This aids clarity because the minor roads would only confuse the issue and it is unlikely that many visitors would use them. All they require is a clear and simple picture of how to get to the castle.

Fig 10.16 is an interesting representation of a route because it combines two forms of travel, coach and train. It shows a journey from Hunstanton to Peterborough and beyond. Peterborough can be reached by travelling through Kings Lynn and Wisbech. It then shows graphically how, having reached Peterborough, trains can be caught to all parts of the country.

All these examples are different methods of showing routes. They have achieved a high degree of **clarity through skilful design**.

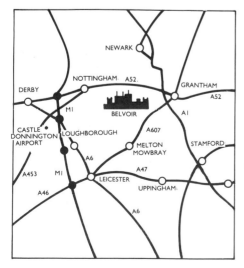

fig 10.15. Route map

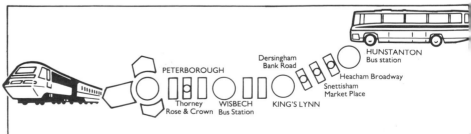

fig 10.16. Representation of a coach and train route

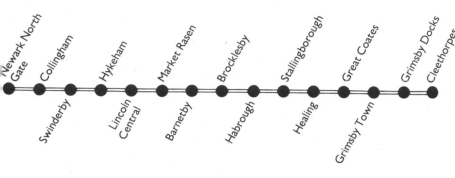

fig 10.17.

The examples on this page have been selected because they have each adopted a different approach to showing one aspect of rail travel. There are many more that you may be able to explore.

Fig 10.17 shows a very simple, but nevertheless effective, way of showing the railway line between Newark and Cleethorpes. Of course the line is not straight, the stations are not equal distances apart and the line passes through other villages too. However, these are of little or no interest to the passenger and would only contrive to add confusion to the situation.

Fig 10.18 shows a route map of the Inter-City routes on which cyclists can take their bicycles free of charge. Again we can see that all the lines are represented by a straight line which, in reality, is not the case. Furthermore, the distances between, and positions of, the stations are drawn with the idea of producing a clear and visually pleasing map. However, they are generally accurate in that Peterborough is north, Brighton south, and Reading west of London.

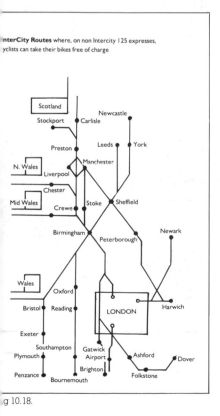

fig 10.18.

fig 10.19.

Fig 10.19 shows a very simple map that is aimed at showing travellers how they can begin their journey to Holland, Germany and Scandinavia. This involves linking up with the train that goes to Harwich. It can be seen that as the lines from Blackpool and Birmingham join the main line it becomes thicker. Of course this train is timetabled to reach Harwich in time to catch ferries to European ports. The arrival of these boats will link in with European railways, meaning that many forms of public transport are in fact interlinked and do not, as one might first think, operate independently.

Fig 10.20 shows a very graphical representation of the electrification of London to Edinburgh line. The drawing of the line has many of the features mentioned in figs 10.17 and 10.18. However, the shape of the map has been determined by the fact that this is a line running from north to south. It would have been wrong to draw this map in a horizontal box that would have been suitable to show the line from London to Bristol, for example. In this case we also have the addition of an illustration for each of the major cities along the route. For instance, York has its cathedral shown and Newcastle the Tyne Bridge, adding a certain amount of interest to the map. The addition of dates also allows one to build up a mental picture of when the electrification of each section of the line is to be completed.

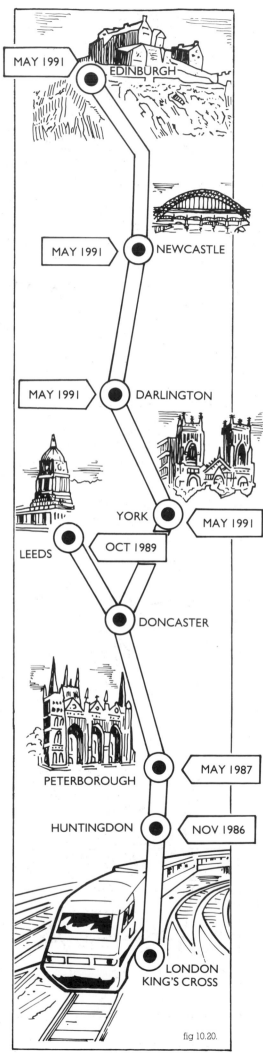

fig 10.20.

DISTRIBUTION MAPS

Earlier in this chapter we saw how maps are often produced to show roads, rivers, towns and similar features of the landscape. However, these are not the only factors that may be displayed. It is sometimes necessary to show the distribution of certain features over an area. This could range from a **climatic** map showing rainfall over a period of one month to a map showing **land use**.

The example given in fig 10.21 shows the distribution of principal crops throughout the British Isles. Trends can be identified clearly from this, with the majority of East Anglia being devoted to such crops as wheat, barley and oats, and a large part of Wales to sheep grazing. Of course this is a map covering a very large area and it can only show general trends, not local detail.

The second example (fig 10.22) shows the average number of days of sunshine enjoyed by different areas of the country during a particular year. This is a climatic map and similar examples could be drawn to show rainfall, temperature, amounts of snowfall and air movements.

It will be necessary to develop a method of colouring your maps so that the different areas can be identified.

PRINCIPAL CROPS
- Wheat, barley and oats
- Barley and oats
- Oats
- Cattle pastures
- Sheep grazing

fig 10.21. Areas growing principal crops

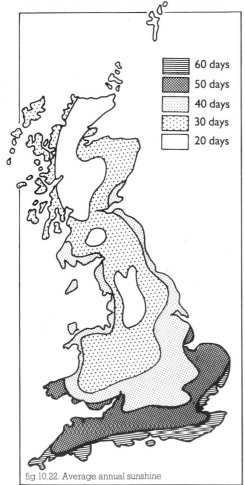

60 days
50 days
40 days
30 days
20 days

fig 10.22. Average annual sunshine

This can be achieved using coloured pens, but it is also possible to use one colour, providing different types of line are used, for example vertical, horizontal and diagonal (fig 10.23). A **key** to show what each of the areas represents must also be drawn.

Further maps can be drawn to show the distribution of the **world's natural resources** such as timber, minerals and sources of power. These must be constantly updated as discoveries and developments are made.

Maps are often drawn to show the distribution of people over the world's surface. This is called **demography**. As one would imagine, people are not spread evenly, but concentrated in certain highly populated areas such as cities. Some areas will be very sparsely populated because the terrain may be very rugged or the climate unfavourable.

fig 10.23. Examples of shading used in keys

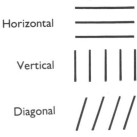

Horizontal

Vertical

Diagonal

THREE-DIMENSIONAL MAPS

Although it may appear that most maps show only two dimensions, they can in fact show three. This is normally achieved by the addition of **contour lines** which show the height of the land above the sea level at intervals.

A true three-dimensional map can be seen by drawing a **cross-section** through the land as shown in fig 10.24. This shows how layers of rock have moved to form geological features.

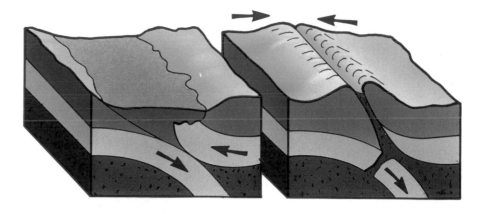

fig 10.24. A three-dimensional map

OVERLAY MAPS

It is possible to show a great deal of detail in a map without it appearing confused by using **overlays**. In the example shown in fig 10.25 the three maps show first part of the coastline of Eastern England, second the outline of the county, and third the main towns.

If this information were all given on the final map, it would be less easy to understand. By presenting it in stages, there is a gradual build-up to the end product.

It is possible to draw the map out each time and add the extra information. However, it is much easier to use clear acetate film for the second and third sheets so that the original drawing need not be redrawn.

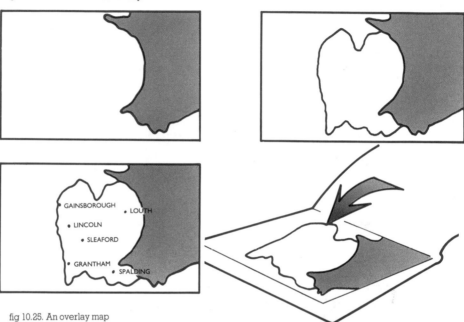

fig 10.25. An overlay map

ILLUMINATED MAPS

An **illuminated map** can prove very effective because it is a means of picking out a particular feature from the background. These types of maps are often used in towns to show visitors where particular features such as the library, the railway station, shopping centres and the museum are situated.

By pressing a button against the feature you wish to locate, a **light-emitting diode** (LED) or **bulb** is lit, bringing the point to your attention immediately, saving you several minutes searching for it.

One possible electrical circuit that can be used to make an LED light is shown in fig 10.27. This will show only one location, but could be repeated to show further points of interest.

fig 10.26. Illuminated map

fig 10.27. Circuit to light an LED

STREET FURNITURE

ROAD MARKINGS

A close examination of the surfaces of Britain's roads will reveal many examples of communication. These usually take the form of coloured lines, or symbols, applied onto the road surface.

An example of this is shown in fig 10.28, which illustrates the markings that are required for a signal-controlled junction. The exact positions and dimensions of the markings have been calculated so that they give the road user the best possible chance of seeing and reacting to the situation. Every mark that is applied to a road surface has been designed with this in mind and its position, colour and shape are vital to the message that is being communicated.

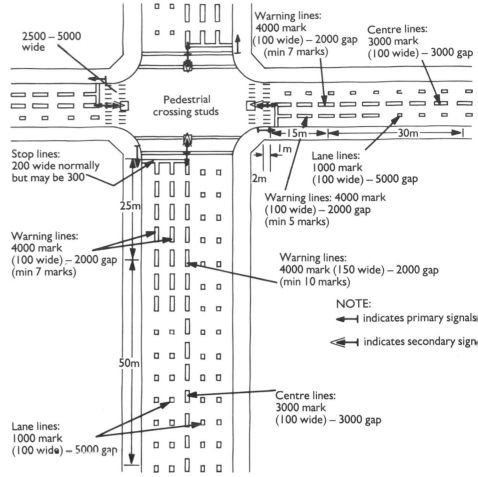

fig 10.28. Layout at signal controlled junction and approaches

ROAD SIGNS

Examples of communication are to be found not only on the surface of the road, but also at the sides and above roads. A full copy of all the road signs used in Britain can be found in the **Highway Code**. It is not necessary for us to look at all of them, but it is essential to look at some of the points that may have been considered during the design.

First, the shape of the sign is important. This is usually circular for **orders** that must be obeyed, and triangular for **warning** signs. A red border surrounds most signs to make them stand out from the environment. **Lettering** or **symbols** on the sign are in black and must be simple and clear so that the passing motorist can understand them quickly. The positioning of these signs is also important because they must be sited far enough away from the hazard to allow sufficient time for the motorist to react.

fig 10.29. Road signs

DIRECTIONAL SIGNS

Not all signs are erected to give orders or warning of an approaching hazard. Some are there to give **directions** (fig 10.30). Without these it would be very difficult for motorists to find their way unless they were prepared to stop and refer to a map.

Once again these directional signs are designed to a system that will make it easy for the motorist to pick out the relevant information. First, all directional signs are rectangular, so that they cannot be confused with the triangular and circular road signs. Second, the colours used are different, with green backgrounds being used on primary routes, white backgrounds on other routes and blue borders showing local places.

Roads in Great Britain are given identification numbers which makes it unecessary for all the places that the road passes through to be listed on the sign. The road number is given instead so that the motorist can identify the required route.

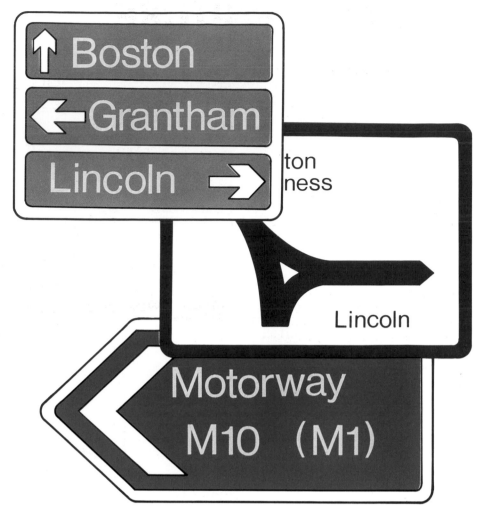

fig 10.30. Directional signs

INFORMATION

Some signs are erected at the sides of roads purely for **information** purposes. These are there to show the way to public amenities such as petrol stations, service areas, hospitals and telephones. These types of signs are mainly blue and rely upon strong symbols similar to those shown in fig 10.31, a selection of information signs that are good examples of communication. The top one indicates the way to a public telephone, using the same symbol as can be found on Ordnance Survey maps. The middle one shows a variety of facilities available at a service area; these are fuel, parking, cafeteria and restaurant facilities. The bottom sign shows the symbol that is used to display the way to a hospital. A clear symbol is important for all of these signs if the idea is to be communicated effectively.

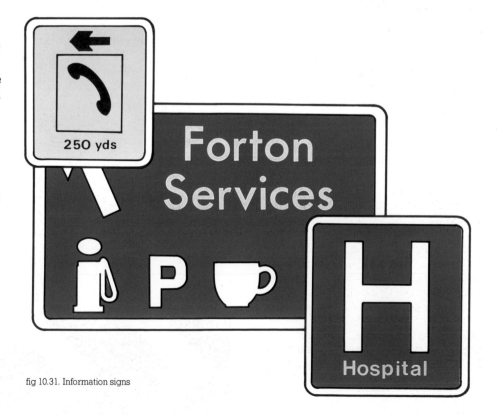

fig 10.31. Information signs

CONTROLLING TRAFFIC FLOW

In addition to the normal restrictions that are placed upon the flow of traffic by road markings and signs, it is also necessary to have an overall **traffic control plan** within a city. This will include methods of monitoring the flow of traffic so that delays, such as the one shown in fig 10.32, can be avoided. It may be designed to take into account the general flow of traffic during peak periods of the day. There will also be provisions made so that emergency services can pass quickly to the scene of an accident.

fig 10.32. Traffic flow problems

A TRAFFIC CONTROL SYSTEM

In any **traffic control system** the production of drawings is essential to the presentation of the information. These drawings may take on many different forms, but all have the common aim of communicating the state of the traffic within a particular area. Clarity is of the utmost importance if the information is to be any use at all.

Fig 10.33 shows a drawing of the city of Lincoln's Urban Traffic Control System. It has many important features that help to promote the smooth flow of traffic, while at the same time enabling unforeseen emergencies to be dealt with quickly and efficiently.

The flow of traffic along the major roads is **monitored** by **close circuit television cameras** that can be remotely controlled to give different views. Vehicle **counters** and **detectors** also measure the volume of traffic and the speed at which it is travelling over selected points.

This information is fed to a central control unit and then through a computer where printouts are made. Using this information modifications can be made to traffic signals, emergencies dealt with, queues reduced and repairs carried out.

Fig 10.34 illustrates a graphical way of showing the traffic flow at a roundabout. In this case the traffic flowing into the junction from the west and the directions in which it then departs are shown. Similar graphical displays can be made for any road junction once the information has been collected by **traffic census**.

fig 10.33. A traffic control system

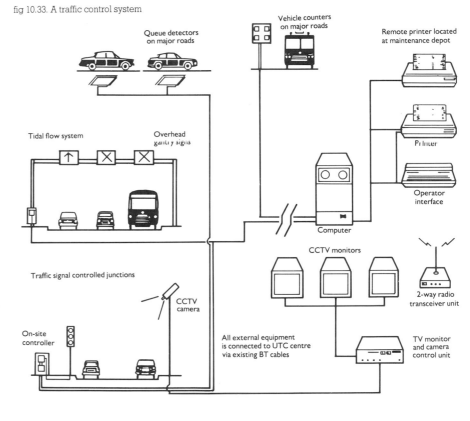

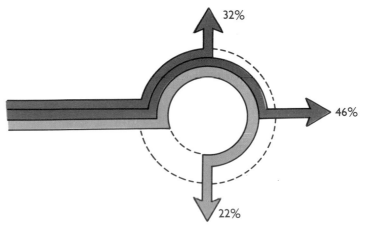

fig 10.34. Traffic flow at a roundabout

TIDAL FLOW SYSTEM

Many cities have to operate a **tidal flow system** to cater for the uneven flow of traffic. As one might expect, the flow into a city is likely to be heaviest during the early morning period when people are travelling to work. In the early evening the effect is the opposite, with the bulk of the traffic leaving the city.

To accommodate this, many cities operate a tidal flow system similar to the one shown in fig 10.35. How this works, is that where three lanes are available, the two outer ones are always used for traffic flowing in opposite directions and the centre lane can be adjusted to take into account the requirements of the traffic flow at a particular time. The function of the centre lane is shown by the overhead gantry signs positioned above the roads.

fig 10.35. A tidal flow system

PREFERENTIAL ROUTES

It is essential that the Fire Brigade (and other emergency services) can travel to the scene of an accident as quickly as possible once the alarm has been raised. This can be a problem in crowded city areas, so to keep this to a minimum a system of **priority routes** is often established.

In the case shown in fig 10.36, the Lincoln Fire Brigade has four alternative routes that can be used. The four spread out from the fire station in different directions so that the most appropriate can be used depending on the location of the emergency.

These routes are stored in the control computer and are called remotely from the fire station to provide fire appliances with **uninterrupted flow** through a series of selected traffic signals. This means that when an emergency call is made the driver will be told the most appropriate priority route with the traffic signals automatically programmed in his favour.

fig 10.36. Fire brigade emergency routes

SERVICES
WATER

A considerable amount of drawing is used to ensure an hygienic supply of water to all users. Great Britain is, in fact, supplied by ten regional water authorities with each maintaining its identity through a **name** and **logo**. The area covered by the Anglian Water Authority and its logo are drawn in fig 10.37. This is a very positive image that is used on all the authorities' vehicles and stationery.

Water must be purified before it is fit for human consumption and the treatment process that it passes through is shown in fig 10.38. The process is very complicated, but the drawing shows it very well through a series of arrows and boxes. This is a very interesting form of drawing because it uses the '**black-box**' technique. This is where a box is drawn and labelled to state what happens there without it being shown in detail by graphical methods. The water begins its journey at the top right-hand corner and travels down to the bottom left-hand corner at which point it joins the household supply system.

There is a vast network of pipes running through the countryside and eventually to each home. The complete **water cycle system** is shown in fig 10.39. This explains that once the water has been used and polluted by chemicals, such as washing powders, it would be harmful to human, plant and animal life to allow it to return to the rivers. It must, therefore, be treated again to ensure that it is not harmful before being returned to the system.

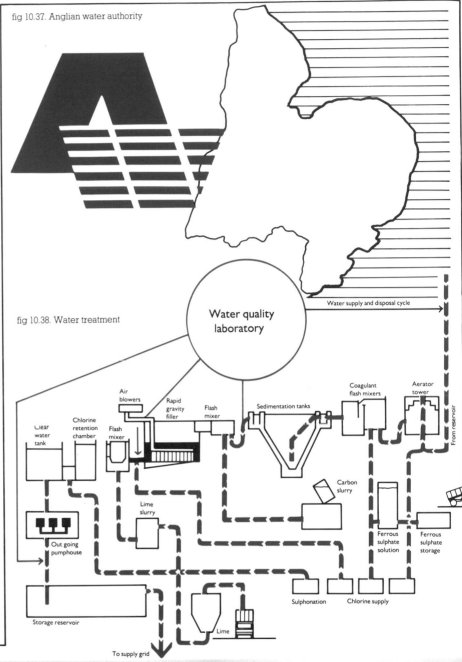

fig 10.37. Anglian water authority

fig 10.38. Water treatment

Water quality laboratory

Water supply and disposal cycle

From reservoir

Air blowers

Rapid gravity filler

Flash mixer

Sedimentation tanks

Coagulant flash mixers

Aerator tower

Clear water tank

Chlorine retention chamber

Flash mixer

Carbon slurry

Lime slurry

Ferrous sulphate solution

Ferrous sulphate storage

Out going pumphouse

Sulphonation

Chlorine supply

Storage reservoir

Lime

To supply grid

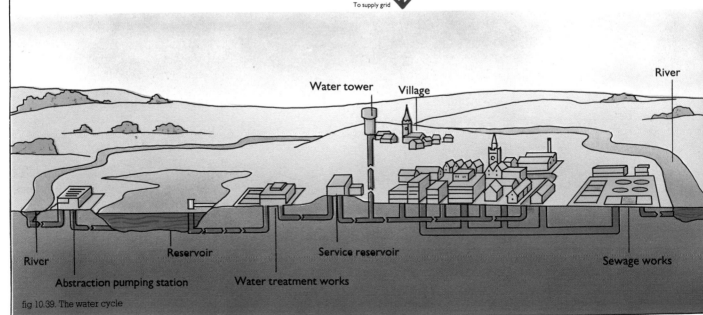

Water tower

Village

River

River

Abstraction pumping station

Reservoir

Water treatment works

Service reservoir

Sewage works

fig 10.39. The water cycle

TELECOMMUNICATIONS

The production of good quality drawings and graphics is vitally important to the Telecommunications service. The logo shown in fig 10.40 is one that is instantly recognizable and widely used. It can be found on all vehicles and equipment used by the industry.

In recent times great efforts have been made to update the image of the service and this is particularly evident in the type of public call boxes produced. The old and the new styles are shown in figs 10.41 and 10.42.

The traditional telephone box was a rather interesting solution to the design problem of housing a telephone. The **specification** would almost certainly have included the following points:

1. The telephone apparatus must be kept dry.

2. The user must be protected from the weather and to a certain extent from external noise.

3. The box must be instantly recognisable.

4. Operating instructions must be displayed in the box.

There may be other points that you could add to this list, but a little careful thought will reveal that the traditional telephone box satisfied all of the points mentioned above.

Today there are several different styles of telephone box in use varying according to where they are to be sited. The new types of telephone boxes satisfy the same specification, but the solutions are different. Most rely heavily upon good quality

fig 10.40. British Telecom logo

fig 10.41. A traditional phone box

fig 10.42. Interior of a modern telephone kiosk

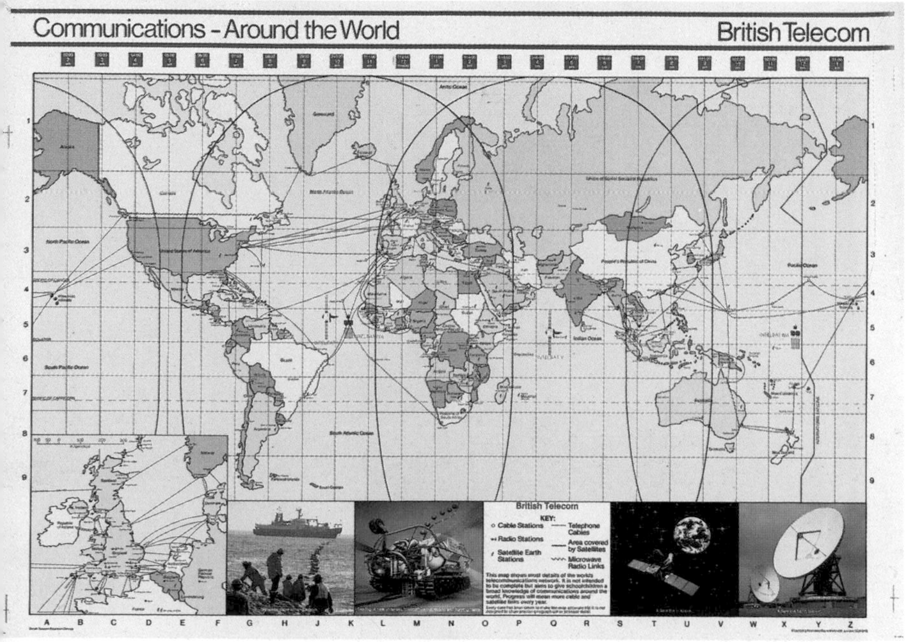

graphics to show how the telephone can be operated. A more subtle colour scheme is used and full use is made of modern materials, such as plastics, to produce a cost effective design with a long life. These combine to give a modern looking telephone box that is functionally very sound.

It is important that the instructions are not only given clearly, but also with symbols that will help people who have reading difficulties or who do not understand English. Public telephone boxes can be found throughout the world, but not all the designers have arrived at the solutions we find in Britain today.

fig 10.43. Communications around the world

ELECTRICITY

Many examples of drawing being used to communicate ideas can be found in the supply of electricity. This can range from the display and advertising material to be found in showrooms, to diagrams illustrating installation procedures for equipment used in power stations. Great Britain's electricity supplies are maintained by a number of electricity boards, each having its own logo similar to that shown in fig 10.44.

Fig 10.45 shows that electricity is generated in power stations situated throughout the country. These may be one of four different types, either conventional (steam), diesel, hydroelectric or nuclear powered. There are many ways of showing their distribution on a map, but the solution used in fig 10.45 clearly solves the problem in a satisfactory manner.

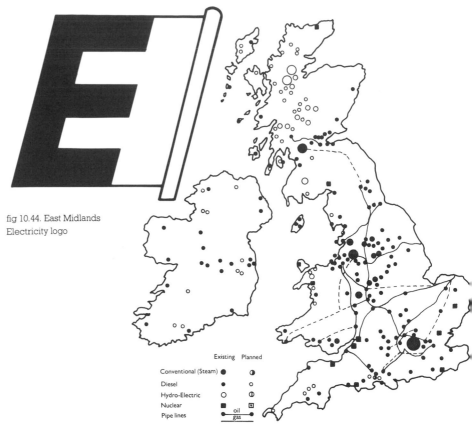

fig 10.44. East Midlands Electricity logo

fig 10.45. Sources of power

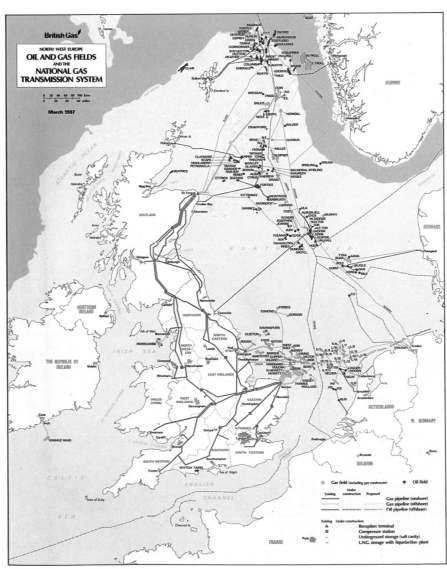

fig 10.47. Sources and distribution of gas

fig 10.46. British Gas logo

GAS

Drawing is used extensively in the gas industry as a means of communication. One of the most obvious forms is in the way all the vehicles are painted to a particular specification. This makes them easily identifiable and creates a professional looking image when they are out maintaining supplies. A drawing of the British Gas logo is shown in fig 10.46. It is clearly designed to represent a flame.

Fig 10.47 shows the major oil and gas fields. The majority of these are in the North sea from where the gas is brought to land terminals and storage, before finally being piped to the consumer.

ARCHITECTURAL DRAWING

PLANS

It is essential that plans are drawn of all buildings before construction begins. An example of this type of drawing is shown in fig 10.48, which includes **front** and **rear elevations**, **plan views** of ground and first floor and three alternatives for the upper floor layout. Plans often include more details of the type of materials to be used in construction than is shown here. However, all materials must be used to the agreed **building regulations** which state such things as what depth the foundations should be laid.

These drawings are usually produced once the site has been surveyed and the local environment considered. This is important because new buildings must blend in with existing ones. The completed plans are then submitted to the local planning department for approval. If they do not comply with the nationally agreed building regulations and requirements of the local environment, they will almost certainly be rejected. Modified plans can then be submitted and may prove acceptable.

Detailed costing also has to be worked out along with a **construction programme (work schedule)** of the type shown in fig 10.49. This includes the order in which work will proceed with a time allocation for each particular task. Finally the plans must be given to the builder so that construction can begin.

Throughout the building stage the detailed plans and construction programme are referred to continually. They must be adhered to in the interests of efficiency and

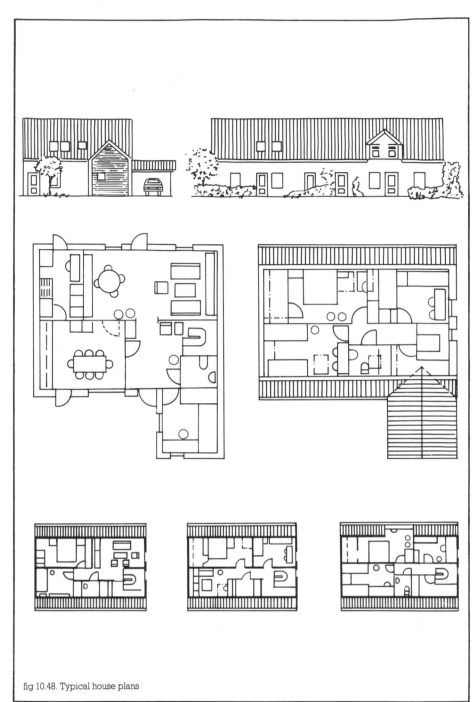

fig 10.48. Typical house plans

accuracy. Clearly some tasks rely upon others being completed first, so good planning is essential. In fact this is the same type of planning that you would use in a design project, but on a much larger scale and with more factors to be considered.

There is also a case for producing a three dimensional drawing of a building. This is most useful when drawn in a **cut-away** form because this shows the interior of the property, while at the same time giving some idea of the exterior and interior methods of construction used. The drawing of plans is an essential part of the building industry before, during and even after construction.

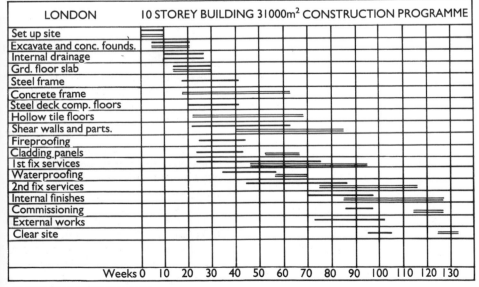

fig 10.49. Construction programme

CONSTRUCTION MATERIALS

Brick

This is a very commonly used material in the building industry. A large variety of colours are available and the addition of coloured **mortars** can produce some exciting effects as shown in fig 10.51.

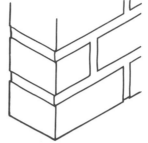

fig 10.50. Brick

fig 10.51. Building with different coloured bricks and mortar

Concrete

Concrete is a very useful material in that it can be mixed and then cast into a mould to set. It has very good compressive strength, but little tensile strength unless reinforced with steel wires.

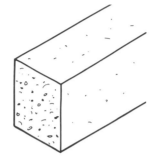

fig 10.52. Concrete

fig 10.53. Concrete structure

Timber

Timber was one of the earliest materials to be used in construction, and is still used extensively today. It has good decorative qualities when stained, can easily be painted, but is subject to fungi attack if left untreated.

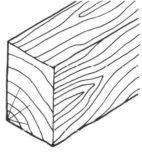

fig 10.54. Timber

fig 10.55. Timber framed building

Steel

Steel is often used to make the rigid structure of a building with the spaces then being filled in with lighter materials. **Girders** such as the one shown in fig 10.57 are designed to give a good strength to weight ratio.

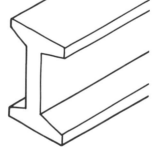

fig 10.56. Steel

fig 10.57. Bridge structure made from steel

Plastic

Plastics are now used extensively in the building trade because they can be easily manufactured in a wide range of colours and shapes. Chipboard is often covered with **melamine formaldehyde** to produce self assembly furniture.

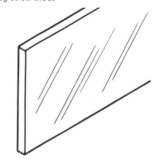

fig 10.58. Plastic

fig 10.59. Plastics used in building

Glass

Glass is often used for windows, making use of its qualities of allowing light to pass through. However, fig 10.61 shows how glass can be applied to modern building design.

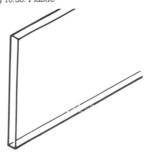

fig 10.60. Glass

fig 10.61. Building using glass as a covering material

This page shows details of a modern building design. The building chosen is the Equitable Life Assurance Society's headquarters at Aylesbury, and was selected because of the imaginative way in which it uses materials to produce a very unusual external appearance (fig 10.62.). The **sectional view** in fig 10.63 shows that the building has four floors with a central atrium stretching from top to bottom of the building. This central area houses many plants and brings together the natural and the man-made to form the focal point of the building.

One of the most striking features of the building is that it goes completely against the **traditional building principles** of ensuring that walls are vertical and opts for a 17° slope. This produces a visually impressive image, as fig 10.62 clearly shows, which is even more striking when one considers that the outer surfaces are covered with azure blue double glazing.

fig 10.62. The Equitable Life Assurance Society's new headquarters in Aylesbury

fig 10.63. Section of Equitable Life Assurance Society Headquarters

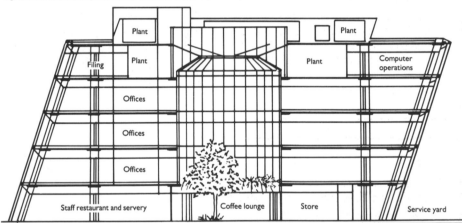

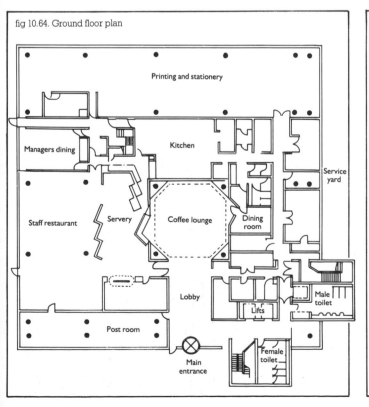

fig 10.64. Ground floor plan

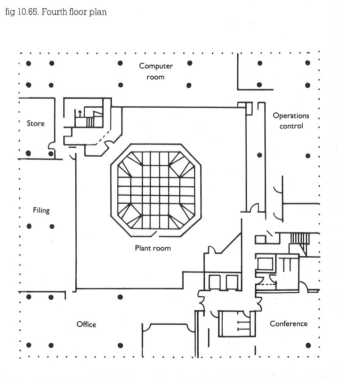

fig 10.65. Fourth floor plan

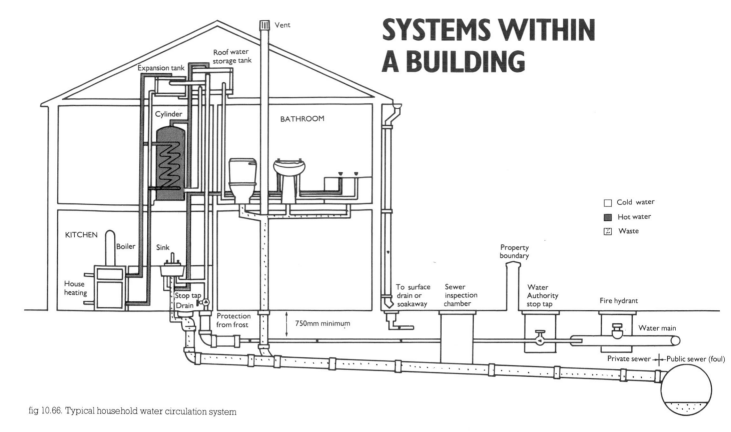

fig 10.66. Typical household water circulation system

SYSTEMS WITHIN A BUILDING

Any building includes a number of **systems** that have to be drawn out in detail. These can be divided into two main areas: the **water system** and the **electrical circuits**. The **heating system** may be connected to either or both. In each case the production of accurate drawings will assist in installing the system and rectifying any faults.

Fig 10.66 shows a typical household water circulation system. It can be seen that there are three interlinking systems to be considered. They are the hot water system, the cold water system and the waste water system. The illustration shows very clearly how these are combined in a house.

In fact, this drawing could be used by anyone building a house or wishing to understand how his own water system works. The cold water supply is taken from the water main which is usually situated underneath the road. Stop taps must be provided so that the supply can be turned off. Cold water must be available for sinks, toilet, cylinder, storage tank, expansion tank and central heating boiler. Hot water can then be supplied to hot water taps and radiators.

Waste water must be taken from the sink, wash basin and toilet and then drained into a public sewer situated beneath the road. In some cases a private sewer is provided that will require emptying at regular intervals.

Fig 10.67 gives one small example of how a drawing can be used in the explanation of a household electrical system. In this case it illustrates the method of wiring a 13 amp plug.

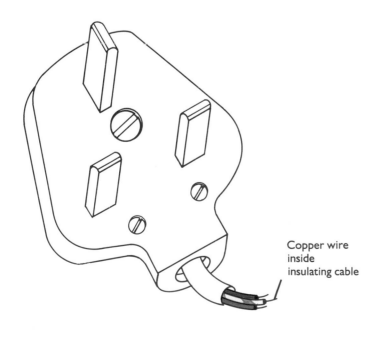

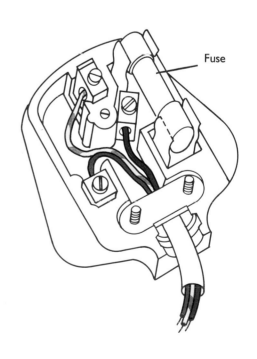

Copper wire inside insulating cable

Fuse

fig 10.67. Wiring a plug

MODULAR FURNITURE

Modular furniture is commonplace in homes today. It is usually made from **chipboard** and covered with a range of **plastic laminates** to give a decorative finish. It can be obtained from large DIY shops and its great advantage is that individual units can be purchased and then combined to give the effect of fully fitted furniture (fig 10.68). Cost and transport problems are kept to a minimum by the fact that the units are usually **'packed flat'** and assembled on site.

The success of ordering the correct number and type of units to fit neatly into a room is largely dependent on the ability to produce a plan view of the room, as shown in fig 10.69. In the first instance this need only be a sketch giving the overall dimensions and shape of the room. Later on it may be refined to a proper working drawing produced to a suitable scale. In some cases an elevation may also be required, and a little imagination will certainly prove useful in visualising the finished room.

fig 10.68. Assembled modular furniture

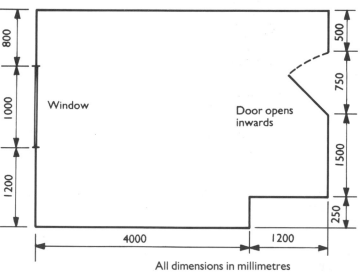
fig 10.69. Plan of a room

The manufacturer will usually provide a catalogue with drawings similar to those shown in fig 10.70, showing sizes of individual units available. Sometimes a computer printout showing the most suitable choice and position of units can be drawn. The room dimensions are fed into the computer and a number of possible solutions tried. It should then be a simple task to assemble the units when they arrive and fasten them into the chosen positions.

Once the modules have been selected, an order can be placed with the manufacturer. If the design work has been carried out correctly, when the modules arrive it should be a simple task to assemble the units and fasten them into the chosen positions.

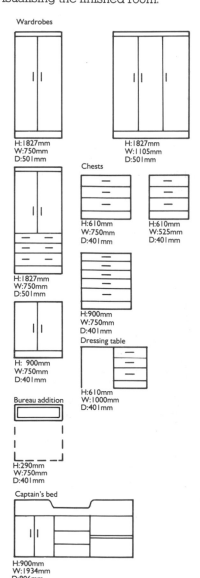
fig 10.70. Units available

fig 10.71. Planning a room

EXERCISES

1. Fig 10.72 shows an aerial photograph of the countryside. Design a map of this area and use graphical methods to represent the features such as the church, woodland, river and roads.

2. It is intended to show the features listed below on a map to be used in a game called 'Treasure Hunt', for children aged between nine and eleven years. Design symbols that you think would be easily understood by children of this age for:

(a) the treasure

(b) a swamp

(c) mountains

(d) jungle

(e) a crocodile infested lake

(f) underground caves.

fig 10.72.

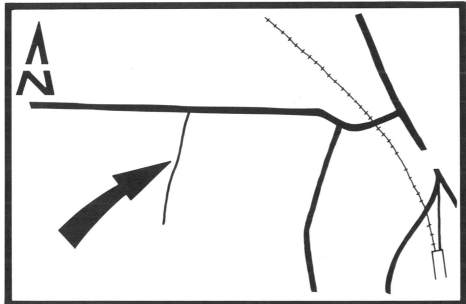

fig 10.73. A route map

3. Imagine that you are holding a party at your home and will be sending postcard invitations. A route map showing the way to your house, time and date of the party is to be printed on the reverse of the postcard. Design a means of communicating this route. It may be similar to the one shown in fig 10.73

4. Conduct a traffic census at a road junction such as a roundabout or a crossroads. You may collect information over a convenient period, for example, one hour. You should collect information of two types. First, the ways in which the traffic leaves the junction, and second, the different types of vehicle that arrive at the junction. Show the results of both surveys in graphical forms similar to that shown on page 10, fig 10.34.

5. Make an accurate ground floor plan of your house, similar to that shown in fig 10.74, taking care to ensure that the scale chosen will allow the finished drawing to fit onto A3 size paper. Do not show any movable furniture in your drawing, only the items that would be left were you to move house. By moving the internal walls only design a second plan which shows an alternative use of the available space.

6. Make a sketch plan of your bedroom with all the necessary measurements included. Select and sketch in the appropriate places, a range of units from those shown on page 19 that would fit nicely into your room making full use of the space and providing adequate storage.

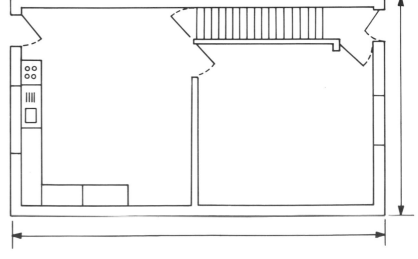

fig 10.74. Ground floor plan of a house

PROJECT WORK

Your design projects will carry a large percentage of the marks in any examination. In order to gain the best possible mark you must learn how to **manage** your project work. The points highlighted on this page, and examples of projects given later in this chapter, will help you develop project management skills.

Different examination syllabuses have different structures for their project work and it is wise to follow the structure set by the examining group if possible. Your teacher may provide you with a great deal of support by telling you exactly what he wishes to see in your design folder and the way it should be presented. However, if no structure is provided, the format set out on page 12 of this book may be helpful.

The nature of project work means that it is very easy to fall behind. Therefore, it is wise to devise a plan for the whole project as soon as possible. A sensible policy is to divide the overall time allocation for your project into small sections so that individual targets can be identified and met. This avoids the embarrassing situation of 'bottle necks' where many things are required at the same time and you have little chance of producing any of them to the required standard.

At an early stage in the project things which may take a long time should be identified and acted upon. These may include letters requesting information or materials and components.

A consistent effort throughout the course nearly always produces the best results because very rarely can a project be neglected for a long period and then revived and completed in the final weeks of the course.

It is useful to lay down a few basic rules before beginning a project so that the time can be used as productively as possible. It will also help the finished folder to take on the appearance of one project and not a whole series of individual pieces of work assembled at the last minute for the examiner. A sensible list of rules might be as follows:

1. Establish the size of paper on which your project will be presented. A number of smaller drawings and photographs can be mounted to make complete sheets. Never throw any work away no matter how insignificant it may appear.

2. Decide upon a common layout for each sheet of paper. This may simply be a border around the edge of the paper but it can be developed to include a personal logo made from your initials.

3. Decide upon the colour, size and style of lettering for the page headings. If these are the same it will help to tie the project together.

4. Be aware of the sections that your project must include. You may use a chart similar to that shown below to plot your progress.

DATE	ACTIVITY	SIGNED
20/1/88	ANALYSIS	CMUA
15/2/88	RESEARCH	J.I.C.
2/3/88	SPECIFICATION	MMMA

5. Make sure all work is kept in a folder and this is stored in a safe place when not being worked upon.

Once the project is underway you may use a checklist similar to the one shown below to establish the level of progress that is being achieved.

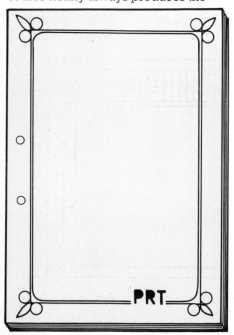

PROGRESS CHECKLIST

- Do you know the date by which the completed project must be handed in?

- Have you divided the time allowed so that you have a realistic time scale for completing all sections of the work?

- Have you a folder in which all your design work is kept?

- Do you know in what format your project is to be presented?

- Are you regularly working on your design folder out of lesson time?

- Have you carried out sufficient research to allow a full range of solutions to the problem to be developed?

- Will the proposed solution satisfy your specification?

- Have you produced working drawings in sufficient detail that will allow the final design to be realised?

- Are the materials or components that you require to realise your design readily available?

- Is the equipment available in school that will the design to be realised?

- What progress did you make during the last lesson?

- What progress do you hope to make during the next lesson?

ANALYSIS AND SPECIFICATION

Before you can begin any design work you will need a thorough understanding of the problem. This understanding is gained by carrying out an investigation or analysis. Your findings or results will then need to be recorded graphically in your folder and used to provide the basis of your specification. Annotated sketches are a good way of presenting your thoughts on a particular subject. Short paragraphs of notes are best illustrated with small relevant diagrams.

For his second project Tim has decided to produce a series of wall charts or posters for use when exercising or body building. They are to be used to show how to do the various types of exercises and to display the progress made by recording muscle measurements at regular intervals. One of the finished charts is shown on the right.

Tim has developed a neat hand-printed style of lettering which he has used for this page. It is a good idea to adopt a similar style yourself as stencilling takes a long time and dry-transfer lettering can prove to be expensive.

He has written his analysis to the problem on the same page as the specification. Can you suggest any ways in which it could be improved or the problems shown more clearly?

ANALYSIS OF THE BRIEF

WHEN EXERCISING THE EXERCISER WILL HAVE TO REMEMBER NOT TO WORK TOO HARD AND OVERSTRAIN.

SUCH WARNINGS OUGHT TO BE WELL PRINTED ON THE WALL CHART.

THIS WILL MEAN A LOT OF RESEARCH AND THE READING OF KEEP FIT AND BODY BUILDING BOOKS WILL HAVE TO BE DONE IN ORDER TO FULLY UNDERSTAND ALL AREAS OF THE SUBJECT.

THERE WILL BE TWO TYPES OF POSTERS COVERING TWO DIFFERENT AREAS OF KEEP FIT -:

ONE AREA CONTAINING SIMPLE KEEP FIT EXERCISES, SUCH AS -

PRESS UP'S, SIT UP'S, SQUATS, STAR JUMPS, E.T.C, ACCOMPANIED BY STRETCHING EXERCISES.

THE SECOND AREA OF EXERCISES WILL BE DIFFERENT EXERCISES WITH BASIC WEIGHT LIFTING EQUIPMENT SUCH AS -:

THE BENCH PRESS, SQUATS WITH BAR-BELL, ARM CURLS, DUMB-BELL PRESSES, E.T.C.

SPECIFICATION

ESSENTIAL CRITERIA

① A NUMBER OF POSTERS ARE TO BE DEVELOPED WHICH, AS GRAPHICALLY AS POSIBLE, ILLUSTRATE A CERIES OF DIFFERENT EXERCISES.

② THE POSTERS MUST WARN AND GUIDE USERS HOW NOT TO OVERSTRAIN AND PULL MUSCLES UNNECESSARILY.

DESIRABLE CRITERIA

① THE POSTERS COULD BE COVERED IN A PROTECTIVE SEE-THROUGH FILM.

② THE GRAPHICS ON THE WALL-CHARTS COULD BE COLOURED WITH A MULTIPLE ARRAY OF BRIGHT COLOURS MAKING THE CHARTS VERY ATTRACTIVE.

③ A SIMPLE LOGO COULD BE DEVELOPED WHICH WOULD IDENTIFY THE DIFFERENT POSTERS AND COULD EVEN BE PRINTED ON T-SHIRTS.

Here the specification has been divided into two parts. The essential criteria section contains those points from the analysis which MUST be included in the design solution. The desirable criteria section contains points which the designer would like to include if possible. It is also a good idea to draw up the points of your specification in order of priority or importance. This will enable you to tackle the important aspects of the problem first.

If you have access to a computer and a printer it might be possible to word-process the text and glue it onto the page. Check with your teacher to find out if word processing facilities are available in your CDT department and also have a look at the computer graphics section in this book.

Research can consist of many things depending upon the project on which you are working. It might involve collecting statistical data or experimenting with a technological principle. It might involve contacting manufacturing companies or retailers in order to find out what is already available. You may need to look into certain industrial processes before you can finalise your own ideas. For example you may need to find out about certain printing methods before you can design a poster or brochure.

Research can take place at almost any stage in the design process. It does not automatically have to follow the specification. You may need to carry out research more than once. For example, you may have to carry out more research at the planning stage in order to find out the best way to realise part of your project.

THIS ITEM GIVES ALL THE INFORMATION REQUIRED TO DO BUSINESS WITH THE COMPANY. ALSO THIS ADVERTISEMENT WILL BE SEEN EVERY TIME THE OWNER PICKS UP THEIR ENQUIRIES BOOKS.

ALTHOUGH THIS 'PAPERWEIGHT' ADVERTISES THE WEIGHT OF PAPER, THE COMPANY'S NAME IS ON THE UNDERSIDE.

Specialists in Recruitment

PER

Executive Selection

BRIEF

A company is hoping to break into new markets with its products. Design and make a piece of fold-flat advertising which can be sent out by post to advertise the companies.

John has been given a brief to design and make a piece of promotional material. He has been asked to make an item of fold-flat advertising which can be sent through the post by a new company to advertise its products or services.

He has written to several companies which specialise in producing this type of promotional graphics and has also collected examples himself from various exhibitions and trade shows. From his collection he has been able to find out what is already available. He has also been able to find out exactly how they fold and study the mechanisms used in cardboard engineering.

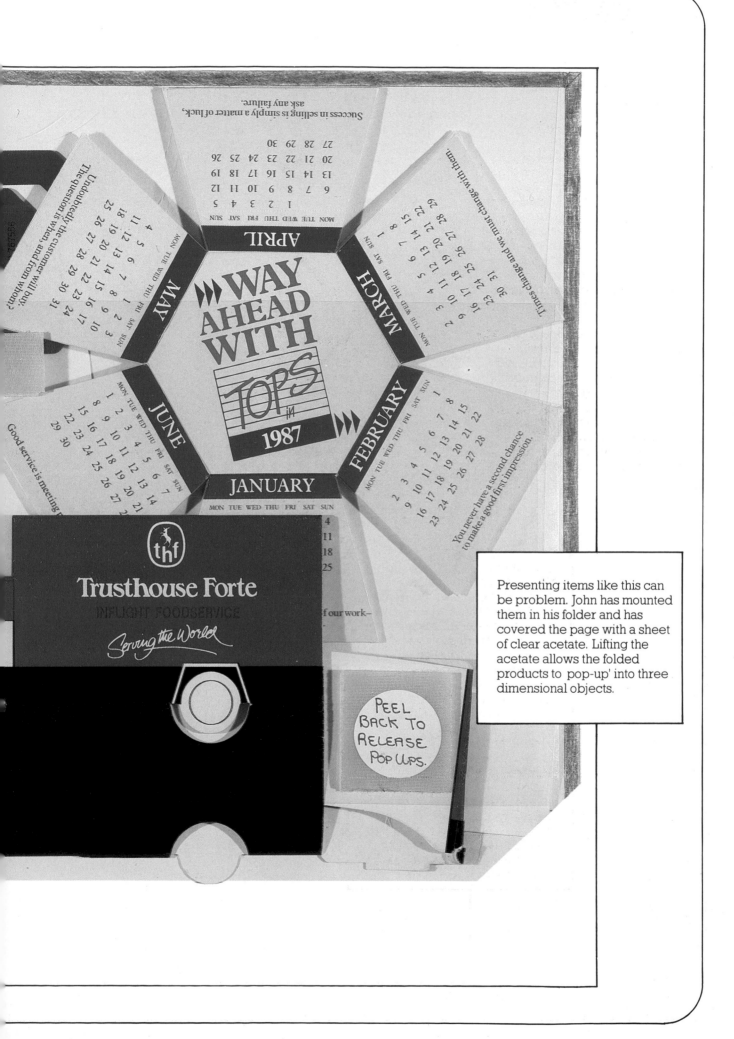

Presenting items like this can be problem. John has mounted them in his folder and has covered the page with a sheet of clear acetate. Lifting the acetate allows the folded products to 'pop-up' into three dimensional objects.

IDEAS

It is important to generate a wide range of solutions to a design problem so that the most suitable can be chosen and developed. By drawing these on paper it is possible to explore a range of solutions fairly quickly and at relatively low cost. These possible solutions are usually presented in the form of ideas sheets.

Each sheet can show a range of ideas. Some of these may appear unimportant at the time but they should be kept because they are an important part of the design process and with some refinement could be developed into an acceptable solution. You may also need to return to the ideas stage of your project if the first solution you have chosen to develop proves unsuccessful.

Many methods of communication can be employed during the production of ideas sheets. These may include isometric sketches, exploded views, sectional views, orthographic views and of course, adequate notes of explanation. Pencils, crayons, paints and felt tipped pens can be used in your drawings but you

must always remember that the main objective is to clearly display your ideas. It is usual for ideas sheets to be drawn freehand.

On the following two pages a number of ideas sheets are shown that demonstrate some of the approaches that you may use to present your ideas.

Here Andrew has produced a design sheet to show a range of ideas for an estate agents sign. This has been produced by taking a number of small sketches, many produced in a notebook at home, and re-drawing them onto a larger piece of paper. This technique can be widened to include glueing sketches and photographs onto a sheet but some attempt should be made to pull the sheet together with notes of explanation.

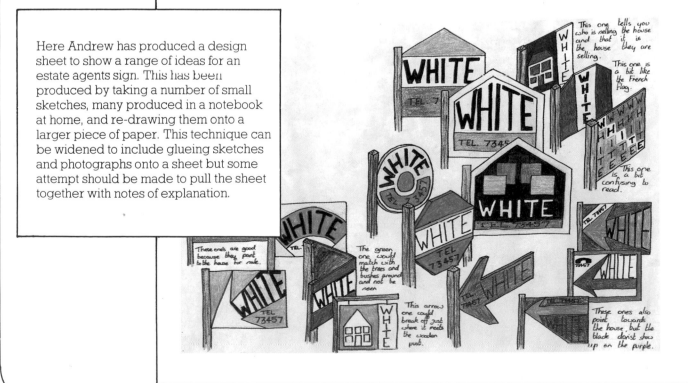

Chris has produced a sheet showing an idea for a model home. He has worked in a very careful way to produce a sheet with adequate detail and explanation of his thoughts. Several similar sheets were produced to show other ideas. Further construction details, including measurements, would be added during the development of the chosen idea.

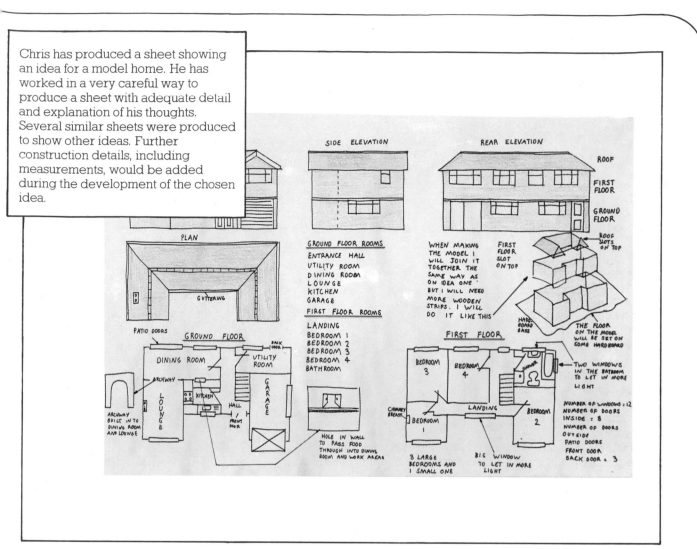

Michael has drawn an ideas sheet showing a range of ideas for packaging a toy. The drawings on this sheet concentrate on showing possible solutions and the shapes of the pieces of cardboard required to make them. Details of lettering and illustrations are omitted as further ideas sheets were produced to explore these factors before applying them to the chosen solution.

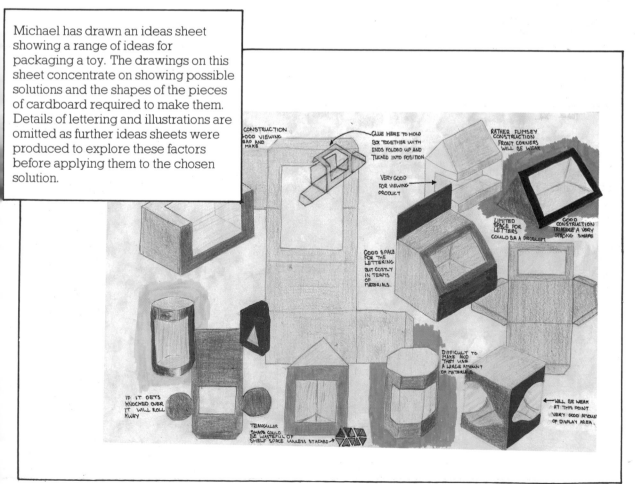

WORKING DRAWINGS

Working drawings in Design and Communication can take many different forms. They do not have to be the traditional three view orthographic drawing. They can take almost any suitable form as long as they convey sufficient information for the product to be accurately realised. An environmental drawing project for example, may require a site plan while a graphic design project may require a detailed layout to be sent to a printer.

The drawings on the right are to be given to a sign-writer. Darren has designed the lettering and logo for his father's new van. He has used a system of dimensioning often found on building and architectual drawings. While one would expect British Standard dimensioning in project work, Darren nevertheless communicates the required information clearly and effectively. It would be impossible to draw the van full size and so he has drawn it to scale. A scale of 1 to 25 has been used. This means that each millimetre on the drawing represents 25 millimetres on the van.

You will notice that Darren has avoided putting the measurements on the drawing itself. This helps to make the drawing clear and easy to understand. He has also only included the necessary dimensions. Look carefully and you will see that the measurements refer only to the sign-writing and not to the overall size of the vehicle.

If you look at the logo you will see that he has dimensioned it according to its proportions rather than its actual size. This means that it can be enlarged or reduced without changing its proportions.

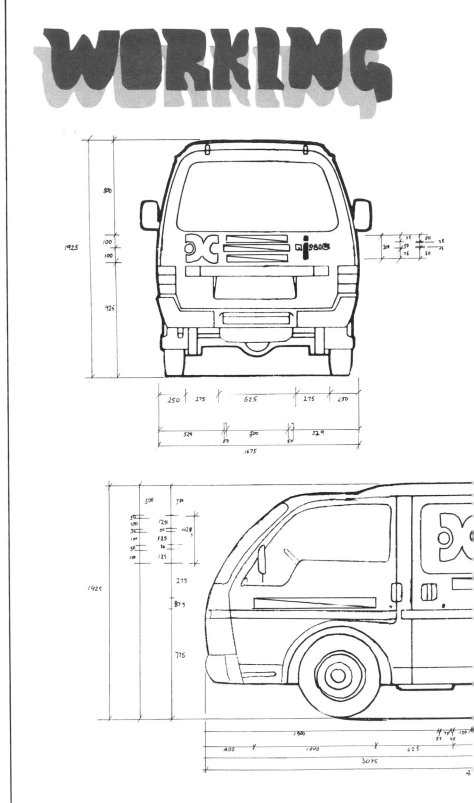

DRAWINGS

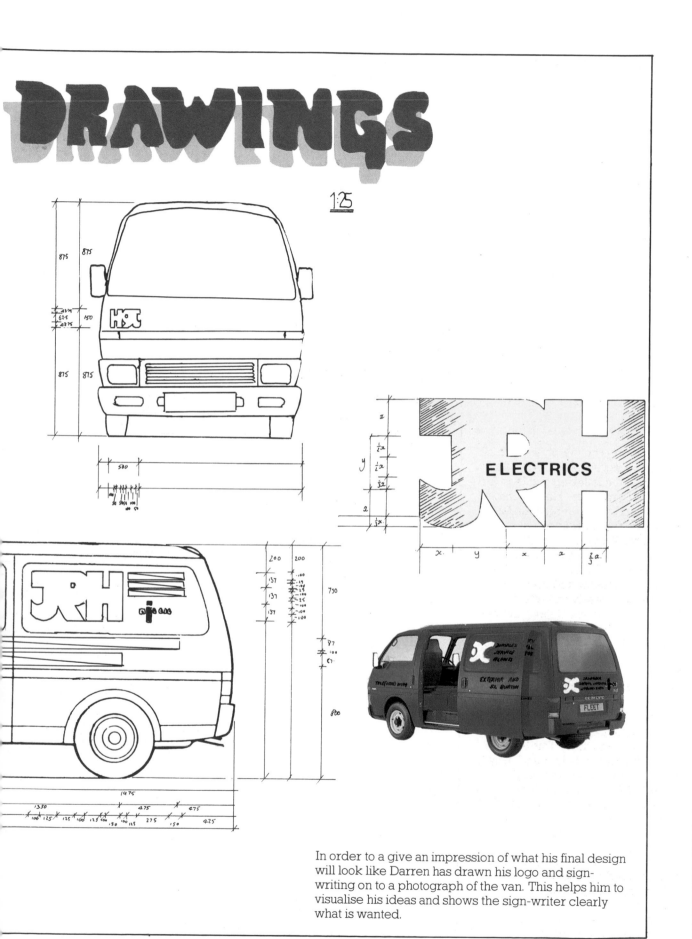

1:25

ELECTRICS

In order to a give an impression of what his final design will look like Darren has drawn his logo and sign-writing on to a photograph of the van. This helps him to visualise his ideas and shows the sign-writer clearly what is wanted.

PLANNING FOR PRODUCTION

There are no set rules for planning the production of a project. The format required will vary according to the nature of the project being undertaken and the skills and ideas of the designer. The examples shown here are not intended to show how it must be done but to show a range of approaches taken by different pupils.

Successful project work requires planning and management or valuable time will be wasted. You will be surprised at just how much time can be lost in gathering materials and deciding what needs to be done. It is very important therefore to know both how much time is available and the exact deadline datc.

Some people prefer to plan their work using a sequential diagram which shows each stage of operation required. Others prefer to draw up a week by week work plan and fill it in each time a task is completed. It is also possible to produce a list of materials required which will save a lot of time at the start of the project. Once you have obtained the materials you will be able to work through without interruption.

It is also important to take into account the time to practise any new skills which may be required. Failing to do this may set your progress back by several weeks. You must also ensure that you have access to all the facilities required in order to realise your design solution. Discuss your production plan with your teacher to ensure that it is possible to produce everything you require in the time available.

When producing your plan you should aim to break the production down into a series of simple operations or stages, taking careful note of your material requirements and keeping the time available in mind.

In the example shown on the right Paul has used a sequential diagram to show the stages of production which he has identified for his project

Shown below are two charts which could be used to plan your work and organise your materials. It is possible to combine this type of chart with a sequential diagram or similar method of showing the stages involved.

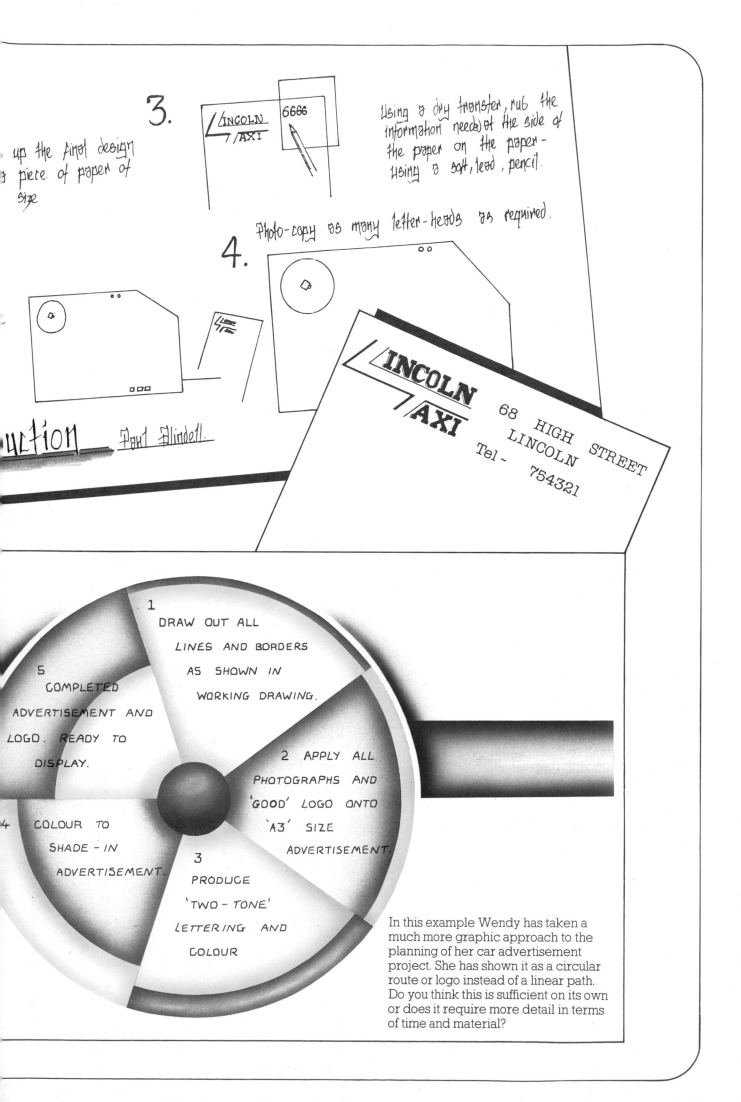

3.

LINCOLN / AXI 6666

Using a dry transfer, rub the information needed at the side of the paper on the paper – using a soft, lead, pencil.

up the final design
a piece of paper of
size

Photo-copy as many letter-heads as required.

4.

uction   Paul Flindell.

LINCOLN / AXI   68 HIGH STREET
LINCOLN
Tel –   754321

1 DRAW OUT ALL LINES AND BORDERS AS SHOWN IN WORKING DRAWING.

2 APPLY ALL PHOTOGRAPHS AND 'GOOD' LOGO ONTO 'A3' SIZE ADVERTISEMENT.

3 PRODUCE 'TWO-TONE' LETTERING AND COLOUR

4 COLOUR TO SHADE-IN ADVERTISEMENT.

5 COMPLETED ADVERTISEMENT AND LOGO. READY TO DISPLAY.

In this example Wendy has taken a much more graphic approach to the planning of her car advertisement project. She has shown it as a circular route or logo instead of a linear path. Do you think this is sufficient on its own or does it require more detail in terms of time and material?

REALISATION

Design and Communication projects can be realised in a variety of ways. Traditional graphic work may be suitable for the realisation of certain projects but in some cases three dimensional realisations may convey information more successfully.

When considering the realisation of your project it is important to consider the nature of the project itself and decide on the most suitable form of realisation. It is also important to consider the materials and facilities available. You may be fortunate and have access to a variety of materials and a well equipped workshop. On the other hand you may be working in a drawing office where the use of resistant materials such as wood or plastic is difficult if not impossible.

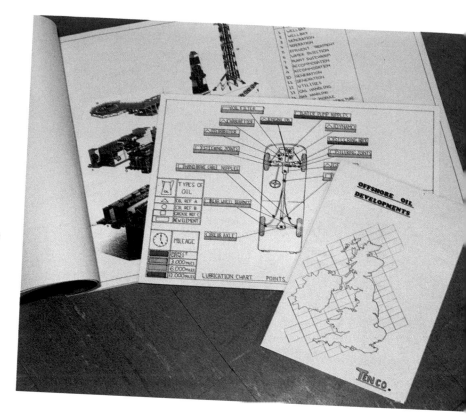

Examples of projects realised basically in two dimensional form are shown at the top of this page. Here is a leaflet produced using coloured paper in a photocopying machine. If available the photocopier can be a versatile tool in Design and Communication. Photocopy masters are produced in black and white and are then assembled using cut and paste techniques. The master is then printed on the copier in the normal way. This type of project also allows the use of computer graphic techniques. There are various desk top publishing software packages available which will allow you to achieve professional results on schools computers.

Packaging can provide a rich area of study for three-dimensional realisation. Products can be packaged using a variety of materials including card and plastic. A quality finish can be achieved by using an air brush. markers or coloured paper to simulate a printed surface. Two examples of product packaging are shown here, one for a chocolate Easter egg and the other for a toy car.

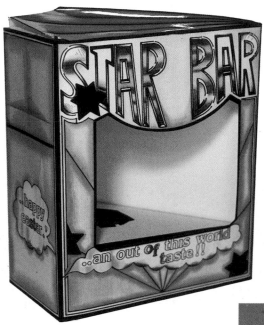

Models are another useful method of conveying information. It is possible to construct models yourself or to use plastic or balsa construction kits where necessary. A model of a railway carriage on this page is cut away to show the design of the interior of the carriage. This model has been constructed using a thin plastic sheet material known as 'Plasticard'. The model below it has been constructed from a plastic kit and has been used to show the design of a ferry company livery and logo. This model has been given the finishing touch by adding a base which gives the effect of the ship being at sea.

EVALUATION AND TESTING

You will not know how successful your solution to a design problem is until you have tested and evaluated it. This can prove difficult because you will not want to be critical of your own work. However, it is important to be able to recognise any limitations or weaknesses and suggest ways in which these can be overcome.

Perhaps the best way to begin is to look back in your design folder and remind yourself of the problem. You must then ask yourself 'How good a solution to the problem is the article that I have made?' It may be a solution that appears to work well but it is very unlikely that you will have produced the perfect answer! You must therefore, evaluate what you have made against your specification and in the light of the analysis and research carried out. Any weaknesses in the function of the product or problems encountered during the realisation and design stages should be highlighted.

Detailed explanations of how these were or could be overcome should be given.

It is usual to produce sheets of drawings and notes, similar to that shown below to visually display your evaluation. These will vary in style according to the nature of the project but wherever possible should include photographs of the article in use.

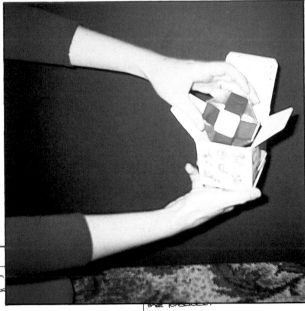

EVALUATION

The solution to my packaging problem is quite successful in that it fulfills my specification. It holds the puzzle and presents it in an attractive manner but there are some problem areas that I will look at in this evaluation.

The solution was developed from the idea shown below. It can be seen that several changes have been made.

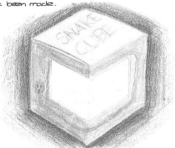

I have decided to consider the following areas in my evaluation:

- Construction of Box
- Design of Lettering and Graphics
- Use of Colour

CONSTRUCTION OF BOX

The construction of the box is basically sound with the thickness of cardboard providing adequate strength. However I have made the front closing flap too small and therefore the lid tends too spring up. I also had

Some problems in ... because the glue ...

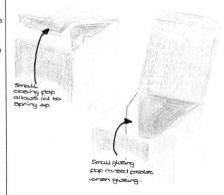

Small closing flap allows lid to spring up.

Small glueing flap caused problems when glueing.

Although the clear plastic window allows good visibility of the product inside the box, it does make the corner rather weak. This may mean that the product may be damaged if the box were dropped on that corner.

LETTERING AND GRAPHICS

I still think it was a good idea to make the lettering look like a snake but it has made it rather difficult to read. It would perhaps been better to simplify it to something

... still ... lettering and the product.

The illustrations on the reverse of the package are rather ineffective because they need more explanation. Perhaps these should have been incorporated in a leaflet enclosed in the box.

USE OF COLOUR

The colours used for the box are reasonably effective because they contrast well against each other. I am not pleased with the colour used for the background colour because it was applied with a pencil crayon which has given a rather textured appearance. Perhaps I should have made more effort to buy some card of the right colour or experimented with other colouring methods, such as felt tipped pens.

CRAYON   FELT TIPPED PEN

The use of black lines around all lettering and drawings does make the colours appear brighter and clearer but I do think that it should have been used more selectively.

INDEX

ACKNOWLEDGEMENTS

The publishers are grateful to the following individuals and organisations for the photographs and illustrations in this book:

AA Picture Library, fig 6.37;
A. B. Designs, figs 8.17, 8.18, 8.59, 8.60, 8.61, 8.62, 8.63, 8.64, 8.65;
A to Z Couriers Ltd, fig 5.69;
Abbey National Building Society, fig 5.66b;
Advanced Memory Systems Ltd, figs 8.24, 8.35, 8.47, 8.48, 8.49, 8.52, 8.53;
Academy Beverage Co. Ltd, figs 2.15, 2.16, 2.17;
Acorn Computers, fig 8.6;
Airfix, fig 7.44;
Aerofilm Ltd, fig 10.72;
All-Models Engineering Ltd, fig 4.23;
Allsport UK Ltd, figs 2.53, 2.54, 5.60, 6.38, 8.2;
Argos Distributors Ltd, figs 1.9, 1.20, 1.23, 1.24, 1.25, 1.27, 1.28, 1.29, 5.89 (microwave), 5.98;
Audi Volkswagen, fig 2.42;
Auto-trol Ltd, figs 8.3, 8.4, 8.27, 8.28, 8.67, 8.68, 8.69, 8.87, 8.88, 8.89, 8.90, 8.91, 8.92, 8.93, 8.94, 8.95, 8.96, 8.97;
Aveling Barford International Ltd, figs 9.3, 9.32, 9.35, 9.51, 9.52, 9.55;
J.C. Bamford, figs 7.1, 7.54;
Barnaby's Picture Library, figs 1.7, 2.48, 6.31, 6.34, 6.39, 6.47, 10.41, 10.42, 10.43, 10.57;
Charles Brereton, figs 3.11, 9.62, 7.1 (book spread), 8.118;
Bridgeman Art Library, figs 5.15 (Bridget Riley), 5.47, 5.57;
British Broadcasting Corporation, figs 2.55, 2.59;
BBC TV, CAL Video Graphics and Graham Kern (Designer), fig 8.102;
British Gas plc, figs 10.46, 10.47;
BSI, fig 7.52;
British Telecom plc, figs 1.11, 1.12, 1.13, 1.14, 1.15, 1.16, 1.17, 1.18, 1.19, 10.43;
Bryan Sears and Associates, fig 10.13
Canon UK Ltd, fig 1.1;
Channel Four Television, figs 8.100, 8.104, 8.105;
Charles Reed School/Lincolnshire Education Authority, fig 2.21;
Christies Colour Library, fig 5.14;
Citroën Automobiles, fig 5.96;
Coca-Cola Great Britain, fig 5.59;
Commotion Ltd, fig 4.3;
Conran Design Group, fig 9.1;
Kevin Crampton, figs 3.1, 10.26;
I.O. Design, figs 8.15, 8.51;
Earls Court and Olympia Group, fig 5.107;
East Midland Electricity Board, fig 10.44;
Electric Image/BBC, fig 2.56;
EMA Model Supplies Ltd, figs 4.1, 4.2, 4.27, 4.44, 4.45;
Equitable Life Assurance Society, fig 10.62;
Ever Ready Ltd, figs 1.22, 1.24;
Ford Motor Co Ltd, figs 2.13, 2.43, 5.91, 7.21, 7.29, 7.31, 7.41, 7.46;
Harry French, figs 8.12, 8.43, 8.44;
Sally and Richard Greenhill, figs 2.11a, 2.25, 2.38, 6.33, 6.102, 10.32, 10.61;
Haynes Publishing Group, fig 7.1 (Ford Sierra book and chart);
HMV Record Stores, fig 5.66c;
Hoover plc, fig 5.89 (washing machine)
M. Horsley, figs 8.22, 8.25, 8.26, 8.37, 8.38, 8.39, 8.40, 8.41, 8.54, 8.55, 8.56, 8.57, 8.58, 8.111, 8.115, 8.116, 8.117;
IBM Computers, fig 8.9;
Institute of Civil Engineers, fig 6.40;
ITN, fig 8.101;
Intervisual Communications Inc, fig 4.31;
Letraset UK Ltd, figs 3.47, 3.48, 3.75;
Levi UK Ltd, fig 5.56;
Linear Graphics Ltd, figs 6.14, 8.10, 8.19;
Lincoln Vulcans Swimming Club / M. Horsley, figs 8.106, 8.107, 8.108, 8.109, 8.110, 8.111, 8.112, 8.113;
A.M. Lock and Co Ltd, fig 1.47;
Lincolnshire County Council, figs 10.10, 10.11, 10.12;
London Graphic Centre, fig 3.39;
London Regional Transport, fig 7.53 (LRT registered user No 88/E/398);
London Weekend Television, fig 2.57;
Magnet Joinery Ltd, fig 10.68, 10.71;
The Mansell Collection, fig 10.2;
Ian Marshall, fig 2.19, 4.4;
Mary Evans Picture Library, fig 5.72;
Yuko Matsuziki, fig 8.1;
Michelin Tyre plc, fig 5.66a;
Mothercare UK Ltd, fig 6.12;
National Trust Photolibrary, fig 6.43;
Nimlok Ltd, fig 5.112;
Norwich Union Life Assurance Society, fig 8.103;
Oracle Teletext Ltd, fig 2.58;
Ordnance Survey, fig 10.3;
Pelltech Ltd, fig 3.39b;
Philips Electronics, fig 5.89 (stereo/CD);
Photoresources, fig 7.57;
Pluto Graphic Systems, fig 8.17;
Prisma Graphics, figs 8.46, 8.50;
R.S. Components Ltd, fig 1.21;
Record Machines Ltd, fig 8.16;
Redwood Publishing, fig 8.11 (from Acorn User magazine)
Research Machines Ltd, figs 8.9, 8.13, 8.16, 8.20, 8.33, 8.34, 8.36, 8.42, 8.45, 8.70, 8.71, 8.72, 8.73, 8.74, 8.75, 8.76, 8.77, 8.78, 8.79, 8.80, 8.81, 8.82, 8.83, 8.84, 8.85, 8.86;
Ruston Gas Turbines, figs 7.1 (colliery), 9.00, 7.90,
J. Sainsbury plc, figs 2.24, 2.28, 5.71;
Science Photo Library, fig 5.45;
Superior Software Ltd, fig 8.5, 8.29, 8.30, 8.31;
Techsoft UK Ltd, fig, 8.66;
Tilcon Ltd, fig 10.51;
The Walt Disney Company, figs 8.98, 8.99;